ID0788700

METHUEN'S HANDBOOKS OF ARCHAEOLOGY

General Editor: ARTHUR BERNARD COOK, LITT.D.

HOMER AND MYCENAE

HOMER AND MYCENAE

BY

MARTIN P. NILSSON
DR. THEOL. ET PHIL.
PROFESSOR OF CLASSICAL ARCHAEOLOGY AND ANCIENT HISTORY IN THE
UNIVERSITY OF LUND
SOMETIME SATHER PROFESSOR OF CLASSICAL LITERATURE IN THE
UNIVERSITY OF CALIFORNIA

WITH 52 ILLUSTRATIONS AND 4 MAPS

A MARANDELL BOOK

COOPER SQUARE PUBLISHERS, INC.
NEW YORK
1968

Originally Published 1933
Copyright Under the Berne Convention
and the United Copyright Convention
Published in Agreement With Methuen & Co. Ltd. London, U.K.
Published by Cooper Square Publishers, Inc.
59 Fourth Avenue, New York, N. Y. 10003
Library of Congress Catalog Card No. 68-54548

Printed in the United States of America
by Sentry Press, New York, N. Y. 10019

THIS BOOK

IS

RESPECTFULLY DEDICATED

TO

H.R.H. GUSTAF ADOLF

CROWN PRINCE OF SWEDEN

PREFACE

WHEN the University of London honoured me with an invitation to deliver the Advanced lectures in Classics in June, 1929, I chose a subject to which I gave the title Homer and Mycenae. In studying the survival of the Minoan and Mycenaean religion, and still more in tracing the Mycenaean origin of Greek mythology, I was constantly brought up against Homeric problems, and I felt it necessary to make up my mind about them. Consequently I picked out for the lectures what seemed to me to be the salient points, first the elements which for historical and archaeological reasons can be dated to certain and widely differing epochs, secondly the probable origin and transmission of Greek epics as viewed in the light of other epics, and thirdly the traces in the epics of an earlier state organization. These lectures appear here enlarged and rewritten as chapters iii, v, and vi respectively.

When Messrs. Methuen & Co. invited me to publish a book with the same title on the basis of these lectures, I agreed, perhaps rashly in view of the difficulties of the extensive and controversial subject. I took the opportunity thus offered of revising and co-ordinating my views and of giving a reasoned exposition of them. This required the addition of further chapters, one on the history of the Homeric question, especially in its most recent phases, another on the history of the Mycenaean age, which is the background of my views, a third on language and style, and finally a chapter on

Homeric mythology, which is in fact a sequel to my book on the Mycenaean Origin of Greek Mythology.

The chapter on language and style was the most difficult, both because of its intrinsic nature and because for many years my work had not taken me much into the philological field. Although this side of the question was indispensable for a survey of the problem, I should not have dared to undertake it if my old teacher, Professor J. Wackernagel, with his accustomed self-sacrificing kindness had not added to the increasing debt of gratitude which I have owed him since my student days by going through my manuscript of this chapter in detail and making most valuable remarks. I have used them freely and some of them are printed in the footnotes.

Mr. T. A. Sinclair of Birkbeck College, London, and Dr. B. F. C. Atkinson, Cambridge, have done me the service of going through my manuscript and correcting my English style. I owe to Mr. Sinclair also valuable suggestions in regard to composition and certain details.

A great deal of the manuscript was written down in the autumn of 1930 during my stay at Berkeley as Sather Professor of Classical Literature. I cannot end this preface without a word of thanks to the University of California and to my then colleagues for a most agreeable time and excellent facilities for studies and research.

MARTIN P. NILSSON

Lund, Sweden
January, 1933

CONTENTS

LIST OF ILLUSTRATIONS AND MAPS

HOMER AND MYCENAE

CHAPTER I

VIEWS AND METHODS IN THE HOMERIC QUESTION

THE reading of Homer raises problems both important and fascinating. Their importance is bound up with the historical conclusions which may reasonably be drawn from a study of Homer. For he stands in the morning twilight of Greek history and looks back to a preceding age, which according to him was an age of much more brilliant glory and valiant men than the age in which he himself lived. The question is whether Homer can help us to bridge over the gulf of the dark ages which separate the historical and the Mycenaean ages of Greece. The fascination of the Homeric question which, in spite of all apparent difficulties and disagreements, has, more than anything else, induced scholars continually to reconsider the Homeric problems, lies in the effort to attain an insight into the creation and the growth of a work of unsurpassed poetical genius. Harsh opinions have been proffered by many scholars concerning certain parts of the Homeric poetry, but nevertheless they admire Homer profoundly and their work was prompted by the lure and spell of Homer's poetical art and undertaken because of their desire to understand Homer better.

The problem is as difficult as it is fascinating. Opinions differ, and not only that but views and methods differ in a most embarrassing manner, so that what is written by one group of Homeric scholars seems hardly to exist for another group striving to interpret the same poetical works. Sometimes the bankruptcy of Homeric scholarship is asserted, and the hopeless disagreement of the results of different scholars is taken to prove that the solution of the problems is beyond reach. But this agnosticism will probably not deter scholars from devoting their sagacity and knowledge to Homeric research even in the future. It would be unjust to deny that progress has been made. If generally acknowledged results are few and meagre concerning the time-honoured points of discussion and dissension, certain hypotheses have been eliminated or reduced to their just proportions, and on the other hand, the materials relevant for the discussion have been enlarged. If they have not afforded any solution of the old problems, they have proposed new problems and opened new vistas, and that is in fact as important as any solution.

Some one has said that it is more important to put a question in the right manner than to solve it, and that is perfectly true in regard to Homer. Questions have been put which may confidently be declared to be insoluble. Their discussion is not therefore idle and useless ; it is important to know even that a problem is insoluble, and the discussion contributes to clearing and broadening our understanding. On the other hand, we may try and see whether there are not questions which can be solved, if not with absolute certainty, at least with sufficient probability. Putting the right questions may be as difficult as giving the right answer ; and errors and mistakes will occur before we can attain either, while the task may take a considerable time.

I. The Separatists

The Homeric question was introduced into the arena of scientific discussion by the famous Prolegomena of Wolf in 1795.[1] Whatever may be said of his originality—it fs certain that his ideas were proposed earlier by d'Aubignac, Wood, and Herder—his merit is that he was the first to treat the problem in a scholarly manner, and the importance of his work is fully testified to by the great excitement it aroused among scholars, poets, and persons interested in poetry and by its long-lasting effects. In fact the form in which Wolf

---

[1] F. A. Wolf, *Prolegomena ad Homerum*, 3rd ed., by R. Peppmüller, 1884.

put the problem determined the lines of discussion for a long time afterwards and still does to a large extent, whilst his arguments seem to be largely superseded.

The problem which we are wont to call the Homeric question in its simplest form amounts to this : Are the Homeric poems a unity, sprung from one brain, or not ? Are the poems as a whole, or the Iliad and the Odyssey respectively, the work of one poet or a composition involving poems of many authors ?

Wolf argued that because writing was unknown to Homer one man would have been unable to compose such an extensive work as either of the Homeric poems. For it would only be possible to hold it together if it were written down. But we know nowadays that the art of writing was used in Greece many centuries before Homer. Whether it was used for recording an extensive poetical work, is another question which, frankly stated, we are unable to decide by purely objective arguments. The answer to this question must depend on the consensus of opinion as to the measure and use of the art of writing in such a cultural stage as that to which the Homeric poems belong. The question of the age of the art of writing does not play so great a part in the discussion to-day as it did a century ago.

Of course, there was a time when Homer was written down, and this was a very important event in the history of Homeric poetry, for thereby the text attained to a much greater stability than before, even if we should not imagine the difference between the handing down of a poem in oral tradition and its transcription from one manuscript into another to be so great as we are apt to do according to our modern ideas, expressed in the Latin proverb : *scripta manent, verba volant*. Oral tradition embodied in versified form and even more in the memory of a minstrel has a greater stability than we are accustomed to think. The use of verse in an early age, even for subjects of purely practical importance, takes this fact into account. Hence the wisdom of the earliest astronomers and of the first Mediterranean pilots [1] and the

---

[1] Cp. my paper Κατάπλοι, " Beiträge zu dem Schiffskataloge und zu der altionischen nautischen Literatur," *Rhein. Museum*, lx, 1905, pp. 161.

lore and rules of the farmers were done into verse. Solon made propaganda for his political ideas in verse because verses were better retained by the memory of men and spread among the people. On the other hand, even the written text was subject to alterations and especially to additions. We know that from the " wild " Homer texts which have come down to us in early papyri.[1] They contain many additional verses, which are, generally speaking, empty and superfluous, only expanding the text usually by means of old, slightly varied stock expressions. They were cut out when the text was established by the Alexandrian philologists.

We do not know when and where the writing down of the Homeric poems took place, nor do we know the purpose of it, whether it was only intended to be an aid to the crafts- man, the minstrel, or whether the written text became ac- cessible to every one who wished to see it. This difference is, of course, of no slight importance. Bréal thinks that somewhere in an Ionian town, a single manuscript was pro- duced for use in a certain festival, in which the poems were recited, that this manuscript was preserved and enlarged in order to be used on other similar occasions, and that it finally was transferred to Athens ; here it was decided that it should be recited at the Panathenaic festival.[2] Gilbert Murray supposes that Homer was a traditional book in the hands of a minstrel or a school of minstrels, and that it was carefully preserved and guarded, but enlarged and extended in the course of time.[3] He compares the traditional books of the Hebrews, but forgets the very important difference that these are in prose whilst Homer is in verse, and that they were rather mechanically pieced together of old and late elements. It used to be thought by some people that a similar piecing together might have been done by Homer, but this view is scarcely now held. Andrew Lang compares the texts of the *chansons de geste* which the *jongleurs* kept

---

[1] Bibliography by A. Ludwich, " Jahrb. f. klass. Philologie " (Fleckeisen's *Jahrbücher*), Suppl. vol. xxvii, 1902, pp. 34. They are adhibited in the edition of Homer by Allen and Munro. Cp. P. Cauer, *Grundfragen der Homerkritik*, 3rd ed., pp. 22, and E. Drerup, *Homerische Poetik*, I, pp. 83.

[2] M. Bréal, *Pour mieux connaître Homère*, 1906, pp. 42.

[3] G. Murray, *The Rise of the Greek Epic*, 1907, 3rd ed., 1924.

very carefully for their own personal use and sometimes trans-
mitted to a son.[1] All this is nothing but guesswork. We
know minstrels also who relied solely upon their memory for
preserving extensive poems. We know young Athenians who
learnt the whole of Homer by heart. We should face things
as they are. These questions can only be answered according
to our subjective opinion of the use and extent of the art
of writing in the early age of Greece.

Wolf believed, however, that these questions were answered
by our knowledge of the fact, handed down by the ancients,
that Peisistratos collected the Homeric poems which formerly
were confused or dispersed in the form in which they now
are read.[2] This information was thought to prove that there
was originally no plan according to which the poem was
built up, but that disconnected poems referring to the same
cycle of events were first collected and brought into an orderly
whole in Athens by the agency of Peisistratos in order that
they should be recited at the Panathenaic festival. This
view is nowadays hardly accepted by anybody except Cauer.[3]
Bethe comes near to it in believing that the Homeric poems
were composed in Athens in the sixth century B.C.[4] The
redaction committee appointed by Peisistratos is mere invention of a late age. Athenians play a very insignificant
part in Homer, and it has been pertinently pointed out that
their rôle is anything but glorious.[5] A single Attic interpolation[6] does not prove anything to this effect. The redaction of Peisistratos is nowadays taken very little into
account in attempting to solve the main problem. Even by
Cauer it is not thought to have affected the idea and the
plan of the poem seriously.

Another question is implied in the fact that Homeric
language shows undoubtedly a slight Attic colouring as Wackernagel proved in a penetrating and searching analysis.[7]

---

[1] Andrew Lang, *Homer and his Age*, 1906, pp. 299.

[2] Cicero, *De oratore*, iii, 137. Concerning the redaction committee, see
the keen criticism of K. Lehrs, *De Aristarchi studiis Homericis*, 2nd ed., 1865,
pp. 462.

[3] Cauer, loc. cit., pp. III.

[4] E. Bethe, *Homer*, ii, 1922, pp. 355.

[5] J. A. Scott, *The Unity of Homer*, 1921, pp. 47.   [6] *Il.*, ii, v. 558.

[7] J. Wackernagel, *Sprachliche Untersuchungen zu Homer*, 1916. Cp.
below, pp. 161.

This proves not that the Homeric poems were composed in
Athens, only that they went through an Attic medium, and
this is easily explained by the dominating influence of Athens
in letters.

The methods of attacking the problem were soon changed.
Wolf had argued with arguments only drawn from external
conditions and circumstances, his followers tried another
way, although they aimed at the same goal. Their method
was the analysis of the extant poems.   Commonly only such
scholars are reckoned as adherents of the analytical school
who through an analysis of the poems try to prove that the
Iliad and the Odyssey respectively cannot be the work of
one man but in one way or another have come into existence by an agglomeration or bringing together of different
poems composed at different times.   But the unitarians who
try to demonstrate the unity of the Iliad and of the Odyssey
rely no less upon an analysis of the poems.   Their arguments
also are drawn from the poems themselves, but their conception and explanation are different, and they bring different
points and different sides of the poems to the fore.

The first question is that of the plan of the poems.   Both
in the Iliad and in the Odyssey there is unquestionably a
central idea which connects the parts and makes them links
of a whole.   Thus the question amounts to this, whether
this idea is carried through in such a manner as may be expected of a poet conceiving and elaborating a plot or not.
If the plan did not originate with a single man, the apparent
connection must have come about in some other manner.
It is to be admitted that there is a containing bond in the
myth itself.   Songs treating coherent mythical events may
have attracted each other and may thus have been agglo-
merated and united.   This is, of course, the standpoint of
the separatists.

In order to demonstrate their case they point to inconsistencies between the poems and the plan and also in the
poems themselves.   To take an example of the first, it is
said that the Iliad puts forward the wrath of Achilles as its
subject, but that its later books do not concern this wrath which
was appeased at the death of Patroclos.   Hence the inference
is drawn that an Achilleïs, a poem treating the deeds of Achilles

and ending with his death,[1] was remodelled and incorporated
in the poem which gives the wrath of Achilles as its subject.
The death of Achilles was cut away, but so much of the Achilleïs
remained that the end of the poem became inconsistent with
what was professed in the beginning to be its theme. The
unitarians reply that the death of Patroclos and the slaying
of Hector in vengeance of Patroclos' death is but a consequence of the wrath. They cannot find any real inconsistency. The voyage of Telemachos is but loosely connected
with the plot of the Odyssey. Hence the inference is drawn
that it is a later accretion.[2] On the opposite side it is said
that this tale serves admirably as an introduction and exposition of the situation.

The composition of the poems offers many points of attack
to the separatists, for inconsistencies and contradictions are
evident. Sometimes the joining together of different parts
is defective. Sometimes the plan seems to be dropped or
thwarted. Sometimes a leading idea seems to be hinted at
which is not carried through properly, e.g. the wrath of Poseidon in the Odyssey. There are long and seemingly superfluous digressions which divert attention from the professed
subject of the poem. Events which have been described are
not referred to in their proper places but seem to be forgotten.
The separatists use the sharpest tools of analysis in order
to detect and to stress such inconsistencies, and they draw
the conclusion that these inconsistencies prove that originally

---

[1] The assumption that the kernel of the Iliad was a poem on the wrath
of Achilles was made by Gottfried Hermann, De interpolationibus Homeri,
1832. G. Grote in his discussion of Homer in his History of Greece,
vol. ii, proposed the Achilleïs. In regard to the contents of the Achilleïs
views differ ; the view referred to in the text is that of U. v. Wilamowitz-
Möllendorff, Die Ilias und Homer, 1916. It may reasonably be objected that
though the poet strikes the key-note with the words " Sing the wrath, etc.,"
these words may not apply to the whole poem, just as Xenophon's work
was called " Anabasis," a title which applies to the first book only. There
are many such inconsistencies in ancient literature. The well-known verse
in the teacher's book in the schoolroom scene, painted by Duris (Furt-
wängler-Reichhold, Griechische Vasenmalerei, pl. 136), Μοῦσά μοι ἀμφὶ Σκά-
μανδρον ἄρχομαι ἀείδειν, is such a key-note, although we are at a loss to know
to what epos it belonged ; perhaps it is a new-made verse. It may be the
prologue of any epos of the Trojan cycle, even the Iliad itself.

[2] The " Telemachia " was stated to be a later addition by G. Hermann,
loc. cit.

independent poems were fused or that alien poems were incorporated ; the joints were not quite smoothed over, but traces of the earlier independence of the parts remain and become apparent in inconsistencies and contradictions. The unitarians, on the other hand, emphasize the general idea which makes the poems a coherent work ; they try to smooth over and explain the inconsistencies and contradictions, and they strengthen their case by calling attention to the fact that even modern authors who were working at their own desks and were able to corroborate what they had written in their manuscript have often admitted inconsistencies and contradictions.

Two things are here brought into play. One is logic, another is sentiment and effect on listeners ; poetical economy is made up of both. The separatists appeal more to logic, the unitarians more to poetical effect. Judgment is in both respects a matter of taste, even concerning logic. For the question is not of logic as such but of what logic may be expected from the poet. In literature in general, we find not only inconsistencies and contradictions due to the unwariness of an author—sometimes he admits such undoubtedly in order to enhance the poetical effect—but also such as have been introduced by others in working over another's work. We are seldom able to settle, on objective grounds, the question how much of this kind is to be conceded to the author and what testifies to an alien hand ; in the case of Homer especially there are no objective reasons at all. Our judgment is necessarily dependent on our subjective opinion concerning the amount of inconsistencies and contradictions which may be conceded to an author or cannot possibly be due to one and the same man.

Style and language too were called to aid for discerning earlier and later parts of the Homeric poems. We have to recur to this subject later ; here some preliminary remarks only will be made. Earlier forms of language are found in Homer which were obsolete at the time when Homeric poetry was still being composed. The most outstanding instance is the digamma discovered by Bentley. Sometimes the metre is correct if F is pronounced so that the preceding syllable is long ; sometimes the metre would be upset, because the preceding syllable should be short. Although F certainly once existed in the Ionic dialect, it has vanished from it as we know it, but it was preserved in the Aeolic dialect. Thus the appearance of the F was connected with the traces of the Aeolic dialect in Homer.

In these traces of an older language and another dialect there seems to be a means ready at hand for discerning earlier and later strata, and this idea was taken up as a working hypothesis by Fick.[1] He thought that the earlier Homeric poems were originally composed in the Aeolic dialect and later translated into the Ionic dialect. In this translation Aeolic forms were kept if the Ionic forms did not correspond to them metrically so that the latter could not be fitted into the metrical scheme without trouble. Fick undertook to retranslate parts of the poems into the Aeolic dialect and thus to demonstrate which parts were the earliest. The attempt was repeated by Bechtel in connection with Robert's work which will be mentioned later.[2] These attempts were admittedly a failure. An Aeolic form does not prove that a passage is old, for it may have been introduced by mere tradition, but even in the parts which are said to belong to the old Aeolic stratum there are Ionic forms which cannot simply be replaced by Aeolic ones and which cannot be removed without violence. The supposition of interpolations must often be called to aid in order to get rid of such Ionisms. And the Iliad made up of those parts which were retranslated into the Aeolic dialect is a very disconnected matter, mere rags. The weight of these objections was so heavy that Bechtel himself had to admit that the language of the earliest parts was composed of mixed Aeolic and Ionic elements : thereby the bankruptcy of this hypothesis was confessed.

Other linguistic arguments were often adduced in order to show that certain parts are late and especially that the Odyssey is later than the Iliad : words occurring in certain parts only, the use of the pronoun ὁ as a definite article, of abstract nouns, of the short forms of the dative plural in -αις, -οις, -ης instead of the long forms, all which evidently

---

[1] A. Fick, *Die homerische Odyssee in der ursprünglichen Sprachform hergestellt*, 1883 ; *Die Ilias*, 1886.
[2] Below p. 20.

belong to a later stage of language as compared with the use
of ὁ as a pronoun, the absence or scarcity of abstract nouns,
and the long forms in -αισι, -οισι, and -ησι. But even these
arguments are fallacious. The statistical inquiry into the
use of these words and forms instituted by Scott proves undoubtedly the conformity of language in both poems.[1]

Another argument which is often used is taken from the
repetition of verses. For when a verse is repeated it is assumed that it is borrowed from another passage in which
it is found. Even this argument is fallacious, for the verses
may be borrowed from a common stock ; and even if a verse
is borrowed it may be somewhat uncertain how far the argument drawn from this fact applies to the passage or poem
in which the verse occurs. It is otherwise with certain passages
which consist of a large number of repeated verses. There
are such centos in Homer largely made up of repeated verses
and phrases. The interpolations in the so-called wild texts
of early Ptolemaic papyri consist precisely of such verses.
But these are to be called interpolations. Such a passage,
made up of verses ready at hand and stock expressions, shows
certainly a falling off in poetical inspiration ; they are too
similar to known interpolations not to be suspect, and the
view that they are additions must be taken into account
seriously. But these passages are not so numerous or extensive as to have any serious bearing on the problem of the
composition of the whole.

These arguments have failed and are repeated very little
by separatists ; but the differences in style are often put
into the foreground. This principle is expressed in condensed
words by Wilamowitz, who states that style much more than
language distinguishes early and late parts.[2] Immisch pointed
to such differences in an interesting pamphlet [3] and made
the striking remark that an outworn and weak style may
be used in songs which show a progress in the deepening
of psychological characterization, e.g. in the description of
Priam's visit to Achilles in the last book of the Iliad. Bethe

---

[1] Comprehensive survey in J. A. Scott, *The Unity of Homer*, ch. iii.
[2] U. v. Wilamowitz-Möllendorff, *Die Heimkehr des Odysseus*, 1927, p. 174.
[3] O. Immisch, *Die innere Entwicklung des griechischen Epos*, 1904.

took such a difference of style as his starting-point for his analysis of the Iliad.[1]

The differences of style are very remarkable, and are strongly felt by every reader of Homer who has a sense for poetical language. The observation of Bethe is just : the rapid, almost breathless progress of the exposition in the first book of the Iliad is very different from the usual epic expansiveness of style. To take another instance adduced by Wilamowitz,[2] in the description of the arrival of Odysseus in Ithaca and his visit to Eumaios in the thirteenth and fourteenth books of the Odyssey there is a style indulging in the details of simple everyday life somewhat reminiscent of bucolic poetry. But it is uncertain how far such differences are due to differences of ages and persons. A great poet may have many strings to his bow. It is to be feared that if these principles were applied to Shakespeare or Goethe some of their works would no longer be considered authentic. This means of discerning different strata in the poems is the most highly subjective of all.

These methods of analysis were perfected and refined during the last century. The tenacious defender of Homeric unity in the early part of the last century, Nitzsch,[3] has very little of them. Gottfried Hermann [4] used them in order to prove the existence of two earlier, smaller poems on the wrath of Achilles and the return of Odysseus respectively, which, according to him, were enlarged and extended partly by parallel poems, partly by poems which did not belong to the original plan. George Grote [5] and many others followed similar lines.

This view of the origin and growth of the Homeric poems acknowledges a plot, a fundamental idea, which holds the various parts together. There is an original plan due to some poet. To quote Grote, the Iliad is similar to a house which originally had a narrower ground plan and by and by was enlarged. This unity too was contested by Lachmann [6]

---

[1] E. Bethe, *Homer, I, Die Ilias*, 1914.

[2] Wilamowitz, *Die Heimkehr des Odysseus*, pp. 17.

[3] G. W. Nitzsch, *Die Sagenpoesie der Griechen*, 1852 ; *Beiträge zur Geschichte der epischen Poesie der Griechen*, 1862.

[4] See above, p. 7, n. 1.   [5] See above, p. 7 and n. 1.

[6] K. Lachmann, " Betrachtungen über Homers Ilias," *Abhandlungen der Akademie der Wissenschaften zu Berlin*, 1837 and 1841 ; new edition, by M. Haupt, 1847.

who goes to the extremes in discerpting Homer. Lachmann was a prominent scholar both in German and in classical philology; he came from the study of Teutonic epics and he tried to prove that the " Nibelungenlied " was founded upon earlier short ballads.   The same idea he transferred to Homer, and in order to show that the Iliad was a conflation of smaller independent poems he stressed the inconsistencies and contradictions unduly, ,But there·is another powerful idea underlying the views of Lachmann, the romantic idea of popular collective poetry which cannot be ascribed to the interference of any individual but which grows up unconsciously as a product of the collective mind of the people, an idea which had a long lasting influence going back to the great German poet and scholar, Herder.   There is something of mysticism in the rôle attributed to the popular mind ; we shall see that, as far as we know, epic songs are always created by certain individuals, the minstrels, even if these are anonymous.   This idea of a collective creation has seriously hampered the research into epic poetry of other peoples which offers very valuable analogies for the understanding of the origin and growth of Greek epic poetry.   For Steinthal, who first took up a comparative study of epic,[1] was obsessed by the idea of a creative genius of the people.

It was, of course, an implicit assumption that only short ballads were able to be preserved on the lips of the people. Lachmann found sixteen such songs in the Iliad.   They were fused, he thought, by the redaction committee of Peisistratos into a comprehensive poem because they treated cognate subjects.   In certain cases he conceded that a poem had appropriated the contents of an earlier poem or was composed as a continuation of another poem.   These concessions show the weakness of his position, for it would be a sheer miracle if independent ballads fluttering about as the leaves of the Sibylla had been able by mere redaction to coalesce into an organic whole, as the Iliad in fact is, in spite of all inconsistencies and deviations.   The *Liedertheorie*, which for a time caused so much excitement and counted so many fervid adherents, is no longer seriously taken into account.   It

[1] H. Steinthal, " Das Epos," *Zeitschrift für Völkerpsychologie und Sprachwissenschaft*, v, 1868, pp. 1.

is one of these working hypotheses which had to be tested, and as it did not correspond to reality had to be put aside. But the discussion was not altogether idle, and served to clear our understanding by eliminating certain views.

The analytical school, if the striving to dissolve the Homeric poems is taken to be inherent in the analysis, had to fall back upon more reasonable ways, and this was done by Kirchhoff [1] who laid down the lines which in the main are still followed by the most prominent adherents of this school. The object of his research was the Odyssey. He discarded the *Liedertheorie*, even if he assumed that sometimes a separate song may have been incorporated into the poem. He thinks that in the sources from which our Odyssey is drawn the old songs had already been worked over so thoroughly that the songs themselves cannot be discovered—only traces of them. The kernel of the Odyssey is taken to be a song of the adventures of Odysseus. Besides this poem there were other connected poems and to these poems a continuation was added. Finally, all these poems were put together by one man and worked up according to a definite plan, but not so thoroughly as to eliminate all discrepancies found in the earlier songs.

The foremost Homeric scholar of the present time, Wilamowitz, started from the principles of Kirchhoff but attained to different results. [2] Bethe has given another account of the earlier poems and the composition of the Odyssey. [3] His poet is an energetic redactor who welded together smaller epics into a firmly united composition. He is said to be somewhat later than the composer of the Iliad. Eduard Schwartz gave another bold reconstruction, suggesting three successive epics which were joined mechanically by a redactor. [4]

In a recent book Wilamowitz has modified his views. [5] The poet of the Odyssey, he says, joined together and worked over earlier poems. The kernel is Odysseus' tales of his

---

[1] A. Kirchhoff, *Die homerische Odyssee und ihre Entwicklung*, 1859, 2nd ed., 1879.

[2] U. v. Wilamowitz-Möllendorff, *Homerische Untersuchungen*, 1884.

[3] E. Bethe, *Homer, I1, Die Odyssee*, 1922.

[4] Ed. Schwartz, *Die Odyssee*, 1924.

[5] *Die Heimkehr des Odysseus*, 1927.

adventures in the court of the Phaeacians to which a continuation had been added ; the work of a later poet who
struck an almost bucolic style, Odysseus' visit to Eumaios,
etc. His poem must have ended with the final victory of
Odysseus. The trying of the bow and the slaughter of the
suitors are told in a different style, resembling that of the
Iliad in being more heroic, and belonging to another epos.
The man who composed our Odyssey united the poem concerning the adventures of Odysseus and another late epos
concerning the return of Telemachos. After the Odyssey
had been thus created some additions were made : the hunt
of the boar, the punished criminals in the Hades, and the
last book.

I do no more than mention the bulky work on the Odyssey
which Bérard published recently on the basis of previous
writings ; [1] even he assumes that the Odyssey was composed
of earlier poems.

A most attractive analysis of the Odyssey was recently
published by Woodhouse.[2] He will probably object to being
taken together with the separatists, for he is strongly convinced that the Odyssey is the work of a great poetical genius,
but we shall see that nevertheless there are certain reasons
for so doing. At least, he is an analytical unitarian. He
distinguishes various components which were used in the
formation of the Odyssey. Firstly, there are the deep-sea
yarns, fantastic tales of adventures on the sea. Secondly,
a series of five folk-tale motifs, not always followed up to
their end but cut and remodelled. For the formation of the
Odyssey, still another component is obviously needed—the
saga of Odysseus, a poetical tradition of the hero's life and
the historical kernel of the Odyssey. The quest and education of Telemachos and the lay of Calypso remain. Telemachos
is vital to our Odyssey, the figure is created by a genius.
Lastly, we have the Poet's Cement, episodes and pieces of
narrative and description inserted as connecting links or for
embellishment.

Thus the Odyssey is composed of pre-existing elements.

---

[1] V. Bérard, *Introduction à l'Odyssée*, 3 vols., 1924-25 ; *Les navigations d'Ulysse*, 3 vols., 1927-29.
[2] W. J. Woodhouse, *The Composition of Homer's Odyssey*, 1930.

The minstrel's choice of a subject within the mass of tradition was limited and directed by the tastes and desires of his audience, and the epic style itself was a part of this tradition created by generations of men. A vast mass of metrical material must have been in existence,—descriptions of real and imaginary localities, similes, schematic narratives of commonly recurring events, handed down from generation to generation, revised, added to and modified according to varying purposes. Homer used these materials, incorporating much that in actual wording was traditional and of an age older than his own, although much was fashioned by himself ; but these different parts can hardly be discerned. He treated the components mentioned with constructive genius, truth to nature, and poetical inspiration. The Odyssey was planned as a romance and is a romance. It is definitely the creation of a single master mind, none other than Homer's.

It is a merit of Woodhouse to have laid stress upon the folk-tale motifs utilized in the Odyssey ; a more detailed comparison with the folk-tales [1] would have brought out this point still more strongly. In regard to the composition his position is definitely analytical, and he emphasizes strongly and justly the rôle of the epic technique and the existence of older chants. But all these components were according to him moulded and welded together by one man, Homer, i.e. the author of the Odyssey. If it is thought that the epic tradition for a long time centred around the story of Odysseus, and consequently that lays concerning Odysseus were chanted for more than one generation and ultimately used by a certain poet for the composition of our Odyssey— and in view of what we know of epic tradition this cannot be said to be either impossible or improbable—we arrive at the separatist standpoint. The profound difference between Woodhouse and the separatists is, however, that he does not enter upon the minutiæ of an analysis of the extant text but analyses the materials only. Thus he discards, in fact, earlier epic versions and is able to attribute the creation

[1] This is done by L. Radermacher, " Die Erzählungen der Odyssee," *Sitzungsberichte der Akademie der Wissenschaften zu Wien,* clxxviii, 1915, No. 1. He adduces parallels from folk-tales of Odysseus' adventures on sea, the web of Penelope, the country of the Phaeacians, and the return of Odysseus.

of the Odyssey to one poet. I do not intend to proffer any opinion in this respect ; we encounter here the dividing line between separatists and unitarians, which is irreconcilable because it depends on subjective conviction.

Three scholars already mentioned have used similar treatment with regard to the Iliad. Bethe calls attention to the rapid and vivid, almost harsh style of the first book of the Iliad and recognizes the same style in certain other parts of the poem also.[1] Thus he makes out the original Iliad to be a small poem of about 1500 verses. It consisted of the kernel of the first book, the defeat of the Greeks, and finally the old form of the tale of Patroclos, the return of Achilles into the battle, the death of Hector and the dirge of Hecuba. It was a poem of a true tragic spirit. This was enlarged by others, and the narratives of Patroclos and of the death of Hector were worked up afresh. A later poet created our Iliad on this foundation, annexing various small epics which had grown up independently around the Iliad having the wrath of Achilles as their premise. Some independent epics, the deeds of Diomedes in Book v, and the lay of Dolon, Book x, were also incorporated by him. He re-worked these materials according to a plan and subordinated them to its leading idea, connecting them by passages of transition and references. This poet was no mere redactor but a real poetical genius. It must, however, be conceded that this is a little difficult to imagine, in regard to the rôle attributed to him by Bethe. The information concerning Peisistratos is taken to be an obscure reminiscence of the fact that the Homeric poems were brought into the form in which we have them in Athens. A certain Attic colouring of language is thought to prove this.

The great book in which Wilamowitz analyses the Iliad [2] comes between his two books on the Odyssey. Bethe placed at the beginning a really great and original poem which in time was surrounded and overgrown by a number of lateral off-shoots ; these were at last welded together by a man whom we perhaps should be more inclined to call a redactor than a poet. Wilamowitz' Homer is much more of a poet. He had, however, predecessors. The origin of the epics were

[1] E. Bethe, *Homer, I, Die Ilias*, 1914.
[2] U. v. Wilamowitz-Möllendorff, *Die Ilias und Homer*, 1916.

long past. The old lays of an early age had already before Homer been converted into epics which treated of different subjects and cycles, e.g. the Theban cycle, the voyage of the Argonauts, the Trojan cycle, etc. Thus there existed a very flourishing poetry of epics which were fairly extensive but much smaller than the Homeric poems. The epic language and technique had attained a full development, and epic poetry had found its home in Ionia. At a certain time a great poetical genius arose who may justly be called Homer. He conceived the plan of a comprehensive epos. In composing it he borrowed freely from the earlier epics, but he was a great and original poet whose creative power found a corresponding expression in artistic composition, poetical imagination and psychological characterization. Homer's Iliad comprehended Books I-VII, 321 and XI-XXIII, but in these certain changes were made later. The end, the death of Achilles, is lost and replaced by parts of Books XXIII and XXIV. Homer incorporated several small epics, sometimes reshaping or reworking them, sometimes only adding connecting passages. Ed. Schwartz follows the same line in regard to the origin of epics, but puts forward another opinion in regard to the small epos which served as materials for Homer.[1]

There are many other works of the separatist school. Some of them will be referred to in another connection. In order to illustrate both methods and result, the selection given of the works of the most recent and able adherents of the separatist view will be sufficient. My aim was to give an idea of methods and results, but for want of space it was only possible to enter upon the reasons adduced by them in a general way ; for estimating them justly a perusal of their books is indispensable. A concentrated review of the results attained by different scholars will, however, bring the uncertainty of the method to light ; for there are more opinions than authors, since authors have sometimes changed their views.

For those who want to know in greater detail what has been written on the Homeric question, there are excellent surveys covering the whole field of Homeric research up till

[1] Ed. Schwartz, *Zur Entstehung der Ilias*, 1918.

the present time ; two written from a separatist standpoint and one from an unitarian standpoint. The latter is Drerup's book to which I shall recur below,[1] the other two are the works of Finsler and Cauer. Finsler's book gives the most handy survey of Homeric materials and problems, including the history of the Homeric question.[2] His standpoint comes near to that of Wilamowitz, although he strives to give an unbiassed account. It is only occasionally that he advances opinions of his own, e.g. that the state organization depicted in Homer is that of the Ionian towns at the beginning of the historical age, and that the different way in which the gods are treated is a means for discerning early and late strata.

Cauer's book [3] served for many years as an introduction to the study of Homer, for he gives an admirable survey of the problems with, at the same time, an extensive appreciation of the archaeological and geographical materials. Cauer has, however, his own axe to grind. He is an adherent of the nucleus theory and the redaction by Peisistratos. The development of epics was, he thinks, a long process and their origins go back into the prehistoric age. His special hypothesis is that their cradle was Thessaly. On the basis of earlier lays, connected by their reference to the Trojan war, an epos was created, the subject of which was the wrath of Achilles. The motif of the wrath was taken from the myth of Meleagros. Its popularity gave rise to many new inventions, all referring to the same fundamental idea, but loosely connected with the main subject. They were handed down by oral tradition. As these poems were recited at the Panathenaic festival, they were written down, and a continuous narrative was created by the addition of connecting passages.

In the decade in which the Mycenaean civilization first came to light in all its marvellous splendour the separatists seemed to have carried the day, at least in Germany. One

---

[1] See below, pp. 18.

[2] G. Finsler, *Homer*, 2nd ed., 1913. A third edition of Part I, " Der Dichter und seine Welt," was re-edited by E. Tièche in 1924, with an additional survey of the works on Homer published between 1912 and 1923.

[3] P. Cauer, *Grundfragen der Homerkritik*, 1895, 3rd ed., 1923. The first volume and the first part of the second are thoroughly reworked by the author himself, but death stopped his work, and the last section, published by E. Bruhn, is taken over from the second edition with some additional matter.

of them was able to boast that the number of those who
believed in the unity of Homer was steadily decreasing. In
spite of vigorous opposition, the same ideas took hold upon
the most prominent English and French scholars too in the
end of the last century—Jebb,[1] Walter Leaf in his early works,[2]
and Maurice Croiset, the author of one of the best histories
of Greek literature which has ever been written.[3] In an
English history of Greek literature from the first decade of
this century, it is stated that time has suppressed the unitarians
and that all scholars are now separatists.[4]

Literary analysis and the reconstruction of earlier poems
which were used for the composition of our Homer, and con-
jectures as to their plots and ideas, seem to exercise a fascination over the human mind similar to that exercised by the
putting together of a zig-zag puzzle or by solving crosswords.
The difference is that in our case the pieces must first be cut
out by dissecting the apparent unity in which Homer has
come down to us, while the lines which serve as guides in
once again putting together the different parts are blurred,
and must be reconstructed from starting-points which are
all but indisputable.   Such literary research seems to be more
fascinating than research which tries to state elements of
culture and environment on historical lines.   For when the
Mycenaean civilization was discovered, and its connection with
Homer was recognized, the new and large vistas opened for
Homeric research were soon applied as a means to the old
end of discerning older and more recent strata and discovering
earlier poems which were the kernel of the Homeric epics or
had been incorporated into them.

2. MYCENAEAN DISCOVERIES AND HOMERIC RESEARCH

In regard to the bearing of the Mycenaean finds on Homer
the pioneer work was done by Helbig who illustrated the
Homeric epics from the monuments,[5] but in doing this

---

[1] R. C. Jebb, *Homer, An Introduction to the Iliad and the Odyssey,* 1887.
[2] Walter Leaf, *A Companion to the Iliad,* 1892.
[3] M. Croiset, *Histoire de la literature grecque,* I, 1887.
[4] W. Wright, *A History of Greek Literature,* 1907, p. 31.
[5] W. Helbig, *Das homerische Epos aus den Denkmälern erläutert,* 1884, 2nd
ed., 1887.

compiled his materials from all ages without much heeding to their historical setting; he adduced Mycenaean monuments as well as those of the classical age and even from the Etruscan civilization. It is Reichel's merit in his important book on Homeric armour and weapons [1] to have made an energetic and sagacious effort to distinguish between the Mycenaean and the later elements in Homer in this respect. He proved beyond doubt that an older kind of war equipment, unknown in historical Greece but appearing in Mycenaean monuments, was recorded in Homer. But there is a certain amount of confusion in the Homeric descriptions of weapons and armour due to the poet's lack of understanding of the old kind of equipment. It may be understood and perhaps pardoned that Reichel, in his joy over his really important discovery, went too far in explaining the Homeric passages along Mycenaean lines, assuming that interpolations and re-modellings were made in a later age in order to fit in the descriptions with the only kind of equipment known after the Mycenaean age.

Such mistakes became very serious when the difference in regard to armour and weapons was applied to discerning earlier and later strata in Homeric poetry. This was done by Robert.[2] His idea was very simple, viz. that Mycenaean weapons and no others were found in the early parts of the Iliad, and to this he added the assertion that the same early parts could be re-translated into the Aeolic dialect, according to Fick's principle. In the philological side of his work he was aided by Bechtel, and an attempt was made to print the original Iliad in the Aeolic dialect. I stated above that the attempt admittedly is a failure, and refer to the objections mentioned.[3] The cutting out of weapons and armour of the later fashion could be achieved only by the same violent and discrediting means as were needed in order to get rid of Ionic words and forms. On the whole, the attempts to distinguish older and later parts of the poems with the guidance of archaeological and cultural elements have proved unsuccessful. Such differences are mostly spoken of in general words when applied to the discerning of strata.

[1] W. Reichel, *Homerische Waffen*, 1894, 2nd ed., 1901.   Cp. below, pp. 143.
[2] C. Robert, *Studien zur Ilias*, 1901.   [3] Above, p. 9.

There was another flow of ideas for which both the ortho-
dox separatists and the unitarians cared but little, confined
as they were to their own circles of reasoning,—the striving
to harmonize the Homeric poems with the archaeological discoveries from the Mycenaean age and with the culture and
historical setting of that age, which, however, was and is a
matter of conjecture and reconstruction. The connection between Homer and Mycenae was there, and the problem had
to be worked through. Schliemann had a dilettante's fervid
and unreasoned faith in the exactness of Homer's descriptions and their actual application to the civilization and the
monuments which he discovered. He took Homer literally
and his faith was rewarded by his brilliant discoveries, a
most exciting corroboration of his views. It can be understood that this had a strong influence upon the minds of many
people.

His helper, the famous archaeologist Dörpfeld, whose merit
it is to have introduced scientific methods into the excavations
of Schliemann, proceeded on the same lines in regard to Homer,
and tried to prove the conformity of Homer's descriptions
with actual reality in Mycenaean times. Concerning Homer
his work was chiefly devoted to geography and topography.
He tried to prove that the indications in Homer correspond
to the sixth city of Troy, and that his description of the battle-
field in the Scamander valley between the sea and Troy was
in conformity with nature only if it is assumed that in that
age Scamander flowed in a bed, still partially extant, near
to the city.[1] He tried to trace the voyage of Telemachos
from Pylos to Sparta which has often been said to be geographically impossible. He was thus led to embrace the
opinion that the Homeric Pylos was situated on the coast
between the rivers Neda and Alpheios, and he found at Kakovatos the remains of an important Mycenaean site which he
held to be Nestor's Pylos, an opinion which is shared by many.[2]
Most famous and most disputed is his attempt to localize
the home of Odysseus on the island of Leucas which he assumes to be the old Ithaca, but this hypothesis has not been

[1] W. Dörpfeld, *Troja und Ilion*, 1902, pp. 601.
[2] W. Dörpfeld, " Alt-Pylos," *Mitteilungen des deutschen archäologischen
Instituts zu Athen*, xxxiii, 1908, pp. 295; K. Müller, *ibid.*, xxxiv, 1909,
pp. 269.

borne out by the finds.[1] He tried to discover the palace
of Odysseus. This striving to identify Homeric civilization
with the finds made by him led him to hold views on Greek
archaeology which are at variance with established results,
and thus led to certain discomfiture.

In Germany the analytical method, chiefly that of the
separatists but in recent years that of the unitarians also,
continued caring little for the bearing of the archaeological
finds on the Homeric problems, except the attempt, already
mentioned, to apply archaeology to the discerning of strata.
Research into the connections between the Homeric poems
and the Mycenaean age was taken up principally by English
scholars, and thus a difference between Homeric research in
England and in Germany was created which, ever widened,
persists to this day. It seems almost as if the two schools
hardly care for or know of each other, although they work
for the same great goal, a better understanding of Homer
and his origins.

I noted that separatism seemed to have carried the day
in England about the beginning of this century. There was,
however, a vigorous and clever opponent, a man whose scholarly merits are hardly justly appreciated because his statements often are sweeping and his writings witty, Andrew
Lang. He was a great admirer of Homer and a sagacious
defender of his poetical genius and unity. His first book [2]
was a criticism of separatism, adding some sweeping comparisons with other epics and a discussion of the archaeological
problems which are now out of date. He recurred to the
last-mentioned topic at greater length in another book,[3] the
main part of which consists of a discussion of the archaeological evidence. He advocates the unity of the civilization
described by Homer, suggesting it to be a transitional stage
intervening between the Mycenaean and the Geometric periods
when there was a knowledge of iron, but without the ability
to temper it properly, so that iron weapons were unreliable.
Consequently bronze was preferred for weapons, being more

[1] This view was propagated by Dörpfeld's adherents in very many writings.
For an account of the excavations on Leucas and a restatement of his views
see his large work, *Alt-Ithaka*, 2 vols., 1927.
[2] Andrew Lang, *Homer and the Epic*, 1893.
[3] Andrew Lang, *Homer and his Age*, 1906. Cp. below, pp. 140.

reliable in the throng of the battle, whilst iron was used for tools.[1] Likewise the Homeric description of the funerals are taken to testify to an intermediate age in which the body was cremated and the ashes covered by a cairn ; in the Geometric period there are both inhumation and cremation.[2] The picture of the political organization is said to be a loose feudalism, and with consistent uniformity the whole Iliad pursues Agamemnon's scheme of character and conduct, guided at once by feudal allegiance and feudal jealousy, and this uniformity testifies to the unity of Homer. It is very easy to fancy such a mixed civilization in a period of which we know next to nothing. We are not able to put the picture to the test, nor are we able to believe that a civilization so brilliant as that depicted by Homer falls in with an archaeological period whose only outstanding feature is its extreme poverty. Occasionally Lang admits that Homer imagines his heroes to have lived in a distant past, but a serious acceptance of this view would ruin his system.

In his last book [3] Lang restated and partially modified his views. I note solely his statement in regard to the question of unity. The Iliad is a work of one brief period because it bears all the notes of one age and is free from the characteristic traits of the preceding Achaean and of the following Geometric ages. That it is in the main the work of one man, is proved by the unity of thought, temper, character and ethos of epics and by the perfect consistency in the drawing of the characters. These are the time-honoured points of the unitarians. I need hardly remark that the alleged archaeological unity is open to controversy.

Between the publication of Lang's two last-mentioned books two important books were published which from both the negative and the positive side have affected Lang's arguments, Gilbert Murray's *Rise of the Greek Epic* and Ridgeway's *Early Age of Greece*.[4] Ridgeway is not primarily concerned with Homeric problems but with the pre-Greek civilization and origin and racial connections of the Greeks,

---

[1] Cp. below, p. 140.   [2] Cp. below, pp. 152.
[3] Andrew Lang, *The World of Homer*, 1910.
[4] W. Ridgeway, *The Early Age of Greece*, vol. i, 1901 ; vol. ii edited by A. F. S. Gow and D. S. Robertson, 1931.

their immigration and settling in Greece. He takes the Mycenaean civilization to belong to a pre-Achaean population
called by the Greeks Pelasgians. These people were dark-
haired and dark-skinned in contrast to the fair-haired Homeric
heroes. These were Achaeans, a Celtic tribe coming from the
north, who brought with them the use of iron, new military
equipment, a new mode of dress and the custom of cremation
of the dead. They took over the language of the conquered
population and were merged racially with them. Ridgeway
expressed his views concerning the origin of Homeric poetry
in a striking chapter. The myths embodied in the poems
are pre-Achaean. He is very severe against the separatists,
accusing them of want of literary appreciation and inability
to project themselves into the past and to place themselves
at the standpoint of men who lived under conditions far
removed from our own. The Homeric critics have failed to
comprehend the difference between a great original work
created by a genius out of old materials fused in the alembic
of the brain and the mere patch-work of a journeyman. The
bards continued to exercise their calling under the new masters
and sung their praises in their old language which became
that of the newcomers. Thus, minstrels lived at every court
in the mainland of Greece, and the Homeric poems were
composed before the Dorian invasion, not later than about
1000 B.C.

Gilbert Murray [1] should evidently be reckoned among the
separatists, for his ideas, especially that of the traditional
book referred to above,[2] would of course be deprecated by
the unitarians. He is very critical, and thinks that the Iliad
has many characteristics of a bad poem and that its subject
is second-rate, but that in spite of this it is a good poem,
which he admires profoundly. As he does not present any
analysis of the poem but relies upon an account of the elements
of civilization, he may conveniently find his place here. He
points to the gap, alike in literature and archaeology, between
the pre-Greek and the Greek civilizations. In this dark age
we must look for the beginnings of Greece. The basis of
Homer is tradition, not fiction. The immigrating Greeks had

---

[1] Gilbert Murray, *The Rise of the Greek Epic*, 1907, 3rd ed., 1924.
[2] Above, p. 4.

their mythical traditions and fostered epic lays, but narratives of the fall of the Mycenaean cities are wanting. There is the gap again. Murray leaves us in the dark in regard to the time when the traditional book came into existence, but it existed during the dark age. It was an heirloom hidden in the hands of some wise man, continually handed down to succeeding generations, and constantly remodelled. With each successive owner, with each successive great event, it was changed, expanded, and enlarged. The analogy on which Murray proceeds is that of Hebrew literature. The differences in regard to archaeology, to social and political life, to the rôle of the gods become, he thinks, clear when it is realized that Homer represents the ever-moving tradition of many generations of men. So changes of custom affected the book unconsciously and even consciously. Much importance is attributed to the expurgation of crude and barbarous beliefs and practices, a process which was continued by the Greek critics. The Iliad is a lay encrusted with additions and which has utterly outgrown its boundaries. This is accounted for by long years of recitation at various great Ionian festivals. Finally the book was transferred to Athens. Murray's book is very suggestive in many ways, but the point in which he differs from the nucleus theory, viz. that the poem existed in a written manuscript, constantly subject to revision, seems to be most improbable.

It has been mentioned that Bérard tried to explain the world of Homer by calling attention to geographical and physical facts,[1] but his attempts to find Phoenicians everywhere discredited his work.[2] The same line was taken up by Walter Leaf on a sounder basis. Leaf, who in the nineties wrote his *Companion to the Iliad* from a separatist standpoint, devoted his later works to proving the reality of Homeric geography, and to testing the underlying historical events from this point of view. In several journeys he made himself acquainted with these localities.

The result of his careful investigations of Trojan geography [3] is not only a corroboration of the correspondence between the

---

[1] Above, p. 14.
[2] V. Bérard, *Les Phéniciens et l'Odyssée*, 2 vols., 1902-3.
[3] Walter Leaf, *Troy*, 1912.

allusions in Homer and the ruins of the sixth city of Troy, but also that the landscape of the Iliad is the landscape of Troy and that the Homeric descriptions are drawn from the knowledge of an eye-witness. He points to the fact that the Trojan allies are arranged according to four lines : in the west the coast of Thracia, in the east the southern coast of the Black Sea, in the south-east the Mysians and the Phrygians, in the south the Maeonians, the Carians and the Lycians. He takes these four lines to represent the four trade routes which converged at Troy. The importance of Troy was due to its situation ; it blocked the mouth of the Hellespont and exacted toll of the traders who gathered to the market held beneath its walls. The Trojan war was due to the economic pressure on Greek trade exerted by Troy and an attempt to free the Greek trade from the control of the Trojans, the only feasible manner of doing so at that time being that implied in the story of the ten years' war, slowly bleeding Troy to death by exhaustion of its economic resources. For the war prevented trade, and the necessity of hiring foreign aid spoiled the wealth of Troy. Leaf takes the war and much of the description of it, and perhaps even the alleged cause, the rape of a Greek princess, to be historical facts.

The hypothesis by which the power of Troy and the war are accounted for is ingenious and certain to win favour in a time in which economic reasons are all important. But there is an initial flaw : why do not peoples from the fertile middle coast district of Asia Minor appear ? That country was certainly addicted to trade not less than the neighbouring peoples. If its inhabitants were Greek they ought to appear among the foes of Troy, and if they were not Greeks they ought to appear among the helpers of Troy. Moreover, the fundamental idea is seriously to be questioned. Trade is of course always important, but to what extent it determines politics depends on the spirit and conditions of the time. The Vikings raided many commercial towns, not in order to crush a trading monopoly of rivals, but simply to take booty. I cannot but think that the early Greek conquerors were much more like the Vikings than, say, the Hansa. Their expeditions to Syria and Egypt were not due to any desire to extend and secure their commerce, but solely to their instincts of migration and rapacity. It is very reasonable to suppose that the wealth of Troy was due to its situation which was most favourable to commerce, and that such a city attracted raids of Vikings fond of seizing booty by their swords. This is the only sound view according to my ideas of the age.

Leaf's second book [1] begins with emphasizing his opinion that the historical character of the Homeric narratives is not at all discredited by the interference of the gods—that is an epiphenomenon—and with an account of the Coming of the Achaeans. The Achaean conquest of Greece was the work of a small number of determined men, the displacement of one ruling caste by another, involving little destruction and slaughter. The invaders were reinforced by new hosts.—I remark in passing that their number cannot in the end have been very small since they were able to impress their language upon the country.—Warded off from the south by the power of the Lycians they turned to open up the way to the Black Sea by an attack on Troy, when the declining power of the Hittite Empire procured an opportunity for expansion in Asia Minor.

The main part of the book is an attempt to clear up the political geography of Greece according to Homer, an inquiry concerning the three main kingdoms of the Homeric world, those of Peleus, of Odysseus, and of Agamemnon. Curiously enough Leaf leaves out the dominion of Nestor which seems to be very well attested.[2] He endorses Dörpfeld's view that old Ithaca is Leucas, and thinks that the Taphians, a nation of traders and pirates located on Corcyra and holding a trade monopoly, shut off Greece from the west. Mycenae guarded the connections with northern Greece by way of the Isthmus. But the opinion of Bérard and Gilbert Murray that Mycenae was a castle built at a juncture of mountain passes for the purpose of levying taxes on all traffic that went through, or to keep open a safe trade route between the northern and the southern seas is rejected. Leaf points justly to the impossibility that an overland trade was carried on between the Peloponnese and Boeotia, the sea being an overwhelming

[1] Walter Leaf, *Homer and History*, 1915.
[2] See my *Mycenaean Origin of Greek Mythology*, pp. 79.

competitor. Mycenae owed its importance to its political
and military position, as it had means of constant and easy
communications with every part of the realm by high-roads.
The Catalogue, however, that curious and sometimes grotesque
product of post-Achaean times, must be put aside. At last
the time came when the forces of the Achaeans were exhausted
and they became fused with the conquered population ; a mixture ensuing which is visible in religion especially. The
foundations of the Greek epos were contemporaneous with
the impulse of Greek migration ; it dates from the century
or so which passed between the fall of Troy and the full
tide of settlement in Asia Minor.

In the problem of the connection of Homeric poetry with
the Minoan and Mycenaean civilization, Sir Arthur Evans
gave voice to his weighty opinion in a presidential address
read to the Hellenic Society.[1] What he has to say, drawing,
as he does, on a life-long and unsurpassed knowledge of these
cultures, is worthy of the closest attention. He is of the
opinion that the dominant factor in Greece was non-Greek
down to the twelfth century B.C., but that there was a subject race of Greek stock which at last got the upper hand,
reinforced by fresh swarms of immigrants. The age in which
the Homeric poems took their characteristic shape was sub-
Mycenaean or proto-Geometric, a period in which the use
of bronze was giving place to that of iron and in which Mycenaean art belonged already to the past. Consequently the
question arises how Homer is able to describe Mycenaean
surroundings, e.g. the huge body shield, etc. In the Homeric
descriptions of, e.g. Achilles' shield, he finds the spirit of
Minoan art and thinks that such works as the siege scene on
a silver vase from Mycenae (fig. 11) and the town mosaic
from Cnossos were the models ; the Homeric similes relating
to animals are kindred with the naturalistic spirit of the same
art.[2] His solution of the problem is that in Mycenaean
times there existed epics in the pre-Greek language which,
in a bilingual medium such as must have existed for some
time, were taken over into Greek when the Greeks became

[1] A. J. Evans, "The Minoan and Mycenaean Element in Hellenic Life,"
Journal of Hellenic Studies, xxxii, 1912, pp. 277.
[2] This point of view had been brought forward by Winter also. See
below, pp. 275.

dominant. In such conditions the taking over and absorption of the earlier materials mentioned were possible. The Homeric poems in the form in which they finally took shape are the result of a prolonged effort to harmonize the old and the new elements. In the nature of things this result was often incompletely attained. The patchwork is frequently evident. Contradictory features are found such as would not have co-existed at any period. Finally, he points to the fact that, apart from oral tradition, we have to reckon with written record and perhaps with a revival of Minoan patterns in the archaic age.

There is much in these views and words to which I gladly subscribe, above all the serious taking up of the problem how the Mycenaean elements came down into Homeric poetry. Evans is, in fact, a separatist, though not in the usual sense of the word. According to him epic poetry was of long duration; it was constantly rehandled, and, in being rehandled, it was remodelled. The Mycenaean elements were preserved by the long-enduring epic tradition and incorporated into the Homeric poems, which took their definite shape in post-Mycenaean days, in the transitional period between the Bronze and the Iron Ages. The remodelling was evidently most effective when the epics were translated from the Minoan into the Greek language. Here Evans put a great obstacle into his own way because of his opinion in regard to the nationality of the dominating population in the Mycenaean Age. The handing down of the epics would evidently be much simpler, if the epics from the beginning were composed in the Greek language. We shall recur to this question, in which I think that Evans errs. His adherence to Lang's view of the creation of the epics, which have come down to us, in the transitional period between the Bronze and the Iron Ages, is by no means vital to his view of the problem. The mixture by which he accounts for the preservation of the clearly Mycenaean elements may explain the mixture in other respects equally as well as this hypothesis.

The scholars who devoted their work to proving the conformity of Homer with actual facts in archaeology, geography, and history were partly unitarians in the ill-considered and unreasoned sense that they took Homer to be wholly

Mycenaean, overlooking the contradictory elements. They were partly separatists but, except for Evans in his presidential address, they did not give a clear account of the growth of the poems, but preferred to discuss the question of the old background, and were content with a general statement of their views as to the origin and development of epics. They entered little upon the problem whether Homer contains elements from various ages, their main concern being the old background of the epics.

I cannot help thinking that there is a certain connection between this tendency of Homeric research and the renascence of unitarianism in recent years. For the research just mentioned tends to prove a consistent cycle of facts underlying the poems. On the other hand, conceding that the general principle of the separatists was right, and assuming that the elements of civilization were a mixture made up of elements from various historical periods, the new lights afforded would reasonably be expected to bring the problem to an issue. When the attempts in this direction proved to be a failure, people were prepared to fall back upon the opposite view, thinking that each of the poems, or both, were a creation of one poetical genius and not a mosaic of songs of various poets, which were cut up and remodelled in order to be adapted to a certain frame.

3. The Unitarians

The unitarians were not done away with, although it would almost seem so, about the end of the last century. In this century their views came to the fore again. The most prominent unitarian in Germany was Rothe.[1] Beginning as an adherent of Kirchhoff he was, through prolonged study of Homer, converted into a fervid unitarian. The unitarians are, as remarked, analysts in a certain sense. In his treatment of the Iliad, Rothe emphasized that it is a work conceived with plan and purpose by one and the same poet. He put forward points of view drawn from the composition of the poem through which he tried to account for and to explain the arrangement of the various parts. He

[1] Carl Rothe, *Die Ilias als Dichtung*, 1910.

did not deny that Homer used earlier sources and even poems, but he considered the attempt to discern these as vain.

The most comprehensive and learned attempt of recent years to defend the unity of Homer is due to Drerup.[1] The analysis of the Odyssey by his pupil Stürmer and that of the fifth book of the Iliad by himself [2] may be put on one side ; they are as open to dispute and objections as such analyses are wont to be. But the introductory volume which reviews the materials of the Homeric problem, its history, and the various views, with a full bibliography, is a very useful book, even if the account given is from an extremely unitarian point of view and contains vivid polemics and dictatorial judgments.

It is to be hailed with special satisfaction that Drerup has collected the materials of the epics of other peoples in a substantial survey with references. But when he comes to the application of the insight into the life and growth of epics which ought to be attained by this survey, he is curiously hampered by his efforts to free Homer from debt to predecessors. He states justly that the unity of the myth and the unity of the epos are two different things and that a tendency towards unity is contained already in the attractiveness of certain central epic ideas ; thus cycles of lays (*Lieder*) came into existence. These popular lays could not, however, spontaneously coalesce into an epic unity, a great epos. The poetical economy of an epos is other than that of lays. The arrangement into episodes and the psychological exposition of the materials mark the progress from separate songs to epics. The last is true, especially in regard to Homer, but not in all cases. Here the influence of the research of Ker and Heusler [3] into the forms of popular literature is visible. In denying the existence of fixed smaller epic chants Drerup runs counter to the evidence collected by himself ; all that can be said is that every word is not

[1] E. Drerup, *Homerische Poetik*, i, " Das Homerproblem in der Gegenwart, Prinzipien und- Methoden der Homererklärung," iii, " Die Rhapsodien der Odyssee," by F. Stürmer, 1921.
[2] E. Drerup, *Das fünfte Buch der Ilias*, " Grundlagen einer homerischen Poetik," 1913.
[3] W. P. Ker, *Epic and Romance*, 1896, 2nd ed., 1908, reprinted, 1922; A. Heusler, *Lied und Epos*, 1905.

invariably laid down. Epic chants are very often repeated
in substantially the same form but with slight variations
in details. His contrary assertion is due to his effort to vin-
dicate the original and creative genius of Homer to the utmost.

The all-pervading idea is that of the self-sufficiency of
Homer's creative genius. He created his language according
to his subjective will ; the so-called aeolisms are but archaisms or at most due to the mixing up of tribes. He abstracted
his cultural milieu partly consciously, partly unconsciously,
mixing up old and new elements.[1] He construed his geography, perhaps using old reminiscences occurring in lays
(*liedhafte Erinnerungen*) and descriptions of travellers. Drerup
makes, however, the valuable concession that Homer used
typical elements and stock expressions which preserved
elements of an earlier civilization, and he thinks that the
Trojan cycle was created in the Peloponnese, perhaps at
the court of Mycenae, incorporating Achilles from an earlier
Thessalian stage of epics. These facts point to a view more
conforming with reality, but they are put on one side.

Drerup turns to what he considers the right way and
what he calls poetic idealism. He asserts that the Homeric
poems are unities written down by Homer himself. The
poems show a certain ethical idea. The economy of events
and its effect in regard to the composition of the poems are
conditioned by the fact that the great epics must be recited
in instalments, the length of which ought not to surpass one
and a half to two hours or at most 1000 to 1200 verses—a
longer recital being physically impossible. Eighteen such
rhapsodies are found in the Iliad ; it is conceded that a like
division in the Odyssey is more subject to doubt. This necessity of dividing the great epos into parts accounts for certain
inconsistencies and breaks. For the rhapsodies must be
rounded off so as to be self-containing to a certain extent,
in the same way as a single lecture of a series on a coherent
subject. The exposition is subordinate to the poetical will
and purpose of the author ; retardations and deviations and

---

[1] This view is shared by E. Belzner, *Homerische Probleme*, i, " Die kul-
turellen Verhältnisse der Odyssee als kritische Instanz," 1911 ; ii, " Die
Komposition der Odyssee," 1912.

even the appearance and the vanishing of personages are to be viewed from this point of view.

There must, even according to Drerup, have been some kind of lays before Homer, in which a part of the materials of his poems was contained; other parts he invented himself. But Drerup has not made clear what he thinks to be the relation between these lays and Homer. He put this question on one side with his verdict of Homer's creative poetical genius. To enhance this the preceding stages are as far as possible neglected, although all analogies from the epics of other peoples would lead us to assume that they had a great influence. Ancient poets and epic poets especially did not think that the greatest possible independence of previous writers increases a poet's glory. They sought their glory, not in creating a new kind of literature, but in creating something better than others. The standpoint of a modified separatism, e.g. that of Wilamowitz, placing Homer in the midst of a rich development of epics, seems to me to be easier to understand than this view which exalts Homer on a lonely pedestal.

Scott began, similarly to Rothe, as an adherent of separatist views and was converted into a most zealous and able defender of the unity of Homer.[1] He follows, of course, the same main lines as Drerup and keenly advocates the view that the Iliad and the Odyssey have the same author. But Scott is a very skilled advocate of Homeric unity and brings up many good points. His special field is statistical inquiry into the Homeric language, and he has put it beyond doubt that the alleged discrepancies in this regard between the Iliad and the Odyssey do not exist. A similar method is applied to the repeated verses which are often quoted as a testimony to the late origin of certain parts. The contradictions are treated fully, with the result that real contradictions are very few and trifling, and due to the lapse of memory of the poet. Others are only assumed, and due to the failure to translate or to understand the meaning of the poet. Finally, other inconsistencies depend on a change of the poetic purpose or a shifting point of view of the various actors in the poem. What is sometimes called inconsistency

[1] J. A. Scott, *The Unity of Homer*, 1921.

is often due to Homer's love for withholding the crisis and
for prolonging the suspense in cases of great excitement.

Especially striking are the chapters devoted to Homer's
characterization of his gods and heroes. Homer is not trying
to arouse a feeling of affection or reverence for the gods,
they are portrayed with the hand of a poet who was not a
teacher of ethics or of religion. The heroes are human beings,
each with his own life and his own problems. Homer creates
and individualizes the characters, not by describing them,
but by exposing the impression they make on others. The
unity of the character of each single hero is considered to
be a proof of the unity of the Homeric poems, especially
when compared with the different characterization in later
myths and authors. A large part of the plot and of the
characters is ascribed to the imaginative genius of Homer.

What Scott states concerning Homeric language seems
somewhat to conflict with the absolute independence of
Homer, for it is recognized that his language is derived from
a poetical art earlier than his. It is said that the grace and
the ease with which the words fall into dactylic rhythm could
have come only after ages of poetical development. Language
so rich and so complicated as Homer's contains within itself
the evidence of the heritage of many generations of poets.
One may think that Homer was influenced not only by the
language of these earlier poems, whose existence evidently
is implied, but by their contents also.

During its best period, antiquity considered Homer as
the author of the Iliad and the Odyssey only ; the current
opinion which ascribes the cyclical poems to him being of
late origin. Homer lived in the ninth century B.C., east of
the Aegean, and he pictures the Mycenaean civilization near
the time of its collapse about 1100 B.C. Scott's treatment
of the archaeological details is very questionable and cursory,
and is due to his wish even here to find the wished-for uniformity. One important remark cannot be passed over, viz.
that the seventh and sixth centuries B.C. were centuries of
short songs ; the great names in literature belong to lyrics.
The different kind of literature follow each other in Greece ;
when lyrics declined, tragedy followed. The bloom of epic
poetry must precede the age of lyrics ; the composition of

the Homeric epics cannot be carried down into the seventh and sixth centuries B.C. I would like to add that in every period and kind of Greek literature we find a number of great poets rivalling one another in genius. Why should the epical age be an exception to this? The solitariness of Homer's genius seems at variance with all our knowledge of Greek poetry and literature.

Bowra also belongs to the unitarians in a recently published and attractive book,[1] but on the other hand, he emphasizes strongly the traditional elements in art and language ; he believes in the Mycenaean background of the epics and proves this by evident examples. There are points of view which come very near to those advanced by the present writer.

4. SUMMARY

There is unanimity on one point, viz. that poetry of some kind existed before Homer on which Homeric poetry drew, but beyond this, agreement ceases. Only the extreme separatist theory is disposed of, the view that this earlier poetry was composed of lays, connected because they referred to the same cycle, and that they almost spontaneously coalesced into a great epos. Then we have the nucleus theory. An original poem based on earlier traditions was devised treating an episode which is central in the preserved epics, the deeds of Achilles or his wrath, the adventures of Odysseus or his return. This poem attracted kindred material and new poems grew up around it. Thus the original poem was extended and enlarged in lapse of time. Even this hypothesis is now abandoned in its simple and original form. But the nucleus theory as well as the little lay theory have left their traces in that more complicated theory which now has replaced them with the separatists. It may be called the compilation theory. It is admitted that the highly refined and perfected handling of the language and metre points to long practice in epic poetry. There were innumerable earlier lays. These lays were collected, reworked and connected by a great poet according to a leading idea, a plot. The popularity of his

---

[1] C. M. Bowra, *Tradition and Design in the Iliad*, 1930.

poem gave rise to other poems which were incorporated and added to the great poem, and likewise other independent poems were inserted. That may seem very reasonable, but the great difficulty is the question in what stage of the development of epics this great poet interfered. Some opinions come near to the nucleus theory, others to the lay theory, the difference in regard to the lay theory always being that the composition of the poem implied a conscious reworking of the earlier songs by a poet. The most consistent representative of this theory is Wilamowitz. It is a premise that so much is left of the original independence of the earlier songs that an analysis can discover them as separate parts incorporated into the great poem.

And what is Homer ? What tradition has to say of him is but legendary. To the lay theory he was a collective name for Greek epic poetry or the eponymous ancestor of a minstrels' guild, the Homeridae. To the nucleus theory he is, of course, the inventor of the original poem around which later accretions crystallized. It is more difficult to say what he is to the compilation theory. As I stated, to this view Homer is a great poet, but according to our views of a poet's creative work his procedure was curious. He simply took over several earlier epic poems and welded them together according to a plan conceived by himself. He cut them up and refashioned them, but to a large extent they were left in their original wording so that they can be made out and recognized by their various styles and by the sutures, for he did not quite succeed in effacing their earlier independency. His creative genius did not achieve a harmonious whole bearing throughout his own stamp. Hence it is not astonishing that many scholars think that Homer was not a great and creative poet but a mere redactor who pieced together already existing smaller epics into a large epos, and that he did this without great poetical skill. The attempts to discover the earlier poems which Homer welded together into his great poem seem, at least from an unitarian point of view, to be somewhat contradictory to the praise of his creative poetical genius. Those who emphasize the poetical genius and achievement of Homer have, in fact, approached not a little to the point of view of the unitarians.

This view may be illustrated by a comparison.[1] One of the most impressive and harmonious works of Roman architecture is the arch of Constantine, but it is pieced together of stones and sculptures from very different ages, from the time of Trajan, of Hadrian and of Constantine himself. The differences in style of the sculptures is seen by everybody, but in spite of this everybody acknowledges the grandeur of the work. Mischievous critics will say that the architect pieced together his work almost as a mosaic of stones from different ages ; in spite of this, he created a masterpiece of architectural harmony. The view on the creation of the Homeric poems sketched above is similar to this example from the history of architecture.

The hotly disputed question whether Homer was a great poet or a mere redactor is conditioned by our views in regard to poetical creation and thus of a highly subjective order. The conception of literary propriety emerged only slowly. In our age the originality of a poet is attested not only by the form which he gives to his materials and by the manner in which he handles it, but even more by his inventing the matter and the plot. Shakespeare and the Greek tragedians had other ideas in regard to the last-mentioned point ; they borrowed their matter freely from others but rehandled it thoroughly. If we turn to epics of an age in which books were written but not read by the general public who knew poetry only by hearing it, we hear that minstrels guarded jealously a book in which their chants were written down. The reason is evident. If the book fell into the hands of others they might use the chants freely. In an age in which oral tradition was prevailing or the only one existing we may infer that the poetical heritage was much more freely, we might perhaps say, unscrupulously appropriated and handled by everybody who happened to acquire it. We shall try to form a conception of this state of things later. Under such circumstances a poetical genius may have expressed itself and asserted itself in a manner quite dissimilar to that which we are wont and apt to think of as the normal and true one.

Given that Homer composed the Homeric poems drawing

[1] I borrow it from Sir Arthur Evans, loc. cit., p. 288.

on earlier poems and granted that our knowledge as to how
he handled his poems is wanting, the one extreme is the view
that he was a mere redactor, the view which emphasizes his
failures in achieving a harmonious whole. The other extreme
is the view which emphasizes the plan commanding the whole,
and converts the inconsistencies into merits explaining them
as means to a poetical end and effect. This Homer is as far
as possible made to approach to the standards now prevailing
of poetical creative imagination, whilst the other Homer is
measured with the same standards, and as he does not correspond to them is called a mere redactor. It is acknowledged
that the unitarian Homer worked on the basis of earlier poems,
but in order to assert his independency these poems are put
on one side and the distance between them and the epos is
enlarged ; they are not allowed to be called epic poems.

5. Mythology in Homeric Research

Even modern poetry and fiction take their materials from
experience, but recast events and characters so that they are
not recognizable. So-called key-novels are justly considered
to be a base form of literature. Thus a modern author invents
and creates not only the plot of his story but also all essential
parts of it, personages and events, even if it is not a *creatio
ex nihilo*. What about Homer in this respect ? Did he
invent and create not only form and plot of his poem but
also his personages and the events described, or did he take
them over from tradition ? If the question was not put by
earlier scholars, treating the Homeric problem, the omission
depended on their innate and almost unconscious opinion
that the myths were of ancient origin, much earlier than
Homer. But by their methods the separatists began to
undermine this opinion. For if the kernel of the Iliad, e.g.,
was a poem on the wrath of Achilles, and still more, if this
motif was taken over from the myth of Meleagros,[1] if the
voyage of Telemachos is a later addition, these motifs are
probably to be ascribed to the invention of the poet who
composed the poems. Their mythical importance is very

---

[1] Finsler, *Homer*, 1st ed., p. 217 ; supported by Cauer, *Grundfragen der
Homerkritik*, 3rd ed., p. 265, and by Mülder ; see below, p. 40.

slight. There is a marked difference between events and scenes which can hardly be called myths in the proper sense of the word, e.g. the voyage of Telemachos, or the meeting of Hector and Andromache, and the traditional myths. Such scenes are of no importance to the myth as such ; they are essentially pieces of psychological characterization, and we have the feeling that they very well, perhaps probably, may be the inventions of a poet. There are certainly both in Homer, both traditional myths and poetical fictions. But where is the dividing line ? What is to be ascribed to tradition taken over by a poet, and what to his own imagination ? Invention is, of course, not to be taken to be absolute in all cases, the poet may have borrowed names and events. The question is whether he remoulded them so that there came about something essentially new in poetry.

As long as the school of comparative mythology prevailed, the question seemed to be idle, for it took the myths without question to be old Aryan heritage. They were thought originally to be nature myths and divine myths which had been converted into heroic myths. A belated adherent of this opinion was the eminent philologist Usener in his treatment of the mythical materials underlying Homer.[1] He tried to prove that the fall of Troy is a reflection of a sacred ceremony enacted at Delphi and that even the shameless Thersites is an old god. In spite of his vast learning and sagacity these hypotheses are too frail and improbable.

Separatists used myths too as tools in their handiwork, and they were consequently driven to take up the problem in its full extent. This was first done by Niese.[2] He proceeded in the usual manner of analytical separatism, exaggerating it not a little. His fundamental idea is that the development of the myths is achieved through the development of Homeric poetry. Originally no other epic poems existed, he thinks, than the Iliad and the Odyssey, and the Trojan cycle existed in these poems only. They were in their origins rather short ; the now existing poems are a

---

[1] H. Usener, " Der Stoff des griechischen Epos," *Sitzungsberichte der Akademie der Wissenschaften zu Wien*, cxxxvii, 1897, No. 3; reprinted in his *Kleine Schriften*, iv, 1913, pp. 199.

[2] B. Niese, *Die Entwicklung der homerischen Poesie*, 1882.

chaos of accretions and additions from various times, but
all are fitted into an already existing situation. They have
the preceding and the following events as their premises.
The Cyclic poets are later than Homer ; they are dependent
on him and only on him.   From hints in Homer which they
connected and supplemented they produced a complete
mythical history. Among the additions in Homer are the
participation of the gods in the battle and even more the
scenes enacted in Olympus, the use of the chariot, and very
many of the heroes. The original poem had only a few
personages. Niese deprecates the old view supposing the
mythical materials of which the Homeric poems are composed to be current among the people before the composition of the poems. It is said to be founded on the view
that the work of Homer is popular poetry, whilst it is, on
the contrary, artistic poetry. Even Achilles, the chief personage of the Iliad, is a figure created by the poet's imagination, for he exists only in and through the Iliad. In the
Homeric poems myth is in a nebulous condition ; we are asked
to see how it is created and how it crystallizes through the
inventions of the poets.

In spite of his new and bold ideas, Niese's book failed
to produce much effect. He proceeded by the usual analytical method ; and the idea that the myths were developed
through the agency of the Homeric poets was but an assertion.
Analysis cannot prove this thesis. It will proceed as con-
sistently, if it is supposed that those who made additions
picked out their materials from current myths, and that
hints as to myths are not accidental inventions but refer
to known myths which sometimes were told in various versions.

It was not feasible to deduce the development of the
Homeric myths from an analysis of the poems only ; there
must be some external evidence which could be used for
this purpose, and the existence of such evidence was presupposed by the literary analysis in so far as it tried to prove
the influence of other epics which had been incorporated into
Homer, or had served as models or inspirations for his poems.
The opinion was mentioned that the key motif of the Iliad,
the wrath of Achilles, was modelled upon an earlier poem
concerning the wrath of Meleagros. Such ideas are the

foundation of the work of Mülder.[1] The Iliad is, he thinks, composed according to a definite plan and the final fruit of a rich development of poetry. The main element of the Iliad is a poem concerning Achilles, who is a representative of the Aeolian colonization in Asia Minor. The model was a poem on the war against Thebes, in which Adrastos was replaced by Agamemnon. The connecting motif, the wrath of Achilles, was borrowed from a poem on Meleagros. The frailty of this construction need hardly be pointed out.

The analysis of the adventures of Odysseus on the sea presents a difficulty remarked long ago, viz. that some of the adventures seem to be localized in the Black Sea, whilst most of them clearly take place in the western sea. This seems hardly astonishing if various sailors' stories were attached to one and the same man, but Meuli's attempt to unravel the relations [2] is interesting. He admits that the narrative of the Odyssey is an artistic unity, but states that the voyages in the two regions just mentioned, the Black Sea and the western sea, are mixed up. Old poems have been reworked, but beneath them is a poem, not of Odysseus, but referring to the voyage of the Argonauts. I do not think it unlikely that the old and celebrated myth of the Argonauts had its share in forming the adventures of Odysseus, but I think that the details must remain uncertain.

These scholars and others tried to prove an influence of earlier epics concerning other subjects upon the development of the Homeric myths, but they did not try to get behind the development of the myths in poetry. If analysis was to be carried further other evidence was wanted, and this evidence was near at hand, if a method were applied which was very widely used in mythological research since K. O. Müller originated it. According to him the heroes belonged to certain Greek tribes, and wandered with them when these tribes emigrated to other localities. Sometimes a cult might survive the emigration or the vanishing of the tribe to which the hero belonged, and might thus give a clue for discovering the locality in which the tribe had been settled in an earlier

---

[1] D. Mülder, *Die Ilias und ihre Quellen*, 1910.
[2] K. Meuli, *Odyssee und Argonautica*, Dissertation, Basle, 1921.

time. The localization of the heroes consequently afforded
proofs for the wanderings of the tribes.

The principle has a sound foundation, especially if heroic
mythology is taken to imply historical reminiscences converted into myths, for then it is evident that a hero was
localized originally among a certain people. The application
of the principle leads us, however, into great difficulties and
shows that it must be used with caution. Firstly, it must
be questioned whether myths always follow the wanderings
of the tribes or if they do not spread independently. The
latter is the case in other countries.[1] Secondly, it has to be
considered whether a localization of a hero, and especially
of Homeric heroes, is early or late. For the fame of Homer
was so great in a later age that people everywhere were inclined to find traces of his heroes or to apply their names
to native cults and curiosities. We remember, e.g. that the
founding of the Greek colonies in Italy, etc., was ascribed
to Homeric heroes roaming about after the destruction of
Troy. Similar inventions occur in Greece.

Mythological arguments are often adduced in Homeric
research in order to localize the country where the poems
or parts of them originated. That the chief personage of the
Iliad, Achilles, is a Thessalian hero is to Cauer a very important argument for his assumption of a Thessalian origin
of the poems which were ultimately developed into our Iliad,
and he adduces a series of other Thessalian elements in order
to corroborate this opinion.[2] He even thinks with Busolt [3]
that Argos is originally the Thessalian district with this name ;
consequently the Argives were originally a Thessalian tribe.
The Thessalian heroes were brought to Asia Minor by Thessalian emigrants and were grafted on to the battles which the
colonists fought with the indigenous population in Aeolia.
In this manner the myth of the Trojan war came into existence. Achilles was in a certain sense made the hero of
the Aeolian colonization of north-western Asia Minor.

It is certain that Achilles belongs to southern Thessaly
and the Spercheios valley which borders it to the south.

---

[1] Such is, e.g., the case of the Teutonic myths ; see below, p. 186.

[2] P. Cauer, *Grundfragen der Homerkritik*, 3rd ed., pp. 241.

[3] Loc. cit., pp. 284 ; G. Busolt, *Griechische, Geschichte*, 2nd ed., i, 1893,
p. 223, n. 1.

But the Trojan cycle has many other heroes, and many of them, and especially the overlord, are said to be Peloponnesians. The problem is, where it is that they were brought together and made personages of the same cycle of myths. Cauer's arguments are rejected by others. Drerup is of the opinion that Achilles was added to the cycle, and that the fact that the most prominent heroes of the Iliad belong to the Peloponnese proves that the uniting of the myths took place in Argolis.[1] He recognizes a primitive Thessalian stage of the formation of the Trojan cycle which he ascribes to very early Mycenaean or pre-Mycenaean times, and another later stage in which the myth of the Trojan war, under the leadership of Agamemnon, was invented and the Achilles myth incorporated into the cycle. This took place probably at the court of Mycenae in the bloom of the Mycenaean civilization. The third stage was the elaboration of the Homeric poems founded upon the earlier Argive lays, and this took place in Asia Minor.

So much for the Trojan cycle as a whole in its relation to the Homeric poems. Scholars who tried to prove that certain parts were additions or lays incorporated into the Homeric poems found welcome arguments in the fact that mention is made of heroes who are localized in various parts of Greece. It is often said that a minstrel when chanting in the court of a certain prince would add the praise of his ancestors and his family. E.g. the Rhodian hero Tlepolemos, a son of Heracles, occurs only once,[2] and this passage is thought to be an addition inserted by some late minstrel in honour of the descendants of Tlepolemos. It has also been said that historical events have been inserted into the Homeric poems. Mention is made of a Spartan influence. Agamemnon and Menelaos are thought to be co-regents as were the Spartan kings, and the promise of Agamemnon to give to Achilles seven Messenian towns is said to reflect the conquest of Messenia by the Spartans.[3]

[1] Cp. above, p. 32.

[2] *Il.*, v, vv. 628-662, not regarding the passage in the *Catalogue of the Ships*, ii, vv. 653-670.

[3] Finsler, *Homer*, 2nd ed., p. 217. The Lycians are also said to have a double kingship, and it is assumed that this is analogous to the Roman consulate by Wilamowitz, *Homerische Untersuchungen*, p. 279, n. 15; cp. Ed. Meyer, *Geschichte des Altertums*, ii, p. 343. The supposition is unwarranted and the comparison is not correct. Cp. below, p. 222, n. 1.

As stated above the problem amounts to this question—
how the heroes mentioned by Homer and localized in various
parts of Greece were brought together into one cycle. To
take an example, Wilamowitz states [1] that Phthiotians and
Magnesians who emigrated to Aeolia brought their Achilles
with them, that the house of Agamemnon originated at Cyme
and on Lesbos, whilst his appearing as king in the mainland
of Greece is due to epic poetry ; that Ionians in whose towns
descendants of Glaucos and Sarpedon were rulers, introduced
these heroes into the epos, and that the Colophonians who
were said to have emigrated from Pylos added Nestor and
his exploits.   According to him the Trojan cycle was brought
together in Asia Minor of elements derived from various parts,
especially of the mainland of Greece. With regard to the
fundamental idea, the war against Troy, he takes this to be
a reminiscence of a historical fact, a vain attempt of the
Greeks at an early date to gain foothold in the Scamander
valley.

The ideas which here come into play were utilized by
Bethe in the third volume of his great work on Homer in
order to explain at one time the growth of Homeric poetry
and the development of the cycle of myths.[2] This attempt
is so comprehensive and so important in regard to the relation between myths and epic poetry that it will be necessary
to dwell upon it at length and to criticize its soundness.
Bethe takes as premises what he thinks to have established
in the first two volumes, viz. that the Iliad was not composed before 600 B.C. and that the Odyssey and the cyclic
epics are still later ; I do not enter upon a criticism of this
very questionable date.   In regard to the question whether
myths are founded on historical reminiscences or are pure
fiction, his answer is that heroic myths on one hand are poetical
fiction, but that on the other hand, they start from a poetical
remodelling of historical events which became more and
more covered up by poetical motifs so that at last a few

---

[1] Wilamowitz, " Die griechische Heldensage," ii, *Sitzungsberichte der
Akademie der Wissenschaften zu Berlin*, 1925, p. 241. Cp. my *Mycenaean
Origin of Greek Mythology*, pp. 45.
[2] E. Bethe, *Homer*, iii, 1927. The fundamental ideas had been set forth
already in his paper, " Homer und die Heldensage," *Neue Jahrbücher für
das klassische Altertum*, vii, 1901, pp. 657.

names only are recognizable as historical elements. But Troy is fictitious. The sixth city of Troy was not destroyed by the Greeks but by Thracian tribes which immigrated to Asia Minor about 1200 B.C. This is quite possible, for it is an established fact that the Phrygians, which were a Thracian tribe, overthrew the Hittite kingdom about this time. A further fact is that certain ceramics of the seventh city of Troy (the *Buckelkeramik*) are non-Greek, and are with probability referred to the Thracian tribe of the Trerians which inhabited this district in the beginning of the historical age.[1] Greek ceramics appear only in the end of the Geometric Age, i.e. c. 700 B.C., and the colonization of Aeolia by the Greeks began at this date.[2] The conclusion that some of the Thracians who destroyed Troy settled there and warded off the Greeks through five centuries is, however, not warranted, for the *Buckelkeramik* belongs to the second layer of the seventh city, the first layer containing finds kindred with these of the sixth city.[3] So Bethe denies any historical kernel of the Trojan war ; to assume that such is to be found in a vain attempt of the Greeks to gain foothold in the Scamander valley c. 1200 B.C. is, he says, a desperate attempt to harmonize conflicting facts. I cannot see that there are any conflicting facts ; for that Thracians destroyed Troy is but a guess which can neither be proved nor disproved, just as the guess that Greeks destroyed Troy ; we know that the sixth city had considerable connections with Mycenaean Greece.

To Bethe's view there is, however, an embarrassing obstacle, the fact that the mention of Troy and its inhabitants occurs even in those parts of the Iliad which, according to Bethe, are earlier than 700 B.C. The answer is ingenious but hardly convincing. Bethe states that the city is called Ilios, Troie in late passages only, but its inhabitants are called Trojans. This tribe, he says, lived originally in the mainland—Hector belonged to it—and emigrated to the southern coast of Aeolia. The information concerning Trojans in the

---

[1] See A. Brückner and H. Schmidt in Dörpfeld, *Troja und Ilion*, pp. 554 and 594 respectively.
[2] This was proved long ago by Ed. Meyer, *Geschichte von Troas*, 1877.
[3] W. Dörpfeld, *Troja und Ilion*, 1902, pp. 183.

mainland ought, however, to be viewed with a critical eye ; their immigration to Asia Minor is not mentioned by anybody and is highly hypothetical. The name of the city, Ilios, is by Bethe connected with the patronymic of Aias, Oïliades. He thinks that Aias' father, Oïleus or Ileus, is identical with the eponymous hero of the city and gave his name to the city and the goddess Athena Ilias. Now, he is a Locrian, and undeniably there is a curious connection between Troy and the Locrians to which the well-known custom of the Locrians of sending maidens as temple servants to the temple of Athena Ilias at Troy testifies.[1] Bethe's inference is that a tribe which venerated Aias settled at the Hellespont and founded the city of Ilios in the beginning of the seventh century B.C. at the time when Greek ceramics appear on this site. The ruling family was the Antenoridae, who are in a certain degree opposed to the kingly family and the war. How slight are the foundations of this hypothesis is evident. It rests chiefly upon a homonymy, with the exception of the very remarkable and much discussed custom of the maiden tribute. Bethe takes Aias' outrage against Cassandra to be an aetiologic myth invented in order to explain this custom. Such myths are frequent, but in this case, there is a serious objection, viz. that colonies very often send offerings, etc., to their mother city, but that an instance is wanting showing that a mother city sent like tributes to a colony. The ancient tradition saying that the custom is due to an injunction of the Delphic Oracle has nothing improbable and is in conformity with the activity of the Oracle in the Archaic Age. This implies that the myth gave rise to the custom—there are instances even of this kind,—and certainly Aias' outrage appears among the earliest works of art, bronze reliefs from Olympia and Delphi.[2] This custom is not sufficient to prove an unrecorded Locrian colony at Troy.

[1] The custom is first mentioned by Aeneas Tacticus in the fourth century B.C.; cp. *Polybius*, xii, 5, 6, etc. The most important testimony is an inscription published by A. Wilhelm, " Die lokrische Mädcheninschrift," *Jahresheft des österreichischen archäol. Instituts*, xiv, 1911, pp. 163, and since then much discussed.

[2] *Olympia*, iv, p. 104, and pl. xxxix, 705a; *Fouilles de Delphes*, v, p. 1231, and pl. xxi.

Thirdly, Bethe derives certain heroes from the Peloponnese, Capys from Caphyae, Dardanos from Psophis, Anchises from Sicyon because Echepolos Anchisiades is said to be a Sicyonian.[1] He thinks that Paris-Alexandros and Helen were at home in eastern Argolis and Aineias in Arcadia.[2] All these were brought to Aeolia by an immigration of Arcadians. The localizations referred to are unreliable, and in certain cases evidently secondary. It is also to be remembered that in naming less important adversaries of the Greeks the poet draws freely on the common stock of Greek personal names.

Consequently, except the well-known emigration of the Aeolians to the north-western corner of Asia Minor, Bethe assumes not less than three different emigrations to the same district which are elsewhere absolutely unrecorded ; that of the Trojans who brought the name of Troy, that of the Locrians who gave the name of Ilios to the city, and an Arcadian immigration which brought Aineias and connected myths. This appears to be a very complicated hypothesis, in fact too complicated to be likely. In this manner Bethe succeeded in bringing together the raw materials of Homeric epics in Aeolia. The kernel of these epics is said to be the duels between certain heroes whose enmity can be understood only if in their native countries where their combats reflect the battles of their tribes. These combats, which were once celebrated in independent lays, have been converted into episodes of the Homeric poems.

The Iliad contains, he thinks, three main themes, the wrath of Achilles and his revenge, the deeds of Diomedes, and the cycle of Helen. Each of these themes has for its kernel a duel : between Achilles and Hector, between Diomedes and Aineias, and between Menelaos and Alexandros respectively. They were remodelled by Homeric poetry, which, moreover, introduced motives for them. The motif of vengeance couples two duels, and the motif of grudge is used in order to introduce a retarding of the narrative. The wrath of Achilles and the rape of Helen being the cause of the war, are consequently the fundamental poetical ideas of the Trojan cycle.

[1] 'Εχέπωλος 'Αγχισιάδης, *Il.*, xxiii, v. 296.
[2] Cp. L. Malten, " Aineias," *Archiv für Religionswissenschaft*, xxix, 1931, pp. 33.

I have already expressed my doubts concerning the localizations of the first mentioned of these heroes, but a few words
must be added concerning the most striking of these re-locali-
zations, that of Hector at Thebes. Certain ancient authors
mention his grave at Thebes and add that his bones were
brought to Thebes according to an injunction of the Oracle.[1]
Dümmler seized upon this information and tried to show that
several adversaries of Hector mentioned in the Iliad had a
tomb cult in Boeotia and Phocis,[2] and Bethe worked out this
idea long ago.[3] Very brisk polemics were directed against his
assumption that Hector was originally at home at Thebes,
and forced him to a modification of his arguments.[4] They
are not convincing, for Hector kills many heroes from other
districts, and I cannot see why the information that his bones
were transferred to Thebes should be unreliable. Such a
translation was fairly common, and in their wars against
the Locrians the Thebans had as much need of Hector's aid
as had, e.g., the Spartans of the aid of Orestes whose bones
they discovered at Tegea.

Bethe's fundamental elements, the duels, are very meagre
and somewhat uninteresting myths. And even if this is only
a personal opinion, still, as Crusius says,[5] the whole context
of the myth ought to stand out clearly in comparison with
the isolated and infinitely varying battle scenes with their
refined but conventional technique which are never deep-
seated in the organism of the poems. The real creation of
myths, and especially of cycles of myths, is attributed by Bethe
to the creative genius of poets. The wrath of Achilles is a
means of poetical technique to join the duels. Agamemnon
and Priamos are inventions of the poet's because the hostile
armies each needed a leader. I have discussed the attempt

[1] *Lycophron*, v. 1265, is the earliest.
[2] Dümmler in an appendix to F. Studniczska, *Kyrene*, 1890 ; reprinted
in his *Kleine Schriften*, ii, pp. 240.
[3] In the paper quoted above, p. 44, n. 2.
[4] References in Bethe, *Homer*, iii, p. 81, n. 6 ; add J. A. Scott, " Hector
as a Theban Hero in the light of Hesiod and Pindar," *American Journal of
Philology*, xxxv, 1914, pp. 309, and W. R. Halliday, " The Cults of Hector
at Thebes and Achilles at Tanagra," *Liverpool Annals of Archaeology*, xi, 1924,
pp. 3.
[5] O. Crusius, " Sagenverschiebungen," *Sitzungsberichte der Akademie der
Wissenschaften zu München*, phil.-hist. Klasse, 1905, p. 787.

to sever Agamemnon from Mycenae elsewhere.[1] Here I only ask : Why precisely was the commander-in-chief made king of Mycenae ? At the time at which this happened, according to Bethe, Mycenae was a quite unimportant town. I confess that for me it is absolutely inconceivable that a poet of the Archaic Age of Greece, wishing to give a town of his own to the commander-in-chief of the Greek army, should have struck upon this decaying spot, as inconceivable as the existence of a war king and commander-in-chief without a town of his own to back his authority. The simple and evident explanation is, of course, the fact that Mycenae was the mightiest and wealthiest city in Mycenaean Greece. The stage of the Iliad being laid before Troy, we have no right to expect that Mycenae should be mentioned more than accidentally. Agamemnon's queen is mentioned in the Iliad only once in passing.

Finally, I give a summary of the development of the Trojan cycle according to Bethe. He discerns two layers of myths. The earlier belongs to the mother country where the original poem on Achilles' wrath originated, and contained the duel of Achilles and Hector and the name of the Trojans, a Greek tribe. It was taken over to Asia Minor by the colonists and localized at Troy. This layer was after 700 B.C. overlaid by a later layer which is termed Ilian. The earlier stratum was remodelled and new strata added. The death of Achilles is a poetical invention, which by the motif of the wrath was connected with the cycle of Helen, belonging to eastern Agolis. Still later Diomedes of Argos and his adversary Aineias were added to the cycle ; the house of Aineias ruled at Scepsis near the Hellespont.

The emigrated Aeolians who had taken with them reminiscences of their old fights, preserved by minstrels, found in these a reflection of their own fights against the indigenous population in Aeolia and regarded Achilles as their

---

[1] See my *Mycenaean Origin of Greek Mythology*, pp. 45. Restating his arguments in a recent paper, " Troia, Mykene, Agamemnon und sein Grosskönigtum," *Rheinisches Museum*, lxxx, 1931, pp. 222, Bethe passes over the god Agamemnon. I remark only that it is no valid objection that the myth knows more kings of Mycenae than Agamemnon, nor that the earlier literature except Homer does not mention Mycenae as the kingly city of Agamemnon, for ancient literature is not the same as ancient myth.

champion in these battles. When they had settled down
on Lesbos and found Trojans in the peninsula north of their
island, they localized their myth telling of the victory
of their Achilles over the Trojan Hector in this peninsula
which they strove to conquer. Ionian minstrels took over
the myths and their localization, and Homer modelled these
materials with the genius of a poet. When the barbarous
Trerians had left Troy and Troas had been opened to the
Greeks by the settling of the Locrians at Troy, Homeric
minstrels came to the courts of the Antenoridae and the
Aeneadae and learnt to know the landscape, the mighty
city walls and the temple of Athena Ilias. They recognized
the city of which their chants told and gave it the name of
Ilios. They added new information remodelling the poems.
The development of the commerce in the Black Sea gave
to the Homeric poems an importance which was more than
local. The Athenians, who early gained a foothold on the
shores of the Hellespont, regarded the Homeric heroes as
representatives of their claims. So the Homeric poems at
last were moulded into their present form in Athens in the
sixth century B.C. Finally, the cyclic epics were created as
a continuation.

Bethe's attempt to unravel the origins and the development of the Trojan cycle is very ingenious, very interesting
and a stupendous effort, but it has failed utterly. His arguments are unsafe and unreliable, and the great hypothesis
built upon them is so complicated and brings so many unknown factors and assumptions into play that it is ruined
by them. The fundamental error is that literary analysis
of the development of the Homeric poems was applied to
the development of the mythical cycles too. Thus two
things were identified which must be distinguished, the development of epic poetry and the development of myths.
The fundamental idea that the cycle of myths was created
contemporaneously with and through the agency of epic
poetry from very meagre and disconnected mythical elements,
is conflicting with the analogies of the epics of other peoples,
for in them the mythical background, the fundamental idea
and containing bond of the myths are earlier than the epics;
the myths are the store from which the epic poets draw,

remodelling and reshaping them profoundly and adding new myths. Such is the case in other epics which are better known in this respect, for example, the battle on the Throstle Field in Servian epics, Charlemagne, his paladins, and the battle at Roncevaux in the French epics, Vladimir the Great and his men in the Russian, and Joloi and Manas in the Siberian epics. Analogies are, of course, no binding arguments, although in this case they seem to be very strong. It is, however, possible to prove that the great cycles of Greek mythology and even the Trojan cycle are much older than the Homeric poetry, and in fact go back in their outlines into the Mycenaean age. We shall come back to this subject in a later chapter.

6. CONCLUSION

We have reviewed the most important contributions to the discussion of the Homeric question, especially those of recent years. The result seems to be distressing. Agreement is as far off as ever ; *quot capita tot sententiae.* In view of this state of things it may well be understood that some are busy proclaiming the bankruptcy of Homeric scholarship. In fact, it may be doubted whether the problem proposed and commonly called the Homeric question is soluble with the means at our disposal.

The Homer of the separatist school is made up of patchwork, even if it is said that the man who devised the patchwork displayed poetical genius in cutting out and mending the patches and in arranging them and putting them together. There is the little lay patchwork, made up of pieces of roughly equal size arranged according to their natural order. There is the nucleus patchwork, in which the patches are arranged around a centre determining the pattern. There is, finally, the compilation patchwork, larger patches being made up of other patches, recut and refashioned in order to be fitted into each other according to a definite pattern. I do not mean to imply any disesteem in using the word patchwork ; I think that work of this kind may be as valuable as more free invention. But I wish sharply to bring out the principle underlying the work of the separatist school. The Homeric poems are cut up into patches which are claimed once to have been independent poems or, at all events, remains of such. The assumption is that these poems were incorporated into Homer unchanged or, if recut and refashioned, not so essentially changed but that their pristine independence can be recognized.

Precisely this assumption is to be questioned. Its weakness appears in the general disagreement of the results of research conducted on these lines. Some scholars seem to have the idea that the poets of the earliest poems were the only geniuses and that poetry was continually deteriorating. This identifying of old and good, of recent and inferior, is, of course, questionable. Almost universally the separatists seem to claim to have had a look into the cards played by the poet and the poets. They know pretty well the plan devised by him which was spoilt by a later poet reworking his poem, and they describe how it would have been carried through. Consequently parts disagreeing with this plan are singled out as later reworking or additions. The reality of this superior insight into the poet's purposes and methods is also to be questioned. It is highly subjective.

The questioning of the separatist principles is carried on very vigorously by the unitarians, and, of course, not without success. To them Homer or, at least, the Iliad and the Odyssey respectively are unities, conceived, composed, and possibly written down by one man. In order to prove this thesis, they refer to the all-pervading dominating ideas and the unity of language, etc., and smooth over apparent discrepancies to the best of their ability. Their views and arguments also are subjective without question. They are hampered by being an opposition party warring against the separatist school, which was dominant until quite recently. Here is an example of the fact which is very often observed, viz. that the position of one of two conflicting parties unconsciously determines that of the opponent. Consequently the concern of the unitarians is to disprove all the separatist arguments and views. In my opinion they overdo their work. Nobody will be able to persuade me that the *Catalogue of the Ships* was written by the man who composed the Iliad, and it will be very difficult to prove that the lay of Dolon is the work of that man, and in the Odyssey the same is true of the description of those who were punished in Hades.[1]

The only point of agreement between the separatists and the unitarians is that there were songs of some kind before Homer which he used in composing his poems, but their attitudes in judging the nature of this poetry and its influence on Homer are very different. Only the nucleus theory gives no consideration to the problem, simply because it had not been put at that time. What the little lay theory thinks about it need not be restated. For this theory as well as for the compilation theory, the earlier songs are smaller epics which were incorporated into the great epos more or less word for word. It is also assumed that epics treating of other cycles influenced the Homeric poems.

At this point of our reasoning we may call attention to a question which comes as a natural consequence of this point of view. How far, in terms of generations, can literary analysis be carried back? I suppose it cannot be seriously suggested that these earlier poems were written down and that Homer used books in composing the Iliad and the Odyssey. The separatists think, of course, he did not. But if the earlier and smaller poems were preserved by the memory of the minstrels and handed down by oral tradition, it is impossible that they survived without being changed more than two or three generations. For my purpose it does not matter if they survived four or five generations, although that seems unthinkable. The unavoidable consequence is that the earliest poems incorporated by Homer and utilized in the composition of his poems cannot be more than, say, a century older than the Homeric poems themselves. This is the limit which literary analysis is unable to transgress.

It is characteristic of the attitude of the unitarians that, although admitting the existence of earlier poems, they are very little concerned with them. They are so obsessed with the magic formula of the creative genius of Homer that the preparatory stages and the materials which he utilized are brushed aside somewhat impatiently. The problem is there, even if their view is accepted, but it is placed on one side.

---

[1] *Od.*, xi, vv. 568-640.

If they touch upon the problem it is only in an evasive manner. E.g. Drerup who has done a real service to Homeric scholars in collecting the materials of other epics, hardly utilizes them at all for his treatment of the Homeric question. He speaks vaguely of earlier chants of some kind, of poetical reminiscences of some kind (*liedhafte Erinnerungen*). He would probably like to think that Homer in composing his epos handled this indeterminate poetry as freely as, e.g., Shakespeare handled the lives of Plutarch in composing his tragedies, and that he owed no greater debt to it.

In fact there is another point of agreement between the separatists and the unitarians, apart from the admission that earlier poetry of some kind existed, viz. that they both take only a very narrowly restricted period of time into account when trying to unravel the origin and development of epic poetry. The importance of this observation appears, if we cast a glance on the matter of the poems, the myths. The final consequence of the separatist methods of tracing the origin and development of Homeric poetry, is to identify them with the development of the myths and the creation of mythological cycles. The attempt was futile, nor has it been accepted by any Homeric scholar. Consequently we may state, generally speaking—there are exceptions which ought not to be forgotten—that the myths are the premises of the Homeric poetry. The question of their age arises. If it is admitted, as I have tried to prove in another book, that the cycles of myths, including the cycle of the Trojan war, go back into the Mycenaean Age, it shows clearly how serious is the problem of the earlier poetry.

It was placed on one side both by separatists and unitarians because they directed their attention exclusively to the form of the problem as they put it, i.e. the separatists were busy with literary analysis reaching back a few generations, and with unravelling the composition or, to speak more justly, the piecing together of the Homeric poems of earlier chants, which precede Homer by a comparatively short space of time. The unitarians used their skill and sagacity in defending their thesis that the Homeric poems are the work of a single man. In treating the Homeric problem, both parties almost forgot the epic problem, viz. the problem of the development of epic poetry and its origins, which may reach much further back than the life of a man or a few generations. It will perhaps be just to say that they did not quite forget it, but that they were earnestly and honestly persuaded that no sufficient means are available for attacking a problem which goes so far back into times of which not the least literary record is preserved, and of which our knowledge is so scarce and uncertain even in regard to their history and culture. In any case, the problem exists and it can no longer be disregarded, since so many points of relation between the Homeric poems and the Mycenaean Age have appeared.

CHAPTER II

THE HISTORY OF THE MYCENAEAN AGE

IN the present state of our knowledge it may seem overhasty to attempt to describe the history of the Mycenaean Age, and such is certainly the case if the word history is taken in its common sense. But as an account of the Mycenaean culture, founded on archaeological materials, is an important part of any history of Greece which deals with the early age, and as the foundations of the Greek people and of Greek history were then being laid, we cannot avoid the attempt to answer from the available sources certain fundamental questions. So, too, in dealing with the origin and development of epic poetry, which ultimately goes back to Mycenaean times, we must try to form some idea of the outlines of the history of that age. Nor am I alone in regarding this attempt as essential, since most English scholars who have inquired into Homeric problems have tried to draw such a picture.

The separatists are very little concerned with this problem, because their analysis of the poems must needs stop at a time when the Mycenaean Age already belonged to the distant past and new conditions prevailed, but if they touch upon the question they generally share the opinion that the Mycenaeans were Greeks. Nor are the unitarians much interested in the problem, assuming, as they do, that the Homeric poems were created during a comparatively short compass of time and that they describe a uniform and fictitious civilization.

1. VARIOUS OPINIONS. GENERAL POINTS OF VIEW

The English Homeric scholars treat the problem as a corollary of the view which they have formed in regard to the genesis of epic poetry, but there are other scholars who, starting from archaeological and ethnological problems, ended in

56

discussing the bearing of the epic problem upon their views. Among these was Ridgeway [1] who thought that the Achaeans described in Homer were a not very numerous Celtic tribe which soon merged in the indigenous population and took over their speech and myths, a most unlikely opinion which is universally rejected ; and Evans [2] who assumes that epic poetry arose among the Minoan conquerors of the mainland, and in a bilingual society was transferred into the Greek speech.

Myres has treated the problem very exhaustively in a recent work from all points of view.[3] His arguments are very complicated, and here a few salient points only can be noted. He rightly thinks that Greece has for long received as inhabitants members of all three primary stocks of the white race, but that it imposed its peculiar geographical control on them all, selecting the strains best fitted for acclimatization. He thinks that peoples with Greek speech first arrived in Greece about 1900 B.C., at a period corresponding to the spread of the oval house and of the grey, so-called Minyan ware through southern Greece. He correlates this with the myths of Hellen and his sons and of Deucalion. Accepting the view that the principal dialects correspond to different waves of immigration he gives a redistribution of the dialects, first of the Arcadian and Aeolic and then of the Doric and western dialects, correlated with a redistribution of families and tribes, as described in the mythical genealogies. An incursion of Phrygian raiders affected the political structure but hardly the dialects, and led to co-operation of mainland peoples in the sea-raids.

Mentioning the Minoans and the Mycenaeans very briefly, and disregarding the differences between them, Myres assumes that the Mycenaean cities of the mainland were Minoan colonies founded after about 1800 B.C., first in Argolis and then in other provinces of Greece, and that the collapse of the Minoan

---

[1] Above, p. 23.   [2] Above, p. 28.
[3] J. L. Myres, *Who Were the Greeks ?* 1930 ; cp. the review by A. J. B. Wace in the *Classical Review*, xiv, 1931, pp. 128. For Myres' principles, see also the summary of his lecture in the *Journal of the Hellenic Studies*, xlviii, 1928, p. xx, and for a criticism of his use of mythology, A. R. Burn, *Minoans, Philistines and Greeks, B.C. 1400-900*, 1931. This interesting book came into my hands after my manuscript was finished. Burn's methodical points of view are sound, his account of the events seems often questionable. He trusts more in mythology than his principles admit.

culture was due to three successive shocks which were of a
very different kind. The first was essentially a quarrel between
the mainland settlements and the Cretan motherland, causing
the fall of the palace régime at Cnossos, but this catastrophe
was attended by, or was perhaps in part the consequence of,
other disturbances which had a profound effect on the redistribution of linguistic and tribal groups. The second shock
was the arrival of the " divine-born " dynasties about 1260 B.C.,
viz. the heroes of Homer and the Age of the Heroes in Hesiod.
The third shock, the coming of the Dorians five generations
later, caused a reorganization, putting an end to Homeric
conditions and spreading the Mycenaean civilization over
wide areas. He says, however, that the colonization of Cyprus
goes back to 1500 B.C. and that of Rhodes to 1400 B.C., and
thinks that these islands were first Minoized and later re-
occupied by a people speaking the Arcadian dialect under the
rule of the " divine-born " dynasties.

Thus Myres gives a very detailed history of the pre-historic
age with names and dates founded on mythical genealogy
and chronology. In spite of his efforts to justify their historical value this is the most questionable part of his work,
and it is at the same time its backbone, determining his views
much more than the archaeological materials which are
thoroughly treated in regard to the pre-Mycenaean age only.
We know how folk memory confuses persons and events,[1]
and how epic poetry which also must be taken into account,
combines heroes and events of different ages. Moreover, the
arrangement of the myths into a kind of history is the
work of the cyclic poets and the logographers, the latter being
especially responsible for the mythical chronology. They remodelled and rearranged the mythological traditions in order
to make them fit in with each other.

Of the Homeric scholars each has his own way. Andrew
Lang is, according to his unitarian standpoint, little concerned
with the problem, noting only that the Achaean epics may
have a basis in the tradition of the earlier and more civilized
population which he calls " Pelasgians." [2]

[1] Cp. my paper " Über die Volksüberlieferung besonders mit Rücksicht
auf die alte Geschichte," in the periodical *Scientia*, xlix, 1930, pp. 319.
[2] Andrew Lang, *The World of Homer*, p. 12.

Gilbert Murray [1] assumes the existence of pre-Greek empires depending entirely upon commerce, which were broken up by the invasion from the north of a great number of tribes with Greek speech. While the great masses of these various peoples were steadily pushing their way southwards in the mainland, small bodies of adventurers or chiefs seem to have gone forth into the Aegean region to carve out for themselves little kingdoms or lives of romance, and settled in various cities. Their power was based partly on sheer plunder, partly on the taxes yielded by a constantly decreasing trade. This state of things was overthrown by further shocks from the north-west. A chaos ensued, and at last the two races were fused.

W. Leaf has a chapter on the Coming of the Achaeans and another on the Fusion of the Races. [2] To him the conquest of Greece is the work of a small body of determined men, the displacement of one ruling caste by another, i.e. the Minoans who had subdued the older population of the mainland were replaced by the immigrant Achaeans. He adduces the Norman conquest of Sicily as an illuminating example of the fact that conquerors do not necessarily change the civilization of the conquered people. That is true, but the Normans did not change the speech of the country, as happened in Greece. As the Achaeans were thrown back from the south-east they had to look for expansion to the east or to the west. But they were shut off from the west by the mysterious people of the Taphians, a people of traders and pirates ; accordingly they turned to the east. The capture of Troy helped to protect the lands which they occupied to the south. The day came when the transient might of this small power and the union maintained by them waned, Greece relapsed into its normal congeries of loosely coherent cantons and in the social reorganization the majority prevailed. The military Achaean and the rustic pre-Achaean religions, the epic heroes and the pre-Achaean daimones were fused. The Hellens were a political and religious syncretism.

Chadwick does not attack the problem from the historical but from the mythical point of view. His denial of the identi-

---

[1] Gilbert Murray, *The Rise of the Greek Epic*, 3rd ed., pp. 50.
[2] Walter Leaf, *Homer and History*, pp. 36 and pp. 243 respectively.

fication of the Achaeans with the Aeolians,[1] and his inference that Achilles belonged to a north-western Greek tribe, are highly improbable. For the north-west Greeks were the last tribe which invaded Greece, coming on the heels of the Dorians. It is the more improbable as Chadwick admits the incorporation of Mycenaean elements into the epics, and thinks that the archaeological evidence of the latest Mycenaean times corresponds to the state of society described in Homer, viz. the eleventh century B.C. Here he comes near to Lang's view.

The picture which he gives of the Heroic Age, viz. the age of epic poetry, is, generally speaking, as follows : [2] first we find a long period of " education," in which a semi-civilized people has been profoundly affected by the influence of a civilized people, e.g. through military service such as the Germans carried out among the Romans. With this the roving sea peoples of the Mycenaean Age are compared. Then came a time in which the semi-civilized people possessed itself of its neighbours' property. This the Achaeans did at the very end of the Mycenaean Age. The effects produced upon the semi-civilized people by these conditions appear as the phenomena recognized as characteristic of the Heroic Age.

We see that even here the sentence applies : *quot capita tot sententiae*, but it would be very unjust to forget that many years have elapsed since the opinions reviewed were written down, except for Myres ; the works quoted are now twenty years old or more. Much new evidence has come to light in the meantime, and the authors would probably revise their views, if they had to treat the subject anew. Moreover, the issue is apt to be obscured if the history and the conditions of the Mycenaean Age and the immigration of the Greeks are adapted to a definite view of the origin and the development of epic poetry inferred from Homeric research. Our best method will be to try and see what can be reasonably stated and inferred in this respect independently of Homer

---

[1] H. M. Chadwick, *The Heroic Age*, 1912, 2nd impression, 1926, pp. 280. Concerning the inscriptions adduced as arguments, cp. C. D. Buck, *Classical Philology*, xxi, 1926, p. 17, n. ; A. Thumb, *Handbuch der griech. Dialekte*, 1909, p. 198 ; A. Fick, "Äoler und Achäer," *Zeitschrift für vergleichende Sprachforschung*, xliv, 1911, pp. 1.

[2] Chadwick, loc. cit., ch. xix, pp. 432, especially pp. 458.

and to apply the results to the understanding of the genesis of the epic poetry.

The questions here relevant are : Who were the Mycenaeans ? i.e. the bearers of the Mycenaean civilization and the ruling people in the Mycenaean Age ? and What can with some measure of certainty be inferred concerning the political and social conditions in the Mycenaean Age, especially concerning the migrations of the Greeks ? I shall try to attack these questions, but would begin with some preliminary remarks on methods and principles.[1] The evidence at our disposal is drawn from three sources, consisting of archaeological remains, of language, including the distribution and relationships of the Greek dialects, and of historical information. Each of these three kinds of evidence has its special peculiarities and insufficiencies. Our historical information is derived from Egyptian and Hittite documents and inscriptions ; the difficulties consist in the localization of geographical names and the identification of personal and tribal names. The linguistic evidence, as Buck justly says, in his clear and circumspect account of the Language situation in and about Greece in the second millennium B.C.,[2] offers the most substantial approach to the question so far as it goes. But it is in some respects scarce and insufficient and its application to inferences of a historical kind is liable to varying interpretation. The archaeological evidence is the most plentiful, but, on the other hand, is also most subject to different interpretation and doubts. Archaeology gives us only the remains of the material civilization—except for the script if it can be read.

In applying this material to historical conclusions there is consequently from the outset a premise subject to doubt, viz. the identification of a certain civilization with a certain people. We know that one people sometimes took over the language of another people, and the same is the case in regard to civilization. The Ostrogoths in Italy and the Normans in Sicily did not leave any imprint of their native civilization. But if a people immigrates in sufficient numbers and if the

[1] I have recently treated these questions in the introductory chapter to my *Minoan-Mycenaean Religion*, pp. 11.
[2] Buck, loc. cit., p. 3.

indigenous civilization has lost part of its attractiveness, traces may appear of the civilization of the immigrants. With the Lombards Teutonic art appears in Italy. Similarly, if a certain civilization is taken over by a less civilized people, certain peculiarities of the inferior native civilization, e.g. barbarism, are liable to remain, as, for instance, in the Egyptian civilization of Nubia. There are many varying forms of this adaptation among the various peoples who took over the Babylonian culture or were influenced by it. In regard to the transmission of culture in ancient times we should realize that the influence of commerce and peaceful intercourse so often referred to works slowly and imperfectly. For example, the civilization found at Phylakopi on Melos is, in spite of the very lively connections with Crete, fundamentally indigenous, although Minoan finds are numerous and the influence of Minoan art is steadily growing. War was the most powerful means of transmitting a civilization as well as the rule imposed by one conquering people upon another. Nubia, conquered and ruled by the Egyptians, was Egyptianized ; Egyptian civilization had a conspicuous influence in Palestine during the time in which that country was an Egyptian province. But the cultural influence of the subjugated people upon its rulers is also marked, and may even be stronger if the subjugated people possesses a superior culture. That is the case, for example, with the Babylonians. Their influence upon the Assyrians dates from the times in which those people were subject to them, but went on when the rôles were reversed. These two peoples were closely kindred, but the Persians were also profoundly influenced by the Babylonian-Assyrian culture. Even Ahuramazda is represented in the guise of the god Assur. The most striking example, however, is the spread of Greek culture to Rome. It began in full force when the Romans acquired Greek subjects by the conquest of southern Italy. A new period of Roman civilization is dated from the war with Pyrrhus.

Thus in drawing conclusions from archaeological materials in regard to ethnical questions we should be well aware of the uncertainty and limitations of the method. The less developed a civilization is, the more difficult is it to discern elements of foreign origin ; they are easier to discern in a more sophisticated culture. In regard to the immigrant Greeks there is a special limitation which makes the matter still more doubtful. The archaeological remains of the earliest times consist chiefly in pottery, and consequently attempts have been made to discern the coming of the Greeks by attributing certain kinds of pottery to them. But a migrating people does not use vessels of a material which is apt to be broken; [1] instead of earthenware pots they have vessels of skin, wood, bark, etc. A survey of primitive nomadic and sedentary tribes proves this to be a common rule. Hence it may be considered as pretty certain that the invading Greeks had no pottery of their own, and thus the hope of discovering their ceramics will wane. If they had a native art the materials were other than clay. From these their art may have been transferred to other materials, even to clay, but such a supposition involves us in very difficult complications.

The identification of a certain people with a certain civilization is always subject to some doubt. The best argument from which the presence of a new people can be inferred is a break in civilization, i.e. when a new civilization cannot be totally or partially explained as organically developed from an earlier one. But even here caution is imposed. There is, e.g., a very marked and deep-rooted difference between the Kamares period and the naturalistic phase of the Minoan art, but as we have the intermediate links and know the development, we can say that the latter was developed from the former. To put it otherwise, such an argument must be founded on a thorough knowledge without any missing links. Or there must be exterior arguments proving the break, such as a general destruction intervening between two periods of civilization. The argument is stronger if we see that in a certain civilization elements of foreign nature appear which are organically unconnected with it ; and stronger still if these elements have an apparent relation to another civilization. Then we may confidently state that the mixture of civilizations depends on a mixture of peoples. We may, for example, refer to the Etruscans who borrowed so much from the Greek

[1] This is the opinion of Myres also, loc. cit., p. 287. I cannot see how this opinion agrees with his argument from the grey and red ware ceramics.

civilization but also introduced their own ideas and customs, to the changes which Greek culture underwent in Rome, to the mixture of Egyptian and even Greek elements with Babylonian in Persian art, etc. These instances from very sophisticated cultures are complicated ; more simple are the specifically Nubian features in the Egyptianized civilization of Nubia. There are mixtures of all kinds.

2. The Pre-Greek Population. The Breaks in Civilization.

From these introductory remarks on the question of methods and principles we turn to our main subject. Our first question is : Which was the indigenous population of Greece ? Here we find the unanimous statement prevailing that it was not Greek nor of Aryan race at all, that it was spread over the mainland of Greece, the islands of the Aegean, and some part of Asia Minor, more especially its south-western part, and that the carriers of the Minoan civilization belonged to this pre-Greek race. The arguments are well known. Firstly, nobody has supposed that the Greeks were indigenous in Greece, because Aryan peoples are immigrants everywhere in southern Europe and their original habitat was elsewhere towards the north or north-east.

Secondly, there is linguistic evidence of a pre-Greek population in place-names. It is well known that place-names deriving from an earlier language survive everywhere in countries in which a change of language has taken place. Kretschmer made the far-reaching discovery, which is a corner stone of the ethnology of prehistoric Greece, that a type of place-names, distinguished by the elements -nth- and -ss- in their endings appear all over Greece, the islands of the Aegean and in south-western Asia Minor.[1] There -nth- appears as -nd- ; in Attica -ss- appears as -tt-. Such names are, e.g., Corinthos, Tiryns, gen. Tirynthos, Lindos, Myndos ; Cephissos, Parnassos, Cnossos, Halicarnassos, etc., etc. These names cannot be explained from the Greek language, and the fact that they appear in Asia Minor too, in a country which never

---

[1] P. Kretschmer, *Einleitung in die Geschichte der griechischen Sprache*, 1896, pp. 401. See the map, fig. 1, p. 66.

was Greek, proves that they are not Greek.   Consequently
they must derive from a pre-Greek population covering the
said area.[1]   There are names of other formation too, which
certainly are pre-Greek, e.g. Mykenai,[2] but not being so easily
accounted for, they may be passed over here.

This discovery led to a recognition of the fact that a number
of Greek words show the same elements.   Among these are
especially names of plants belonging to a southern climate,
e.g. *terebinthos*, tamarisk, *olynthos*, unripe fig, *hyakinthos*, etc.,
and a few culture words, e.g. *merinthos*, thread, *asaminthos*,
bathing tub.   It is evident that these words were borrowed
by the Greeks from the indigenous population, for they came
from countries where these plants and things were unknown.
The Greeks certainly borrowed many other words from the
earlier inhabitants of the country, but this is difficult to prove,
if the formation is not characteristically non-Greek, as it is
in the quoted examples.   The number of such loan-words is
admittedly great,[3] and among them are such words as βασιλεύς.[4]
Lists have been drawn up of such loan-words ; [5] they are
useful but questionable in details and must be used with
caution.

To this pre-Greek population the Minoan people belonged.
The said place-names are frequent in Crete.   The Minoan
language was certainly non-Greek, for if it had been Greek
the efforts of the most competent and sagacious scholars to
decipher the Minoan script would certainly not have failed.
Moreover, a non-Greek language survived in Crete until the
fourth century B.C.   Some fragments of inscriptions written

[1] These names were especially collected by A. Fick, *Vorgriechische Orts-
namen als Quelle für die Vorgeschichte Griechenlands,* 1905, and *Hattiden
und Danubier in Griechenland,* 1909, with many doubtful materials and
hypotheses.   They were usefully arranged in a map by J. B. Haley, *American
Journal of Archaeology,* xxxii, 1928, pp. 141.   Brief surveys in A. Meillet,
Aperçu d'une histoire de la langue grecque, 2nd ed., pp. 45, and in A. Debrunner,
" Die Besiedelung des alten Griechenlands im Lichte der Sprachwissenschaft,"
Neue Jahrbücher für das klass. Altertum, xli, 1918, pp. 441 ; and in Ebert's
" Reallexikon der Vorgeschichte," s.v. *Griechen, B. Sprache,* iv, pp. 510.
[2] See my *Minoan-Mycenaean Religion,* pp. 419.   H. Lamer, " Über einige
Wörter des ʻ Ägäischen ʼ," *Indogermanische Forschungen,* xlviii, 1930, pp. 228.
[3] A. Meillet, loc. cit., pp. 40.
[4] J. Wackernagel, *Sprachliche Untersuchungen zu Homer,* p. 212.
[5] J. Huber, *De lingua antiquissimorum Graeciae incolarum,* Vienna, 1921,
Debrunner in Ebert, loc. cit., p. 524.

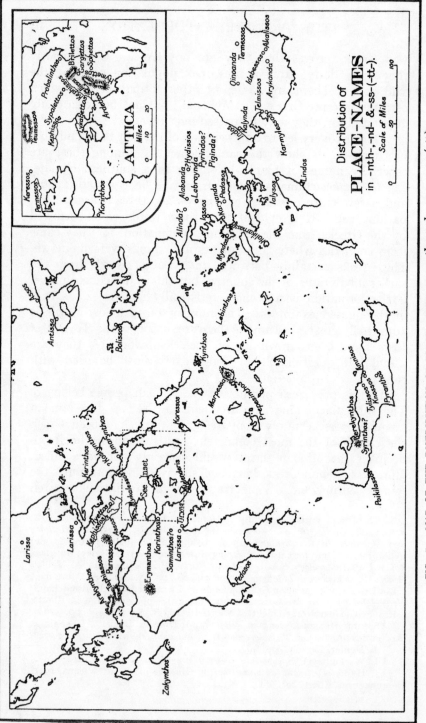

FIG. I.—MAP OF THE DISTRIBUTION OF PLACE-NAMES IN -*nth*-, -*nd*-, AND -*ss*- (-*tt*-).

with Greek letters in an unknown language were found at Praisos in Crete,[1] and this is the more notable as Praisos is said to have been inhabited by the Eteocretans, the true Cretans who are mentioned in the Odyssey as one of the many tribes inhabiting Crete.[2] Most probably they were the last remnant of the pre-Greek inhabitants of Crete.

The next problem is to assign this pre-Greek race to a certain period of pre-historic civilization as shown by archaeology. This problem was recently taken up by Blegen.[3] That civilization must cover the same area as the place-names cover. This is the case with the Late Mycenaean and the Early Helladic civilizations, although it is to be conceded that we know next to nothing of the south-western corner of Asia Minor. The former period is out of the question, coming as it does after the downfall of the Minoan culture, and consequently Blegen states that the population which spoke the pre-Greek language from which the place-names and words mentioned are derived, evolved the early civilization of the Bronze Age in its different but closely kindred branches of Early Minoan, Early Cycladic, and Early Helladic. Blegen's view is well founded, although other opinions have been put forward.[4] If we reject it we must needs fall back upon the Stone Age as the civilization of the pre-Greek population. But this is impossible, for the Stone Age does not correspond to the area covered by the place-names in question. It is blank in the Cyclades and shows great differences in the mainland and in Crete. The spread of a red-on-white ware, closely akin to

---

[1] Published by Conway, *Annual of the British School at Athens*, viii, 1901-2, pp. 125, and x, 1903-4, pp. 115. His attempt to prove the Aryan character of the language has failed completely.

[2] *Od.*, xix, v. 176.

[3] C. W. Blegen, " The Coming of the Greeks," *American Journal of Archaeology*, xxxii, 1928, pp. 146.

[4] F. Matz, *Die frühkretischen Siegel*, 1929, assumes that the Thessalian-Danubian style was originally spread even over the Peloponnese, and that it was ousted by the early Helladic style which immigrated across the Straits of Naupactos and from the south spread to Central Greece also. The immigrants who introduced the early Helladic style were the forerunners of a second stronger wave of immigrants, who brought the middle Helladic style and caused the break between the Early and the Middle Helladic Ages. They were the ancestors of the Mycenaeans. This elaborate hypothesis rests on slight foundations, and implies a very questionable reasoning concerning the principles underlying the early art of different races. See my review in *Göttingische gelehrte Anzeigen*, 1930, pp. 126.

the Thessalian, south of the Isthmus, shows that during the Stone Age the mainland had northerly connections.[1]

Thus we conclude that in the Early Helladic Age Greece was inhabited by a non-Greek population and that the Greeks immigrated after the close of this age, i.e. *c.* 2000 B.C., and before the historical age, at the beginning of which they were already settled in their historical habitats.   The next task is to determine more precisely the date of the immigration and its course. Our guide must needs be archaeology, and consequently we have to look out for breaks in civilization and the introduction of foreign elements of culture, indicating the presence of a foreign people.   There are three such breaks.   The first break intervenes between the Early and the Middle Helladic Ages. The pottery of the Middle Helladic Age, the matt-painted ware and the unpainted Minyan ware, yellow or grey bucchero, differs strikingly from the Early Helladic ceramics of every kind, unpainted, slipped, or varnished ware.[2]   The break is stressed by the fact that in certain places a layer of ashes is found between the Early and the Middle Helladic strata,[3] and that certain Early Helladic sites were not inhabited during the Middle Helladic Age,[4] but the burnt layer is wanting in other sites,[5] and it is doubtful whether it is accidental or derives from a general destruction wrought by foes sacking the Early Helladic sites.   More important is another fact. In Early Helladic, at all events in its late period, connections between the mainland and Crete are testified to not only by the use of the black varnish, which certainly is a Minoan

[1] Only through Blegen's latest researches, which have not been published as yet but with which I am acquainted through his kindness, the Stone Age of the Peloponnese begins to emerge more distinctly.   The first style is very similar to the Thessalian red-on-white ware, and there is a second style derived from this.   Rich finds were made at the Argive Heraion and at Ageorgitiko near Tegea, and these ceramics seem to bè spread all over the Peloponnese. Cp. Blegen, *Gonià, Metropolitan Museum Studies*, iii, 1930, pp. 55.

[2] The classification is due to Messrs. Wace and Blegen, " The Pre-Mycenaean Pottery of the Mainland," *Annual of the British School at Athens*, xxii, 1916-18, pp. 175.   The principal publications are C. W. Blegen, *Korakou*, 1921 ; and *Zygouries*, 1928.

[3] Blegen, *Korakou*, p. 2 ; *Zygouries*, p. 221.   Also at Asine.

[4] J. P. Harland, " The Peloponnesos in the Bronze Age," *Harvard Studies in Classical Philology*, xxxiv, 1923, p. 13, enumerates H. Gerasimos, Yiriza Kenchreai, and a settlement on the Isthmus, referring to Blegen in *American Journal of Archaeology*, xxiv, 1920, pp. 4, 6 and 8.

[5] E.g. at Tiryns.

invention, but also by Minoan seal impressions found on mainland sites.[1] These connections were interrupted with the Middle Helladic Age and were taken up again only later.

The second break is the sudden appearance of the Minoan culture in the mainland in the transitional period between the Middle and Late Minoan Ages, c. 1600 B.C. The Late Helladic Age may justly retain its traditional name of the Mycenaean Age, the difference in regard to the preceding civilization being especially striking.

The third break is the cataclysm of the Mycenaean civilization. The subsequent sub-Mycenaean and proto-Geometric periods are the poorest and darkest of all in the history of Greek civilization except, perhaps, for the Stone Age. Finds are pretty scarce, a fact which is not due to lack of interest and research, but to the extreme poverty of art, viz. decoration of ceramics and the poverty of the contents of the graves.

There have been certain attempts to obliterate the second of these breaks, which ought to be mentioned, although they have not been successful. Harland [2] assumes that between the Early and Middle Helladic periods Greece was invaded by a people whom he labels Minyans, referring to the Minyan ceramics, and he does his best to obliterate the break consisting in the introduction of the Minoan civilization into the mainland by styling the first and second Late Helladic or Mycenaean periods Middle Helladic III and IV, most confusing terms which fortunately were received by none. Instead, he postulates a break between the second and third Late Helladic (Mycenaean) period, but this so-called break is but, in reality, the rapid and vigorous development of Mycenaean culture which sets in with the beginning of the Late Mycenaean period, the extensive building activity at Mycenae and somewhat later at Tiryns, and the subsequent wide expansion of the Mycenaean civilization. The features collected by Harland in order to prove the break partly go back to earlier times and are partly a normal development or deterioration, especially in ceramics.

---

[1] A. W. Persson, " Quelques sceaux et empreintes de sceaux d'Asiné," *Bulletin de la Société des Lettres de Lund*, 1923-24, pp. 162 ; Blegen, *Zygouries*, fig. 91, 1.

[2] In the paper quoted below, p. 84, n. 2.

Another line is taken up by Holland,[1] who, like many other archaeologists, thinks that the break between the Early and Middle Helladic Ages is due to the immigration of the Greeks, but denies any other break until the final collapse at the end of the Bronze Age. He admits, however, an abrupt intrusion of certain new elements, partly of northern and partly of " Aegean " origin, viz. the tholos tombs, the walled city, and c. 1400 B.C. small terra-cotta figurines of a deity. There is no need to refute this view ; in spite of the assertion to the contrary the break between the Middle and Late Helladic Ages is evident.

We have the choice between the three breaks mentioned, and we have to consider which of them best falls in with the given circumstances. The third break is the most significant because of the wholesale cataclysm of culture, but very few scholars ascribe the immigration of the Greeks to the end of the Mycenaean Age. Such an opinion encounters overwhelming obstacles and is out of account. Mythical tradition concerning the conquest of the Peloponnese by the Heracleidae reflects the immigration of the Dorians. This tradition has been said to be worthless and fictitious,[2] but it agrees so well with known facts that a corresponding hypothesis would have to be accepted if tradition were wanting. The west Greek dialects of the Peloponnesian provinces and of the Dorian islands, Crete and Rhodes, show more or less traces of a dialect of the Arcadian type. The Dorians possessed themselves of regions which already had a Greek population with a speech of the same type as Arcadian. The period of time available for two different waves of immigration will be too restricted, if both are assumed to have taken place in the interval between the end of the Mycenaean Age after 1200 B.C. and the beginning of the historical age. The Dorian immigration can hardly be pushed on later than 1000 B.C.

---

[1] L. B. Holland, " The Danaoi," *Harvard Studies in Classical Philology*, xxxix, 1928, pp. 59. I do not enter into his fanciful explanation of the alleged circumstances, viz. that a considerable part of Greece was ruled by foreign conquerors after the later part of L.H. I ; by L.H. III the culture of Argolis was different from L.H. I and exactly similar to that described by Homer. His speculations concerning the wanderings and origins of the tribes deduced from mythology are quite wild.

[2] K. J. Beloch, *Griechische Geschichte*, 2nd ed., i, 2, pp. 76 ; in regard to his views cp. my review in *Göttingische gelehrte Anzeigen*, 1914, pp. 522.

Moreover, such an opinion must needs reject the identification of the tribes attacking Egypt, c. 1200 B.C., with the Achaeans, not to speak of the empire of Ahhijava in the fourteenth century B.C.[1]

3. THE NATIONALITY OF THE MYCENAEANS

The received opinion is accordingly that the Greek immigration took place, or to put it more justly, commenced at an earlier date ; for the Dorian immigration cannot be moved from its place at or after the end of the Mycenaean Age. But the question of identifying the coming of the Greeks with one of the earlier breaks is not so simple. Here we meet the main question : Who were the Mycenaeans ? or more justly, Who were the ruling classes in the Mycenaean Age which created the Mycenaean civilization, taking over the Minoan culture from Crete ?

It seems very reasonable to suppose that the Minoans went over to the mainland, subjugated it, held sway over the native population from strongholds which they built, and introduced the Minoan civilization. This view is supported by Evans and others.[2] They assume that the Greeks had already begun to immigrate in the Mycenaean Age, but that they were part of the subjugated population and only later, reinforced by new waves of immigrants, got the upper hand. No hint is given as to the probable date of this reversion of conditions except that it ought to be rather late.

This view accounts very well for the wholesale taking over of Minoan culture, but it is not the only satisfactory explanation of this fact. There is another : Greek tribes, barbarous but open-minded, and very subject to the lure of a superior civilization, as Aryan peoples always have shown themselves, warlike and fond of booty, may have occupied Greece and come into contact with the Minoans. Roving and pillaging they may have raided Crete and taken booty, and they may also have carried on some trade with the Minoans. They may have acquired a taste for the rich and splendid Minoan culture, and they may have brought not only valuables but men also and among them craftsmen to their strongholds in the mainland.

---

[1] See below, pp. 102. [2] See above, pp. 28.

Their own civilization was of a low standard, consequently they became wholly Minoized, at least in regard to the external and material side of life. We may compare the Persians. If we had the Persian monuments only and no other tradition, we should not be able to imagine the outstanding proper character of old Persian culture.

Which of these two alternatives is the true one, can be shown through an inquiry into the components of the Mycenaean civilization. If, in spite of its wholly Minoized aspect, there are some elements which cannot be derived from Minoan civilization, and especially if these elements have northern connections, the latter explanation must be the correct one. For they can only be understood as elements which a non-Minoan people of northern origin kept and introduced into the Minoan civilization, which they took over and in other respects wholly appropriated. There are such elements. I have treated them more exhaustively elsewhere,[1] and here I restate them briefly.

1. The megaron of the Mycenaean palace is a house type foreign to the Minoan architecture. The word megaron is by modern scholars applied to a room with certain definite characteristics : a room of rectangular ground plan with a forehall or porch formed by a continuation of the sides of the house, with no other opening than a door in the middle of the wall protected by the porch, and with a fixed hearth in the middle. Porch and room may be supported by columns or not ; if there are columns, they are always of an even number leaving the centre free. An ante-room may be inserted between the porch and the room. Nor is this an essential part of the plan. This megaron is isolated from the surrounding rooms, if there are any—this is especially conspicuous in the two megara at Tiryns (fig. 2)—and it is in close architectural relation to the court which is always found before its entrance. The court is organically connected with the megaron, being dominated by its façade. Each of the two megara at Tiryns has its own court. This is a very definite architectural idea in striking contrast to Minoan architecture which groups the rooms around a court without any apparent plan (fig. 3). Nor have the rooms any definite

---

[1] In my *Minoan-Mycenaean Religion*, pp. 12.

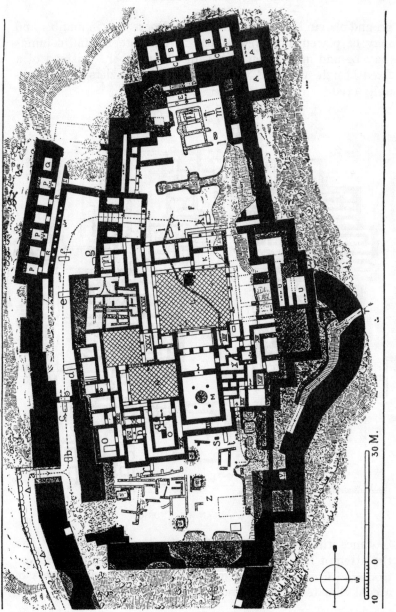

FIG. 2.—PLAN OF TIRYNS

30 M.

0

10

ground plan in Minoan architecture.   Doors vary in number and may be placed indifferently, e.g. at the corners, and columns may be and more often are of an odd number.   Instead of a fixed hearth, which is wanting, portable braziers were probably used.

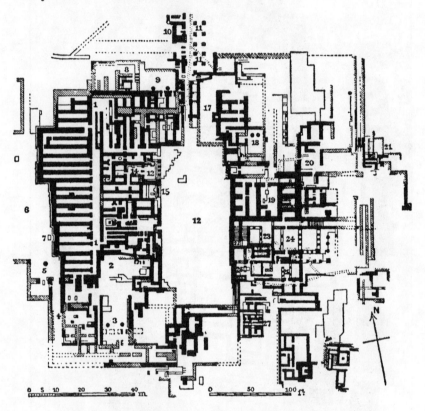

FIG. 3.—PLAN OF CNOSSOS

Since this fundamental difference was pointed out [1] and the attempt has failed to show that the megaron had evolved from the Cretan room in order to meet the requirements of a cool climate,[2] it is generally recognized that the megaron is

[1] F. Noack, *Homerische Paläste*, 1903.
[2] D. Mackenzie, " Cretan Palaces and Aegean Civilization," *Annual of the British School at Athens*, xi-xiii, 1904-7. Cp. G. Leroux, *Les origines de l'édifice hypostyle*, 1913.

FIG. 4.—PAINTED TOMB STELE FROM MYCENAE, SHOWING WARRIORS
WITH SMALL SHIELDS AND CHITONS

FIG. 5.—LADIES DRIVING IN CHARIOT: FRESCO FROM TIRYNS

of non-Minoan origin. The problem of its origins and the question whether it came to Greece from the north or from the north-east are very interesting,[1] but for our purpose the statement suffices that the megaron is non-Minoan and has northern or north-eastern connections. Another important fact is that houses were different in Greece in the Middle Helladic Age, oval, apsidal, or even rectangular, but without any definite arrangement of the megaron type. It may further be observed that the megaron is a single-room house of a primitive type found among several less developed peoples. The court has its origin in the area enclosed by a fence in order to protect the inhabitants from men and wild beasts. The megaron with its court was superimposed upon a Minoan room complex in the Mycenaean palaces, because their lords wanted to live in a room such as that to which they were previously accustomed. It was also very well suited for a chief surrounded by retainers and table companions,[2] and is identical with the hall of the old Scandinavian kings.

2. The dress of the Mycenaeans was different from that of the Minoans. Men are occasionally represented wearing the Minoan loin-cloth, e.g. in the bull fresco from Tiryns, and that is very natural because the artist copied Minoan models, but in other paintings representing special Mycenaean subjects, e.g. warriors and hunters,[3] the men wear a short and short-sleeved chiton (figs. 4 and 51). Even ladies driving to the hunt are wearing it on another fresco from Tiryns (fig. 5). But the ladies of the court took over the elaborate Minoan women's dress (fig. 32). Other women wore, however, probably another garment covering the upper part of the body (fig. 6).[4]

---

[1] See my *Minoan-Mycenaean Religion*, p. 12, n. 1. Cp. the article by A. Boëthius, " Mycenaean Megara and Nordic Houses," *Annual of the British School at Athens*, xxiv, 1919-21, pp. 161. Evans, *Palace of Minos*, i, p. 24, thinks that the megaron came from the east because the megaron is found in the second city of Troy.

[2] Cp. below, p. 230.

[3] The most remarkable examples are furnished by the wall-paintings at Tiryns and at Mycenae, the painted stele (fig. 4), and for a very late age by the Warriors' vase (fig. 47). The latest treatments of the wall-paintings are by G. Rodenwaldt, *Der Fries des Megarons von Mykenai*, 1921 ; and by W. Lamb in the *Annual of the British School at Athens*, xxv, 1921-23, pp. 162.

[4] Rodenwaldt in *Tiryns*, ii, p. 7, n. 6, and *Der Fries des Megarons von Mykenai*, p. 48.

3. Together with the dress goes the fibula or safety pin (fig. 26), for it served to fasten the dress. It is absent in Minoan Crete and not needed for the Minoan dress. It appears only in the Late Mycenaean period, and as the mainland influence was strong there at that time, its distribution is not of fundamental importance, though illuminating. Of the localized finds belonging to Mycenaean times [1] fourteen come from Mycenae, four from Thebes, and single specimens from Tiryns, Korakou near Corinth, Thermos, Therapnae, Cephallenia, and Delphi.   As to Crete a single specimen of the simplest form comes from the cave of Psychro, and two with a flattened bow from the same place, and another from Vrokastro. Here two fibulas were found of a more unusual and evidently later shape—the bow is higher at the one end—and another similar fibula was found near Cydonia.   The fibula is evidently an invention made in the mainland in Late Mycenaean times and spread from there to Crete, where the examples found, generally speaking, are less numerous and later.   It must have been invented for a kind of dress other than the Minoan.

4. The arguments mentioned apply to the Late Mycenaean period only, to which the objects in question belong, and it has been said that the change in house type and dress was caused by the requirements of a cooler climate.   We come to an argument in regard to which no such objection can be made, and which applies even to the earliest Mycenaean times, the distribution of amber. Amber is found frequently and in great quantities in many Mycenaean tombs of the mainland, e.g. in the earliest shaft-graves at Mycenae, in the bee-hive tombs at Kakovatos-Pylos, which belong to a transitional stage between the Early and Middle Mycenaean periods, and in many other tombs ; it is found in almost every new excavation of Mycenaean cemeteries.[2]   The curious fact is, that it is especially found in earlier Mycenaean tombs, whilst it is scarce or altogether absent in later tombs.   The extreme

---

[1] Chr. Blinkenberg, " Fibules grecques et orientales," R. Danish Academy, Historisk-filologiske Meddelelser, xiii, 1, 1926.

[2] Kakovatos, Mitteilungen des deutschen archäologischen Instituts zu Athen, xxxiv, 1909, pp. 278 ; Kalkani, The Times Lit. Supplement, Oct. 26th, 1922 ; Asine, Bulletin de la Société des Lettres de Lund, 1924-25, pp. 43 ; Menidi, Das Kuppelgrab von Menidi, 1880, p. 24 ; Nauplia, Mitteilungen, etc., v, 1880, p. 160.   Delphi, Bulletin de correspondance hellénique, xlvi, 1922, p. 501.

FIG. 6.—FEMALE IDOL FROM
MYCENAE, SHOWING DRESS
COVERING THE WHOLE
BODY

FIG. 7.—BOARS' TUSKS HELMET:
IVORY RELIEF FROM MYCENAE

FIG. 8.—BOARS' TUSKS, CUT AND PERFORATED,
FROM THE IVTH SHAFT-GRAVE AT MYCENAE

FIG. 9.—ORNAMENTS OF GLASS PASTE IN FORM OF BOARS' TUSKS,
FROM THE THOLOS TOMB AT DENDRA

scarceness of amber in Crete is in striking contrast to the abundant finds on the mainland. Only five stray pieces are known from Crete, of which three were found in the tomb of the Double Axe at Cnossos from the end of L.M. II and two in another tomb belonging to the early part of L.M. III.[1] This is all. Further, some pieces were discovered in a late Mycenaean tomb at Ialysos on Rhodes. There is in this unquestionably a radical difference between the mainland and Crete. If the amber had been carried by the usual oversea trade and the peoples of the mainland and of Crete had been of the same stock, it is impossible to see why amber is limited to the mainland with few exceptions. There is only one explanation of the difference, viz. that a people immigrating from the north brought the taste for and the use of amber with it. When the connections northwards gradually grew weaker amber became scarce. Thus it is explained that finds are more numerous in the early than in the late part of the Mycenaean Age.

5. There is another fact of a similar kind. It will be mentioned that the Homeric description of Meriones' helmet is explained by the Mycenaean boars' tusks helmet.[2] Such a helmet is represented by sculptures from tombs in the lower town at Mycenae·(fig. 7), Cyprus and Spata in Attica, by a silver plate from the fourth shaft-grave at Mycenae, by a button seal from the Kalkani necropolis at the same place, and by a gem from the Vaphio tomb.[3] Boars' tusks cut and perforated for attachment were found in the fourth shaft-grave at Mycenae (fig. 8) and in the Kalkani necropolis, and in tombs at Menidi, Spata, Dimini, and Asine, and glass plaques imitating them in the bee-hive tomb at Dendra (fig. 9).[4] Crete has no example in art, but a certain number of boars' tusks were found in a tomb at Zafer Papoura near Cnossos belonging to

---

[1] Evans, " Tomb of the Double Axe," *Archaeologia*, lxv, 1914, p. 42.

[2] Below, p. 138.

[3] References in my *Minoan-Mycenaean Religion*, p. 19, n. 2, and p. 20, nn. 1-7. Boars' tusks, some of which were perforated at the end, were found in the neolithic settlement at Olynthus, " Excavations at Olynthus," i, G. Mylonas, *The Neolithic Settlement*, p. 82, and fig. 94, 3. As some of them have no perforations and others one only they cannot have been used for a helmet, but perhaps for a necklace. The find proves, however, that this kind of ornament came from the north.

[4] A. W. Persson, *The Royal Tombs at Dendra*, p. 36, and pl. xxv, 1.

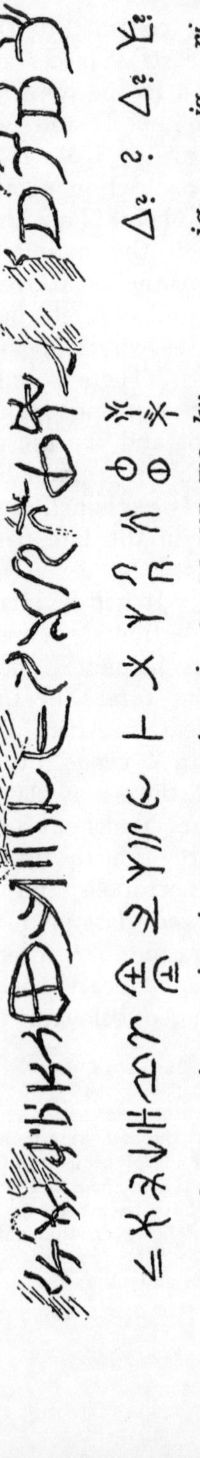

li me ke te e mi u si ni se no vo ta i se po va mo ku ja ja ri

The bottom line represents the corresponding signs in the Cypriot syllabary. The transcription in Greek, from right to left, is as follows:—

- - - ΚυμοϜα (Κυμώ) ΠοσειδάϜονος ἐνσί ὐμὶ ἔθηκέ με λε - - -

Translation: "- - - and Kymo in the precinct of Poseidon, to you [- -] dedicated me - - -".

FIG. 10.—THE MYCENAEAN INSCRIPTION FROM ASINE

L.M. III. This difference of taste falls in with the distribution of amber, and testifies to the different warlike spirit and a more primitive taste of the Mycenaean people.

6. In regard to the art of writing the case is just the reverse. It is common in Crete and in fact very scarce in the mainland. It cannot be accidental that thousands of inscribed clay tablets have been found on Crete but not a single one in the mainland. This cannot be explained by saying that other materials were used for writing, for a number of jars or handles have been found at Mycenae, Tiryns, Orchomenos, and especially Thebes, with short inscriptions scratched or painted on the clay, and there is a special mainland variety of the Minoan script.[1] These inscriptions have from one to three, rarely four or five signs. The script was seemingly used only to put brands on vessels. If the Mycenaeans had been Cretan colonists we could not imagine them allowing the art of writing to fall into disuse, but if

[1] A. W. Persson, *Schrift und Sprache in Alt-Kreta*, Programm, Uppsala, 1930, and "Die spätmykenische Inschrift aus Asine," *Corolla archaeologica*, pp. 208. I. Lindqvist, "A propos d'une inscription de la fin de la période mycénienne," *Bull. de la Société des Lettres de Lund*, 1930-31, pp. 111. His reading ΠοτοιδάϜονος seems improbable to me.

they were barbarians who invaded Greece it is quite natural. The art of writing is the most difficult to a barbarian people ; the great Theodoric was not able to write his own name.

There is one very notable exception to what has been stated above, a long inscription of nineteen signs scratched on the rim of a large clay bowl found in the Late Mycenaean sanctuary at Asine ; [1] some signs have, moreover, been lost, and others seem to be mere scratching. If Persson's interpretation and reading are right—and it is strongly recommended by its simplicity—no more words are needed, for the text is Greek and, moreover, not Doric, as the form Ποσειδά-Fονος proves, for the Doric dialect has τ instead of σ.

7. In the Mycenaean civilization a different spirit is found from that in the Minoan. War was, of course, not absent from Crete, weapons and representations of warriors and of fights are found in art, but they are little prominent. The Cretan palaces were not fortified. Conditions were evidently regularly peaceful on Crete. It was quite otherwise in the mainland. Every city is fortified, and some fortifications are extremely strong. Life was bound up with battles and fighting. Representations of warriors and fights are very numerous in art on all kinds of monuments, wall-paintings, gems, etc. (fig. 11). It may be objected that the latter often are of Minoan workmanship, but it may also be said that gems and other portable objects were made in the mainland—a gem-cutter's workshop has been found at Mycenae—and that the artists had to conform with the taste of their masters. This difference may, however, by those who think that the Mycenaeans were Cretan colonists, be explained by the assumption that when the Minoans colonized the mainland the conditions prevailing in the subdued country metamorphosed them into a warlike people, and they may perhaps add that they had to fight with and to strengthen their fortresses against the invading Greeks.

8. In this connection it may be added that the representations of the horse found in art in the mainland are earlier in date and more numerous than those from Crete.[2] It is always said that the horse came to Crete from the Orient where it appears at the beginning of the second millennium B.C., evidently

---

[1] References in my *Minoan-Mycenaean Religion*, p. 20, n. 8.

[2] References in *Göttingische gelehrte Anzeigen*, 1914, pp. 525 ; cp. R. Paribeni, *Monumenti antichi pubbl. dell' Academia dei Lincei*, xix, 1908, p. 56

introduced from Aryan tribes. Now the horse was bound up with the nomadic or semi-nomadic life of the early Aryan peoples. The word for horse is common to almost all Aryan languages : ἵππος, *equus*, *ašva* in Sanskrit, *jor* in the old Norse are the same word.[1] It is most probable that the horse was introduced into Greece by the immigrant Greeks. The distribution of the monuments falls in with this view.

9. Like the culture the religion of the mainland was wholly Minoized in regard to its exterior aspects, but a close inquiry shows characteristic differences. I have expressed the view that the great antitheses in the Greek religion are of a racial character, the emotional and mystic forms of religion being of pre-Greek origin.[2] This general difference cannot, however, be referred to a certain period of the pre-Greek Age, but there are elements in the religion of the mainland which are definitely Mycenaean and opposed to the Minoan religion. The Mycenaean sanctuary at Asine contained a series of female idols and vessels, just as Minoan house sanctuaries do, but among these were a male head of much larger size, and a stone axe, which in religious connection can be understood only as the thunderbolt. It is very tempting to think that this head and this axe are the earliest representations of Zeus, the Greek god of thunder.[3] A most striking difference between Minoan and Mycenaean burial customs is the richness of female idols in Mycenaean tombs and their scarcity in Minoan tombs. On the whole the cult of the dead was more elaborate and sumptuous in Myceaean Greece than in Minoan Crete. This falls in with the fact that the Greek hero cult originated in the Mycenaean Age, and this is proved by the fact that the cult of the dead at certain tombs continued into the historical age. The dead were venerated in Crete, too, but not as heroes ; according to the Hagia Triada sarcophagus they were deified.[4] The hero cult is an outcome of the Heroic Age, the Mycenaean Age.

A very important discovery was made in a chamber tomb at Dendra.[5] It seems to have been a cenotaph. In the

---

[1] O. Schrader, *Sprachvergleichung und Urgeschichte*, 3rd ed., ii, 1906, pp. 154 ; S. Feist, *Kultur usw. der Indogermanen*, 1913, p. 156.

[2] In my *Minoan-Mycenaean Religion*, pp. 559.

[3] *Ibid.*, pp. xx.   [4] *Ibid.*, chs. xvii and xiii.

[5] A. W. Persson, *The Royal Tombs at Dendra*, pp. 100 and 110. According to Blegen and Wace, "Middle Helladic Tombs," *Symbolae Osloenses*, ix, 1930, pp. 28, the cult of the dead springs from roots already growing in the middle Helladic period.

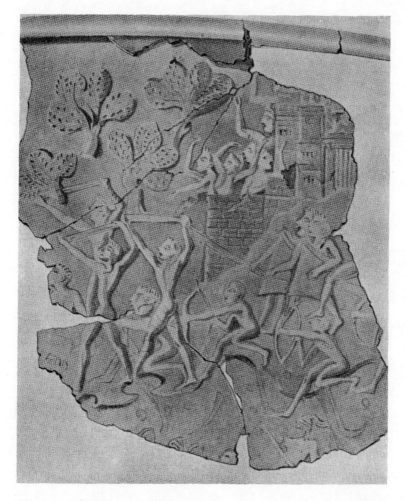

FIG. 11.—RELIEF OF A SILVER RHYTON, FROM THE IVᴛʜ SHAFT-GRAVE
AT MYCENAE, SHOWING A BELEAGUERED TOWN

tomb there was a hearth, and a sacrificial table, and two stone slabs were found there ; these slabs were rectangular with a projection of the same form on one small side and covered with small, shallow cavities (fig. 11). Their similarity with the menhirs, known from the Bronze Age of Central Europe, is striking, and their identity with these sacred stones seems hardly possible to deny. If this is so, it is a very striking corroboration of the northern origin of the Mycenaeans and part of their funeral customs.

10. If we take it for granted, as many scholars do, including Evans, that Greek mythology goes back into the Mycenaean Age, and that a large part of the heroes and myths were created in this age, we have to consider the consequence of this view for the question here treated. Mythological names which, with certainty, can be referred to the pre-Greek language are extremely rare, in fact two only, Rhadamanthys and Hyakinthos. If the myths were created by the pre-Greek people, as Evans thinks they were, we should expect that with the pre-Greek myths many pre-Greek names of heroes would have survived. But even if there may be more pre-Greek names which cannot strictly be demonstrated to be such, the scarcity of pre-Greek mythological names shows that the myths are not derived from the pre-Greek people. To avoid this conclusion it may be said that the names have been Grecized. There is a lengthy series of earlier mythological names with the ending -eus, belonging to heroes of an earlier generation, but many of these also are evidently derived from Greek elements. It is not possible to admit a Grecizing of the pre-Greek mythological names to such an extent as would account for the pre-Greek origin of the mythological heroes. The fact that these names with rare exceptions are Greek, and that to a large extent they go back into the Mycenaean Age, proves that the dominating population in this age was Greek.

11. There is different spirit in Mycenaean to that in Minoan art, in spite of the many and obvious similarities (fig. 14). Minoan art is always essentially small art. It does not know any sculpture of great size, and even the vastness of the palaces is not qualitative but quantitative, achieved by adding one room to the other as the cellules in a bee-hive. There is

no grand architectural idea. In the megaron type with its courtyard, on the contrary, there is such a well-marked idea, the impressiveness of which we feel ; the Greek temple, the propylaea, and the temple courts and imperial fora show its practical uses.[1] The great bee-hive tombs are imposing structures ; we feel their intrinsic grandeur when standing beneath the cupola of the tomb of Atreus, the largest and stateliest dome erected until the Pantheon in Rome was built a millennium and a half later. The Mycenaean Age has created the only monumental sculpture of the Bronze Age, that of the Lion Gate at Mycenae. Scheme and subject are Minoan, though the type is foreign to the spirit of Minoan art and is probably borrowed from the Orient ; [2] Mycenaean art has here created a really vigorous monumental sculpture.

To me, personally, the difference in spirit is the most striking and convincing. I concede, however, without circumlocution that this is subjective. But apart from this, so many differences exist between the Mycenaean and the Minoan civilizations which cannot be explained by an organic development of the Minoan culture under different conditions, and which very definitely point northwards, that we may state confidently that they were brought in by a people with northern connections who overtook the Minoan culture but mixed it up with elements of their own.

4. Archaeological Evidence for the Date of the Greek Immigration

If thus the ruling classes in the Mycenaean Age and the bearers of the Mycenaean civilization were Greeks, we have in regard to their immigration, or, to put it more exactly, to the beginning of the Greek immigration, to consider the

[1] It is commonly denied that the temple court is a Mycenaean heritage, because intermediate links seem to be wanting. The idea was, however, not quite forgotten. This is proved by the fifth century palace on Vouni, near Soloi in Cyprus (fig. 51), the plan of which is essentially Mycenaean, with a megaron, its court, and additional rooms ; plan in the *Journal of Hellenic Studies*, xlix, 1929, p. 237 ; E. Gjerstad, " The Palace at Vouni " in " Corolla Archaeologica," *Acta Instituti Romani regni Sueciae*, vol. ii, pp. 145. Concerning the whole question, see the circumspect discussion by K. Hanell, *Das mykenische Megaron und der Tempelhof, ibid.*, pp. 228.

[2] See my *Minoan-Mycenaean Religion*, pp. 329.

FIG. 12.—THE CONTENTS OF THE MYCENAEAN SANCTUARY AT ASINE

(ARRANGED FOR PHOTOGRAPHING)

FIG. 13.—MENHIRS FROM THE IIND CHAMBER TOMB AT DENDRA

alternatives offered by the break between Early and Middle
Helladic and between Middle and Late Helladic, i.e. the
introduction of the Minoan civilization to the mainland.
In the latter case the assumption would be that the Greeks,
as soon as they had possessed themselves of the mainland,
proceeded to build ships and make sea expeditions, and that
they thus came into contact with the Minoan civilization.
In the former case the assumption would be that the Greeks,
having immigrated into Greece and brought about a change
of civilization, lived there without proceeding further for about
four centuries, until at last they took to the sea and came into
contact with the Minoan civilization. Since they had learned
to know this culture they very rapidly took it over. Such
a process would be quite possible ; during the Middle Helladic
Age the Greeks may have been reinforced by natural increase
in population and by fresh immigration, until the pressure
drove them to make expeditions overseas.

Our ability to decide between these alternatives is limited ;
moreover, it is not certain that the contrast is clearly defined.
It may be that the Greeks continued to pour in during the
Middle Helladic Age or some part of it. Our chief limitation
is due to the fact that the arguments must be taken almost
exclusively from the history of pottery, and, as I pointed out,
it is doubtful to what extent changes in pottery testify to
ethnical changes. It is the more doubtful if, as seems to
be practically certain, the Greeks did not bring any pottery
with them.

The break between the Middle and the Late Helladic Ages
is not complete. Middle Helladic traditions are continued
in Late Helladic. Their extent is slight, but that is only
natural because of the great superiority of the Mycenaean
civilization. Towards the end of Middle Helladic the so-
called Ephyraean goblets appear, two-handled goblets of
Minyan shape but treated in Mycenaean technique. The shape
continues to be common in Late Mycenaean ware. Middle
Helladic elements appear in the earliest shaft-graves.

The most characteristic and finished Middle Helladic
ware is the so-called Minyan ware, a grey bucchero. The
centre of its distribution is evidently Boeotia ; in Argolis
there is an imitation in yellow clay. Its origin has been

vigorously discussed, and as usual hypotheses have been made assuming that it was brought to Greece by an immigration from some other country. Because prehistoric bucchero ware is found in Asia Minor certain scholars assume that it came with a people immigrating from the East.[1] According to another opinion the people who brought the Minyan pottery came from the North.[2] But no pottery similar to the Minyan ware is found in the North.[3] We do not know for certain where the Minyan ware originated : I cannot see why this should not have been in the place where its centre of distribution is found. For our purpose it is very unsafe to rely on hypotheses concerning the origin of the Minyan ware.

It is of importance that two elements which connect the Mycenaeans with the north are absent in Middle Helladic. One is the true megaron type which is not found in this age. The other is that amber is wanting, whilst it appears in great quantities with the very beginning of the Mycenaean Age. Unfortunately the distribution of amber in Central Europe is too little known, and the chronology of the prehistoric periods in these countries is more or less guess-work.

Physical anthropology is often called in to aid in solving the race problems of the prehistoric ages.[4] One might reasonably expect that the actual remains of men's bodies would give definite information. But this science has its limitations, and its conclusions are often very much at variance. We know too little about the races of mankind, and moreover, the remains are scanty, chiefly skulls, and besides in a bad state of preservation. Greek soil has a very destructive influence upon bones, and the archaeologists are not always to be blamed for want of interest and carelessness. It is a matter of great satisfaction that a famous and skilled anthropologist, Professor Fürst, has recently published a work on the human

[1] J. S. Forsdyke, *Journal of Hellenic Studies*, xxxiv, 1914, pp. 155 ; A. W. Persson, *Bulletin de la Société des Lettres de Lund*, 1924-25, pp. 78 ; W. K. Prentice, " The Achaeans," *American Journal of Archaeology*, xxxiii, 1928, pp. 206, supposing that the Achaeans were a non-Greek tribe which' immigrated from Asia Minor *c.* 2000 B.C., first coming to Thessaly, and mixed with the Greeks who took over its myths.

[2] J. P. Harland, " The Peloponnesos in the Bronze Age," *Harvard Studies in Classical Philology*, xxxiv, 1923.

[3] Remarked by Buck, *Class. Philology*, xxi, 1926, p. 25.

[4] For an account see Myres, *Who Were the Greeks ?* pp. 26.

FIG. 14.—TOMB STELE FROM THE Vᴛʜ SHAFT-GRAVE AT MYCENAE, SHOWING NORTHERN INFLUENCES IN ART

remains from Asine, Dendra, the Kalkani necropolis at Mycenae, and the graves near the Argive Heraion.[1] He expresses his opinions with due caution. They may be summarized thus : The twenty-seven Middle Helladic skulls from Asine—two from Mycenae do not count—prove that the population was very mixed, a mixture somewhat similar to that of the people of Crete at the same age ; it is very interesting that one of the skulls is definitely Armenoid. In regard to the twenty-one skulls from the Kalkani necropolis the verdict is that it would be possible to refer the skulls of the women to the Mediterranean race, but that the skulls of the men have a larger capacity than is usual in this race, and that no objection can be made if they are thought to belong to men of Nordic race. The same difference is observed between the King and the Queen from Dendra. The fourteen skulls from the Heraion are more varying. From Asine there are only two skulls from this age. Consequently anthropology does not oppose but seems to corroborate the opinion that the Mycenaeans were immigrants from the north. They may often have taken indigenous wives, as immigrant peoples frequently do ; [2] the result was certainly an extensive cross-breeding. But until we have more materials from other places than the harbour town of Asine, we cannot regard it as certain that peoples of northern origin were not in Greece in the Middle Helladic Age.

I may summarize the situation thus : the opinion embraced by many scholars, especially those of a later generation, that the first immigration of the Greeks coincides with the break between Early and Middle Helladic cannot be definitely disproved nor can it be proved. At all events the population of the Middle Helladic Age seems to have been mixed and there are as yet no definite traces of a people of northern origin. In the Mycenaean Age the dominating people was a people with northern connections, i.e. the Greeks, because their immigration must have begun before the end of this age. The anthropological evidence supports this inference. This being so, the next step is to try to see whether any more

[1] C. M. Fürst, " Zur Anthropologie der prähistorischen Griechen in Argolis," *Lunds Universitets Årsskrift*, N.F., Avd. 2, vol. xxvi, No. 8, 1930.
[2] Plenty of examples are adduced by Ridgeway, *The Early Age of Greece*, i, pp. 647.

detailed knowledge of the Greek immigration is forthcoming, and for this purpose it is not of vital importance whether the Greeks immigrated just at the close of Middle Helladic or lived in the country a certain time before they succeeded in transplanting the Minoan civilization to the mainland.

5. THE PROGRESS OF THE GREEK IMMIGRATION. THE EVIDENCE OF THE DIALECTS

For this purpose we have to turn to the Greek dialects, their distribution, and their relationships. The first question is this : At what age was the Greek language split into dialects ? The neat separation of the areas of the three dialects in Asia Minor does not imply that the dialects were formed there, since the colonists must have brought their speech with them. The dialects are established in the mainland too, although in that area there are intermediate links. The question whether the separation into dialects was brought about after the Greeks had settled in Greece or before their immigration can only be decided through general reasoning. Indo-European speech had dialectal differences before the time at which the different Indo-European speaking peoples by their migrations and contact with different foreign peoples evolved separate dialects. Most philologists agree that the differences even of the Greek dialects are so deep-seated that their beginnings probably go back to the time before the immigration.[1] This view is supported by the natural and well-attested fact that different tribes immigrated at different times.

According to the closeness of their relationships the Greek dialects may be arranged in a series beginning with Ionic, proceeding with Arcadian and Aeolic, and ending with west Greek including Doric and north-west Greek.[2] There is no doubt as to the closer relationship of Doric and north-west Greek, and that these may rightly be included in one group. The same is claimed for the Arcadian and the Aeolic dialects, and they are often included in one group to which certain

---

[1] Cp. my statements in *Göttingische gelehrte Anzeigen*, 1914, p. 528.
[2] C. D. Buck, *Introduction to the Study of the Greek Dialects*, 2nd ed., 1928 ; A. Thumb, *Handbuch der griechischen Dialekte*, 1909. Survey in A. Meillet, *Aperçu d'une histoire de la langue grecque*, 2nd ed., 1920, pp. 45.

scholars give the name of Achaean dialects, but this fact is disputed. We shall recur to this question later.

The provinces of the Peloponnese invaded by the Dorians were already inhabited by a Greek population speaking a dialect of the Arcadian type, for traces of such a dialect appear in the Doric dialects of the Peloponnese. They are especially conspicuous in the Laconian dialect, e.g. the name of the god venerated on Cape Tainaron Ποοιδάν is the Arcadian form in which σ became h according to the Laconian pronunciation ; the Doric form is Ποτειδάν. Like traces appear, though in a lesser degree, in the Doric dialects of the islands of Crete and Rhodes. In the Greek settlements of Pamphylia we find a dialect made up of a mixture of Doric with Arcadian and Aeolic elements.[1] Then we come back to the notable fact that the dialect of Cyprus is Arcadian. In historical times the Arcadians were shut off from the sea on all sides, but it appears that they must have extended to the coast at the time when they colonized Cyprus. This colonization consequently took place before the Dorian immigration, viz. in the Mycenaean Age. The archaeological facts agree with this. For Cyprus, like Rhodes, is a secondary centre of Mycenaean civilization with very numerous finds from this age,[2] and the bulk of the finds belong to the Late Mycenaean period ; it is questionable if anything is much older.[3] It appears that the Dorians invaded countries which were already inhabited by Arcadian-speaking Greeks whose speech to some degree coloured the Doric dialects. In the Peloponnese they subdued this people or drove them up into the mountains of the interior. In the footsteps of the earlier Arcadian-speaking people they proceeded to the islands in the southern Aegean and to Pamphylia, but did not reach Cyprus. In their rear came the north-west Greek tribes and occupied Elis, whose dialect shows slight Arcadian traces, and probably Achaea whose dialect is very little known.

The Ionic dialect also apparently once covered a larger

[1] A. Meillet, " La place du pamphylien parmi les dialects grecs," *Revue des études grecques*, xxi, 1908, pp. 413, emphasizes the relations to the Arcado-Cypriot dialect.

[2] Cp. below, p. 97.

[3] Concerning the finds from Enkomi, which are from different periods, ese F. Poulsen, " Zur Zeitbestimmung der Enkomifunde," *Jahrbuch des deutschen archäol. Instituts*, xxvi, 1911, pp. 215.

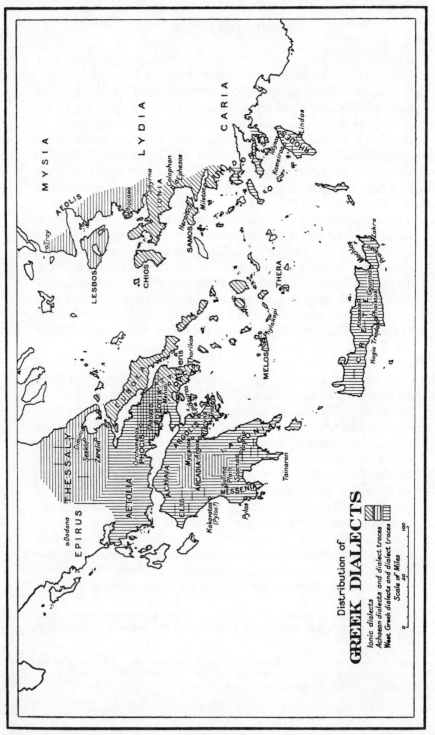

FIG. 15.—MAP OF THE DISTRIBUTION OF GREEK DIALECTS

area and was ousted to a certain extent. According to old tradition Achaea, Megara, and Epidauros were at one time inhabited by Ionians who were expelled by the Dorians,[1] and the same has been asserted of Troizen because of its conspicuous connection with Attic myths, but this town seems to be a post-Mycenaean foundation. [2] Herodotus says that Ionians inhabited Cynuria, the strip of coast south of Argolis, but had been Doricized.[3] That Achaea once had an Ionian population may be questionable, but the remains of an earlier Ionian population in the north and in the south of Argolis makes it very probable that the main part also of this province was once inhabited by Ionians.

The question is : What people drove out the Ionians ? The old tradition says the Dorians, and that is, of course, possible, but the fact that the Dorians elsewhere superseded an Arcadian-speaking population suggests that the process may have been more complicated. Hence Kretschmer [4] has tried to show that the Ionians were the oldest Greek population which once occupied the main part of Greece, and were ousted by the Achaeans.[5] He thinks that Attica was too small and too poor to have been able to colonize such vast districts as the Cyclades and the middle part of the western coast of Asia Minor, and he points to the fact that the noble families of Ionia derived their descent from various parts of Greece, e.g. the Neleidae from Pylos.[6] He deals with the possibility that such characteristics of the Arcadian dialect as agree with the Ionic dialect, are due to an old influence of the Ionians who were subdued by the Achaeans. The immigration of the Ionians cannot have taken place after that of the Achaeans, for there are no Achaean traces in the Ionic dialect, such as the Arcadian traces found in the Doric dialects, although there are some coincidences inherited from earlier times. Hence it seems probable that the Ionians once occupied those

---

[1] Achaea, *Herodotus*, i, 145 *et seq.* ; Megara, *Strabo*, ix, p. 392 ; Epidauros, *Pausanias*, ii, 26, 2 ; cp. vii, 2, 4. Cp. Busolt, *Griech. Gesch.*, 2nd ed., i, p. 216.

[2] See my *Mycenaean Origin of Greek Mythology*, pp. 166.

[3] *Herodotus*, viii, 73.

[4] P. Kretschmer, "Zur Geschichte der griech. Dialekte," *Glotta*, i, 1909, pp. 9.

[5] Concerning the use of this word, see below, p. 91.

[6] Cp. my *Mycenaean Origin of Greek Mythology*, pp. 153.

provinces of the mainland which opened on the Aegean around the Argive and the Saronic gulfs, and that they immigrated before the Achaeans and were ousted by them and retired to the more protected and less fertile parts of their area, Attica and Euboea, and finally emigrated to Asia Minor.

The Arcadian and the Aeolic dialects take up an inter-mediate position between the Ionic and the Doric dialects, the Arcadian showing more affinities to Ionic and the Aeolic more affinities to west Greek, but it is an open question whether Arcadian and Aeolic should be grouped together into one unit or should be taken as separate units. At least the areas of the two dialects are separated geographically, the Arcadian dialect being spoken in the interior of the Peloponnese and on Cyprus and the Aeolic dialect in Thessaly and in the north-western corner of Asia Minor. This country was colonized at a late date, in the seventh century B.C., by the Aeolians. The Boeotian dialect holds an intermediate position between Aeolic and west Greek. This mixture is explained by the historical information that the Dorians who had occupied Thessaly from there proceeded to Boeotia.[1] Thus it seems more likely that the Boeotian dialect is a product of fusion than that its intermediate position is an old inheritance.[2] If we take this fact into account it appears that the Aeolic and the Arcadian-speaking peoples once covered a coterminous area, all eastern Greece except Attica and Euboea which were outlying districts. The fact that the non-Doric components of the dialect of Pamphylia are Aeolic as well as Arcadian certainly speaks to a close connection between Arcadian and Aeolic, for it is hardly likely that the Greeks who settled in Pamphylia emigrated from Thessaly; it is more probable that they were an early side-branch of the wanderings which brought Greeks speaking the kindred Arcadian dialect to Cyprus.

It is well known that Homer ignores the Dorians. They are mentioned only once in the enumeration of the many tribes inhabiting Crete.[3] Homer pictures a pre-Dorian Greece. Nor has he much to say of the Ionians. The Ionians, trailing

---

[1] *Thucydides*, i, 12.

[2] Meillet, *Aperçu d'une histoire de la langue grecque*, 2nd ed., p. 65.

[3] *Od.*, xix, v. 177.

the tunic, are mentioned together with other tribes of the mainland, evidently referring to the Athenians.[1] Athens plays an insignificant rôle in the Homeric poems. He ignores Ionia and the Ionian islands; but Delos and its sanctuary are mentioned once.[2] Homer pictures a pre-Dorian Greece disregarding the Ionians. The most usual designation of the Greeks in Homer is the Achaeans. This is the reason why the name of the Achaeans by modern scholars is applied to the pre-Dorian Greeks except the Ionians, viz. the Aeolic and Arcadian-speaking tribes. This usage has been vehemently attacked and even said to be a falsification of history.[3] Beloch assumes that the Achaeans who invaded Greece early in the second millennium B.C., were Doric-speaking tribes, but he must needs allow the Spartan invasion to remain at the end of the millennium. It is an impossible attempt to obliterate the well-attested difference between the Achaeans and the Dorians, and the Dorian invasion which accomplished the catastrophe of the Mycenaean civilization is thus reduced to a comparatively unimportant raid, which does not account for the fundamental change.[4]

It is much more of a falsification of history to attribute Doric speech to the Achaeans. The reason adduced for this attribution is quite insufficient, viz. that the two provinces which are called Achaea, the southern coast of the Peloponnese and Achaea Phthiotis in Thessaly, were in historical times inhabited by peoples speaking a west Greek dialect. The dialect of Achaea was west Greek but is very little known, as early inscriptions are almost wanting,[5] and that of Achaea Phthiotis shows Aeolic traces.[6] There is nothing at all improbable in the suggestion that these provinces have changed speech and inhabitants but have retained the name of their

---

[1] *Il.*, xiii, v. 685.   [2] *Od.*, vi, v. 162.

[3] By Beloch, *Griech. Geschichte*, 2nd ed., i, 2, pp. 90 ; cp. my review in *Göttingische gelehrte Anzeigen*, 1914, pp. 522. Kahrstedt's attempt to defend this idea, *Neue Jahrbücher für das klassische Altertum*, xliii, 1919, pp. 71, is more confident than convincing.

[4] For a detailed criticism of Beloch's opinions see my review, loc. cit., with which such a competent scholar as Buck, loc. cit., p. 16, n. 1, agrees.

[5] There are only two very short early inscriptions from Achaea ; those from the colonies in Italy are Doric.

[6] See Buck, *Class. Philology*, xxi, 1926, p. 17, n.

earlier inhabitants. E.g. Bohemia owes its name to a Celtic tribe which vanished some two thousand years ago, and Lombardy to the Lombards, etc., etc. There are other arguments proving independently that the modern usage of the word Achaeans is well founded and correct ; the empire of the Ahhiyava in southern Asia Minor and the appearance of the Aqaiwasha in the Delta of the Nile ; to these we shall come presently.[1]

We have seen reason to surmise that the Ionians came first. This corresponds to the geographical fact that, in historical times, they retain only the eastern extremity of the mainland, and to the linguistic fact that their dialect forms the one extremity of the series of the Greek dialects. In agreement with the old tradition it is to be assumed that they once occupied more of the mainland and especially Argolis ; of Boeotia, which is another chief site of the Mycenaean civilization, I have inferred that the Minyans perhaps were Ionians.[2] Just as the wandering Teutonic tribes of the great migrations were drawn towards Italy and Rome, so also the immigrating Greeks were drawn towards the centre of civilization of that age, Crete and Cnossos. Therefore the Ionians settled in Argolis and Attica, whence the islands showed the way to Crete. After the Ionians, the Achaeans came and ousted them from Argolis to outlying districts of this province, allowing them to remain in Attica and Euboea. The Achaeans took possession of the whole peninsula. Traces of their dialect are found not only in Laconia but also in Elis, and the province on the southern coast of the Corinthian Gulf testifies by its name to their presence. In central and northern Greece they occupied Boeotia and Thessaly. At last the Dorians came and at their heels the north-west Greeks. In the Peloponnese they subjugated the Achaeans or drove them up into the mountain country of the interior. In Boeotia the outcome was a mixture of the two dialects, in Thessaly the west Greek conquerors were not numerous enough to impress their speech upon the population ; they took over the Aeolic dialect of their subjects.

[1] Below, p. 102.
[2] See my *Mycenaean Origin of Greek Mythology*, pp. 155 ; cp. below, p. 96.

6. THE PROGRESS OF THE GREEK IMMIGRATION. THE EVIDENCE OF ARCHAEOLOGY

This is the issue of a study of the relationships and the geography of the Greek dialects, and we may now set these results over against certain archaeological facts which may be correlated with them, and certain historical information given by eastern peoples with which the wandering Greek tribes came into contact. If the Greeks attacked Crete, the traces of their attacks will be recognizable only in general and wholesale destruction. Although Crete on the whole seems to have enjoyed peaceful conditions, protected by the sea and by a strongly organized government, war and feuds were certainly not absent even there, and they may, of course, have caused destruction. Catastrophes may be due also to other causes than war, general conflagration, earthquakes, etc. These possibilities must be reckoned with when we try to account for the destruction of the Cretan sites which is often thought to have been caused by invasions of mainland peoples from across the sea.

Ever since Cretan palaces were first erected they were destroyed at the end of almost every period. This was particularly so at Cnossos. The floor levels with the deposits covered up in the rebuilding are the clues to the archaeological periods. At the end of Middle Minoan II a catastrophe occurred both at Cnossos and at Phaistos which caused a temporary set-back of culture, c. 1700 B.C. ; its connection with the invasion of the Hyksos in Egypt is justly doubted by Evans.[1] Nor is there any sufficient reason to refer this catastrophe to mainland tribes. At the end of Middle Minoan III a great catastrophe again befell the palaces of Cnossos and Phaistos, but the assertion that a general catastrophe overtook Crete is not well founded.[2] This catastrophe is contemporaneous with the appearance of the Minoan civilization in the mainland, and thus it is tempting to interpret it as the first sign of the raids of the mainland tribes.[3] But this is uncertain.

[1] A. J. Evans, *Palace of Minos*, i, p. 300.
[2] Karo in Pauly-Wissowa's *Realenzyklopädie der klass. Altertumswiss.*, xi, p. 1767.
[3] I did so with some reservations in my *Minoan-Mycenaean Religion*, p. 33 ; Karo, loc. cit.

Evans, who received a very strong impression of the earth-quake in Crete in 1926 which wrought so much damage, thinks to have found evidence that the catastrophe in question was due to a terrible earthquake.[1]   It is of course possible that the Greeks raided and plundered Crete for a time without leaving marks which are still visible.

The case is otherwise at the end of Late Minoan I, for at that time a catastrophe overtook not only the palaces of Cnossos and Phaistos but also many other Cretan sites. It is even said that the end of this period is marked by a wholesale destruction of the smaller towns.[2]   The most remarkable and important fact is, however, that the Cretan towns did not recover from this catastrophe except Cnossos ; they lay waste during the following period and were re-occupied to some extent only in Late Minoan III.   Only Cnossos was rebuilt and flourished again in Late Minoan II, its last period of bloom, the period of the Palace Style.   The civilization of this period seems to be isolated and limited to Cnossos alone.   Whilst the linear script of the preceding period, class A, is found on many Cretan sites, that of late Minoan II, class B, is found at Cnossos only.[3]   The mainland variety of the script fits on rather to the earlier system than to that of Late Minoan II,[4] and so also do the wall paintings [5] and ceramics.[6]   Motifs of Late Minoan I reappear in Late Minoan III, and the Mycenaean vase painting seems to have been separately derived from the naturalistic phase of the Minoan ceramic art, i.e. Late Minoan I.[7]   This isolation of Late Minoan II and the concentration of life at Cnossos is most naturally explained by the view that the Minoans were afflicted by repeated hostile attacks of the mainland tribes which severed the connections and compelled them to fall back on one principal site in order to defend themselves.

At the end of Late Minoan II about 1400 B.C. or perhaps

---

[1] A. J. Evans, *Palace of Minos*, ii, pp. 286.

[2] Forsdyke in the *Journal of Hellenic Studies*, xxxi, 1911, p. 116.

[3] A. J. Evans, *Scripta Minoa*, i, p. 38.

[4] Loc. cit., p. 58.

[5] Rodenwaldt in *Tiryns*, ii, especially pp. 200.

[6] Concerning the pottery from Kakovatos, K. Müller, *Mitteilungen des deutschen archäol. Instituts zu Athen*, xxxiv, 1909, pp. 302.

[7] A. J. Evans, *Journal of Hellenic Studies*, xxxi, 1911, p. 114.

somewhat earlier Cnossos was sacked, plundered, burnt, and destroyed never to rise again. The collapse of the Minoan civilization ensued. Poverty and decay are conspicuous everywhere on the island, even if the old sites were reoccupied to some extent. The centre of gravity was shifted to the mainland. There the main centre was Mycenae whose most flourishing period is contemporaneous with the final destruction of Cnossos. A great building activity set in with the beginning of Late Minoan III ; a large palace, the ring wall of the city with the Lion Gate, the Grave Circle, and the stateliest of the tholos tombs were erected at this date.[1] About the same time the first ring wall and the first Mycenaean palace at Tiryns were built—the well-known remains are generally speaking still later ; [2] and further the palace at Thebes ; for the wall paintings prove that these two palaces belong to the same time as that of Mycenae. No doubt seems to be possible as to the correlation of the fall of Cnossos with the bloom of the Mycenaean centres of the mainland. It points to a vigorous and successful attack of the mainland tribes on Cnossos. This is justly the general opinion. The people to whom this war is to be ascribed are, of course, the Achaeans who certainly were the dominating population of the mainland in the late period of the Mycenaean Age.

We may imagine that the Ionians who immigrated before the Achaeans and probably before them inhabited the provinces opening on the Aegean and Crete, played the foremost rôle in the early part of the Mycenaean Age and that the first raids on Crete and the transference of the Minoan civilization to the mainland is due to them. Such an opinion is founded on the fact that the Ionians came earlier, but it is, of course, uncertain in view of the uncertainty of the date of the immigration of the different tribes. Certain corroborating

[1] This is Wace's opinion set forth in the *Annual of the British School at Athens*, xxv, 1921-23. His dating of the tholos tombs gave rise to acute dissension, Evans advancing the opinion that the tholos tombs are earlier than the shaft-graves; A. J. Evans, *The Shaft-graves and the Bee-hive Tombs of Mycenae and their Interrelation*, 1929. I cannot enter into details but I am bound to remark that I find the evidence brought forth by Wace conclusive for the dating of the tombs of Atreus and Clytaemestra to L.M. III, and I think that the theory advanced by Evans, that the contents of the tholos tombs were removed to the shaft-graves, is most improbable.

[2] *Tiryns*, iii, 1930.

evidence for this view is, however, to be found in the myths. For almost the only myth which contains clear reminiscences of the time when the palace of Cnossos was still standing in all its splendour and when Minoan power and wealth was flourishing is an Ionian myth, the Theseus myth, whilst the myths localized in Argolis only have a single and somewhat meagre trace of that time, the capture of the Cretan bull by Heracles.[1] This fact is easy to explain if the Ionians belonged to the early period when Cnossos still flourished and its power was feared, but the Achaean power set in with the destruction of Cnossos. The revolution thus brought about in the relations between Crete and the mainland, the final decay of Minoan culture, and the full-fledged bloom of Mycenaean power and wealth, will thus be explained by the reinforcement of the Greeks about the transitional period between Late Minoan II and III by the immigration of a new and numerous Greek tribe, the Achaeans.

Some difficulty as to this view may be said to result from my opinion concerning the myths of the Minyans. From certain indications I inferred that the Minyans were an Ionian tribe.[2] It seems, however, more certain that the great rôle played by the Minyans as seafarers and traders, inhabiting the eastern shores of Boeotia with the inland centre of Orchomenos and the southern coast of Thessaly with the Mycenaean centre of Iolcos is to be attributed to the end of the Late Mycenaean period. This late date seems to disagree with the opinion that the Minyans were Ionians, if the Ionians came before the Achaeans at the beginning of the Mycenaean Age. An immigration is, however, usually divided into separate waves, and the first immigrants proceed farthest. So the north-west Greeks came at the rear of the west Greek immigration the first wave of which, the Dorians, proceeded farthest. Similarly, a second wave of the Achaean immigration may be assigned to some two hundred years later and have ousted the Ionians from the eastern part of north and central Greece which the first Achaean immigrants had passed. This view would also account for the apparent difference between the two dialects comprehended under the Achaean name,

[1] See my *Mycenaean Origin of Greek Mythology*, pp. 175, 180, and 217.
[2] Loc. cit., pp. 155 ; cp. above, p. 92.

the Arcadian dialect of the Peloponnese and Cyprus, once spoken in the islands in the southern Aegean also, and the Aeolic dialect of central and northern Greece.

With the third period of the Mycenaean Age, which is identical with Late Minoan III, not only the full bloom of the Mycenaean civilization appears but also its widest distribution. Whilst the Mycenaean civilization of the first and the second periods was limited to Argolis and certain sites on the coasts of Greece, it now penetrated the country almost entirely [1] and is found to some extent in almost all its provinces. It spread outside Greece also. Here we must not take into account such finds of Mycenaean vases, sherds, and other objects which may have been carried by trade, e.g. those found at Troy, in Sicily, and in Italy, and in many other places around the Mediterranean, but relevant for our purpose are such cases where Mycenaean remains are so numerous and rich that we must speak of secondary centres of Mycenaean civilization and of Mycenaean colonization. This is true of the islands of Rhodes and of Cyprus. Mycenaean tombs and vases are very numerous on Rhodes [2] and a slight local factor is observable in their workmanship, the clay generally being not well baked. Still more extensive and numerous are the Mycenaean finds on Cyprus.[3] In lapse of time local peculiarities appear partly influenced by Oriental art.[4] Taken together with the Arcadian dialect of the Cypriot Greeks these archaeological facts testify to a Greek or rather Achaean colonization of Cyprus in the Mycenaean Age. In Cilicia Dr. Gjerstad discovered Mycenaean settlements, and he is inclined to think that part of the Mycenaean pottery found on Cyprus was imported from Cilicia.[5]

[1] This will be seen even in the brief surveys of the finds given in my *Mycenaean Origin of Greek Mythology*, ch. ii.

[2] E.g. the great necropolis at Ialysos where Mycenaean vases were discovered for the first time by Salzmann and Biliotti; other cemeteries at Lardos, Staphylia, Vathi, etc.

[3] Cp. above, p. 87.

[4] This is apparent in vase painting and especially in the ivory mirror handles of which specimens were found at Mycenae, Dendra, Menidi, and Minet-el-Beida (see p. 101, n. 2). They were certainly imported from Cyprus.

[5] I have to thank Dr. Gjerstad who has recently travelled in Cilicia, for this important information. It may be noted that according to *Herodotus*, vii, 91, the Cilicians were called Ὑπαχαιοί in old times. Wainwright localizes the Keftiu in Cilicia separating them from " the Peoples of the Islands in

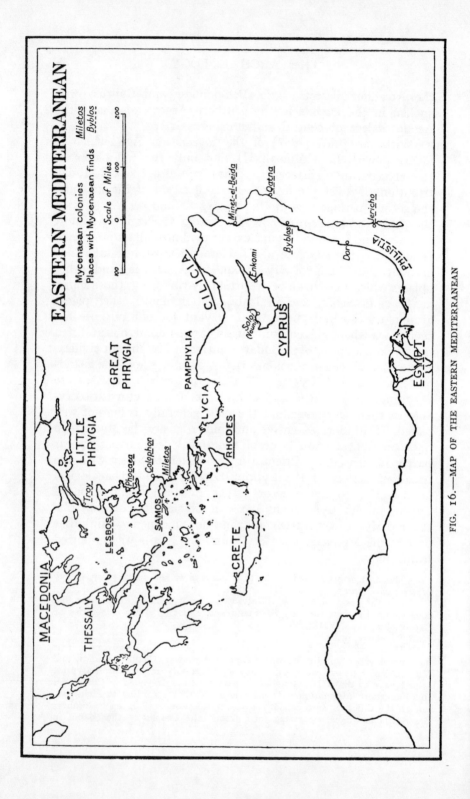

FIG. 16.—MAP OF THE EASTERN MEDITERRANEAN

Thus Mycenaean civilization expanded far towards the east. On the other hand, it is noteworthy that it did not reach the much nearer coast of western Asia Minor except on few and isolated points. Mycenaean vases and sherds are found at Troy, Phocaea, and Miletus only, a small tholos tomb at Colophon, on the islands a single tomb was found at the Heraion of Samos, plenty of rough cups and fragments at Tigani on the same island, and sherds at Mytilene and Antissa on Lesbos.[1] The civilization of the sixth city of Troy is native and wholly dissimilar to the Mycenaean civilization; the Mycenaean objects found there can only have been carried by trade. The only site where so many Mycenaean vases and sherds have been found that the existence of a Mycenaean settlement can be supposed with certainty is Miletus.[2] It has been objected that our archaeological knowledge of Asia Minor is insufficient, but if there were Mycenaean tombs in Ionia, it cannot be doubted that their contents would have appeared in the hands of the dealers, as they did, e.g. on Rhodes. The absence of Mycenaean remains in Ionia is not accidental and it agrees with the fact that Ionia is almost void of myths too. On the other hand, southern Asia Minor, Lycia, with Bellerophon, Sarpedon, and Glaucos, and even Cilicia, have a prominent place in Greek mythology with myths handed down from the Mycenaean Age.[3]

The Greeks did not settle on the western coast of Asia Minor before the very end of and just after the Mycenaean Age, but they expanded eastwards along the southern shores of the peninsula, passing along Rhodes, Lycia, Pamphylia,

midst of the Sea " which are Minoans ; see his papers, " The Keftiu-people of the Egyptian Monuments," *Liverpool Annals of Archaeology*, vi, 1914, pp. 24, and " Keftiu : Crete or Cilicia ? " *Journal of Hellenic Studies*, li, 1931, pp. 1, with Sayce's note, *ibid.*, p. 286. Dr. Gjerstad is of the same opinion, *Studies on Prehistoric Cyprus*, p. 209.

[1] Phocaea, *Compte rendu de l'académie des inscriptions*, 1921, p. 122 ; Colophon, *Art and Archaeology*, xiv, 1922, p. 259 ; Wace, *Annual of the British School at Athens*, xxv, 1921-23, p. 395, n. 10. Samos, Heraion, *Gnomon*, iii, 1927, p. 189 ; W. Technau, " Griechische Keramik im samischen Heraion," *Mitteilungen des deutschen archäol. Instituts zu Athen*, liv, 1929, p. 7 ; Tigani, *Gnomon*, vii, 1931, p. 101. Lesbos, Fimmen, *Die kretisch-mykenische Kultur*, p. 15 ; *Journal of Hellenic Studies*, li, 1931, p. 202.

[2] Miletus, Wiegand, " Sechster Bericht, usw.," *Anhang zu den Abhandlungen der preussischen Akademie der Wissenschaften*, 1908, p. 7.

[3] See my *Mycenaean Origin of Greek Mythology*, pp. 57.

Cilicia, and Cyprus. This route is the old highway from Greece to the old civilized countries of the Near East, and the explanation of this eastward movement of the Greeks is evident. Like the Teutonic tribes which attacked the Roman Empire, they followed the lure of civilization and wealth, and taking the old trade route towards the east and south-east

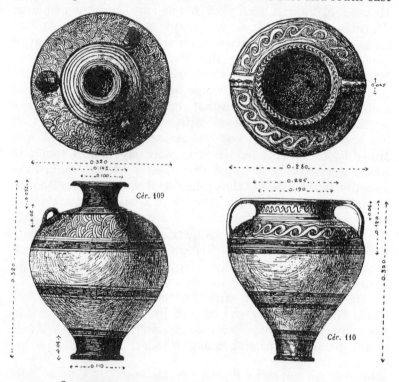

Cér. 109

Cér. 110

FIG. 18.—MYCENAEAN VASES FROM THE TEMPLE OF NIŃ-EGAL AT MISHRIFE-QATNA

they directed their attacks against the rich and highly civilized countries of Syria and Egypt.

We consider first the archaeological evidence. The trade route was old. A tomb at Byblos dating from the Middle Egyptian Empire contained one, perhaps two, Minoan silver vessels.[1] In the tomb of King Ahiram, which is dated by two

---

[1] The tomb of King Abishemu which contained an obsidian vase with the name of Amenemhet III (1850-1800). The date thus given seems to be

FIG. 17.——IVORY MIRROR HANDLE REPRESENTING THE MISTRESS OF
ANIMALS, FROM MINET-EL-BEIDA

vases with the name of Ramses II, Late Mycenaean sherds
were found.[1] Excavations in a necropolis at Minet-el-Beida,
a small harbour town on the Syrian coast, *c.* 8 miles north of
Laodicea ad mare, yielded, in addition to objects of Egyptian
and Syrian origin, so many Mycenaean vases that the site
is called an " Aegean " or more justly an Achaean trading

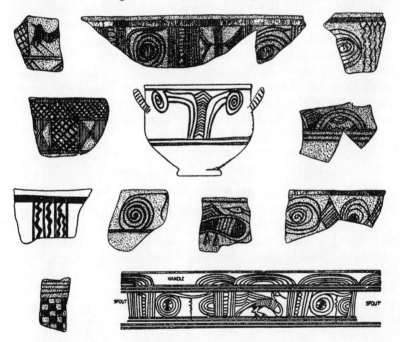

FIG. 19.—PHILISTINE POTTERY FROM TELL-ES-SAFI

station. Mycenaean ceramics were also found in the neighbouring tell of Ras-el-Shamra.[2] Mycenaean vases were found

very early, for the spiral decoration is exactly similar to that of a gold jug
from the fourth shaft-grave at Mycenae.   See *Syria*, iii, 1922, pl. lxiv, and
pp. 298 ; P. Montet, *Byblos et l'Egypte*, 1928, pl. cxi ; the comment, pp. 189,
is very insufficient.   Cp. Dussaud in *Syria*, xi, 1930, pp. 177.   F. Chapouthier,
" Byblos et la Crète," *Revue des études anciennes*, xxxii, 1930, pp. 209, insists
justly on the relations to the Minoan civilization.

    [1] Montet, loc. cit., pp. 218, and pl. cxliii, and Dussaud, loc. cit., p. 179,
fig. 8.
    [2] *Syria*, x, 1929, pp. 285, especially p. 298 ; xii, 1931, p. 5, pl. iii, 2, and
iv, 4.   Most remarkable is a Cypriot-Mycenaean ivory representing a woman in
Minoan costume between two goats : *Syria*, x, 1929, pp. 285, and pl. lvi (fig. 17).

in a temple at Mishrife, Old Qatna, N.E. of Homs in Syria (fig. 18),[1] a stirrup jug is said to have been found in recent trial excavations at Jericho, and it is stated that Mycenaean sherds are found in several places.[2] Further it is a most remarkable fact that not only Mycenaean pottery is found in Philistia but that also a debased native variety was manufactured there (fig. 19).[3] Egypt has yielded many finds of Late Mycenaean date as well as of earlier periods. Late Mycenaean vases were especially plentiful in the capital of Echenaton, Tell-el-Amarna, and its art, especially its paintings, are thought to show the influence of Minoan art, differing by its naturalism from Egyptian conventionalism. These numerous finds, marking the route along the Syrian coast to Egypt, prove the connections with the Minoan and Mycenaean world.

7. The Progress of the Greek Immigration. Hittite and Egyptian Evidence

At last we come to the written information given by Hittite cuneiform documents and hieroglyphic inscriptions. It is much disputed and the reasons for the uncertainty ought to be stated. What we read are names of countries, tribes, and sometimes of men. But old forms of script, hieroglyphs as well as cuneiform script, are very unsuitable for an exact phonetic rendering of names ; for the actual sounds, especially of a foreign language, can only be very incompletely expressed. Further, forms may have been changed in passing from one language to another, and the identification of the countries mentioned is mostly a matter of uncertainty and hypotheses.

Great excitement was caused some years ago by Forrer's announcement that Greeks were mentioned in some cuneiform tablets found in the Hittite capital, Boghaz-keui.[4] The dis-

---

[1] *Syria*, ix, 1928, pp. 20, nos. 109-112, and pl. xviii ; pp. 133, they are said to be Rhodian and date from the first quarter of the fourteenth century A.D.   This is hardly possible if they are Rhodian products.

[2] Cp. Dussaud in *Syria*, xii, 1931, pp. 92.

[3] It was recognized by H. Thiersch, *Archäologischer Anzeiger*, 1908, pp. 378, and 1909, pp. 384.

[4] E. Forrer, " Vorhomerische Griechen in den Keilschrifttexten von Boghazköi," *Mitteilungen der deutschen Orientgesellschaft*, No. 63, 1924.   The texts are now published by A. Götze, *Keilinschriftliche Urkunden aus Boghazköi*, xiv, i and iii.   F. Sommer, " The Ahhijava-Urkunden," *Abhandlungen*

covery was hailed as the most important contribution to our knowledge of early Greek history, but soon criticism set in and seemed to reduce it to almost nothing.[1] Nobody who is not a specialist in Hittite languages can speak with any authority on details, but it seems that on one hand Forrer proceeded without due caution and on the other that criticism went too far.[2] What is of interest here is the presence of Achaeans in southern Asia Minor and on Cyprus, and the existence of an Achaean empire.

In a ritual text from the early years of the Hittite King Mursil, who ascended the throne in 1336 B.C., the gods of the Hittite king and of the countries of Ahhiyava and Lazpa are invoked and a king of Ahhiyava, Antaravas, is mentioned. Another document, a letter addressed by the Hittite king to a " brother," i.e. to another king, relates some events probably from the time of the same king. The people of a district which seems to be situated in southern Asia Minor invoked the aid of the Hittite king and of a certain Tavakalavas against a hostile invasion. This man was a brother of the King of Ahhiyava, and he is said to be an Ayavalash king, i.e. according to Forrer an Aeolian. The district which he possessed seems to be identified with Pamphylia. He would become a vassal of the Hittite king but he takes up an independent position.[3] The fact that the King of Ahhiyava is styled " brother " by the Hittite king implies that the latter acknowledged him as a Great King. The kings of Ahhiyava,

der Bayerischen Akad. der Wissenschaften, phil.-hist. Abt., N.F., vi, 1932, pp. 350, a work which came into my hands after this book was set up, contests vigorously the identity of the Ahhiyava, and even of the Aqaiwasha, with the Achaeans. My views are, however, primarily founded on the archaeological materials. They were conceived long before Forrer's pamphlet appeared and have been corroborated strongly by the great discoveries of Mycenaean objects in Syria in the last years.

[1] J. Friedrich, " Werden in den hethitischen Keilschrifttexten die Griechen erwähnt ? " Kleinasiatische Forschungen, i, 1, 1927, pp. 87. Forrer's reply, " Für die Griechen in den Boghazköi-Inschriften," ibid., i, 2, 1929, pp. 252. He has restated his arguments in his paper, " La découverte de la Grèce mycénienne dans les textes cunéiformes de l'empire Hittite," Revue des études grecques, xliii, 1930, pp. 279.

[2] Cp. P. Kretschmer, " Zur Frage der griechischen Namen in den hethitischen Texten," Glotta, xviii, 1930, pp. 161.

[3] The difficulty that Tavakalavas was at the same time Great King of Ahhiyava and vassal of the Hittite King has been removed by a new reading proving that Tavakalavas was a brother of the Great King ; see Forrer in Kleinas. Forsch., loc. cit., p. 254.

and of Egypt, Babylonia, and Assyria are explicitly mentioned together in a later letter as being on the same footing as the Hittite king.

The salient point is the identification of Ahhiyava, the earlier form of which is said to be Ahhayiva with Achaia (ἈχαιϜία or Ἀχαίϝα) the Empire of the Achaeans (ἈχαιϜοί). This identification does not seem to be subject to reasonable doubt, and has been admitted as possible even by the severest criticism. There is, of course, no place for this great empire in Asia Minor, not to speak of the narrow coastal strip of Pamphylia. It must be the Achaean Empire of Mycenaean Greece, members of which had taken possession of part of the southern coast of Asia Minor. The information given by these Hittite documents is in such complete agreement with what we know from archaeological sources that it seems reliable. Forrer went further, identifying Antaravas and Tavakalavas with two mythical kings of Orchomenos in Boeotia, Andreus and Eteocles (earlier form Ἐτεϝοκλέϝης), identifications which were hotly disputed. They may be possible from a phonetic point of view ; from a mythological point of view they are extremely doubtful, because these two kings are insignificant personages without any myths of their own, such as are common in secondary inventions,[1] and if Tavakalavas was not Great King of Ahhiyava himself the basis of the identification is undermined, as Forrer himself concedes. These identifications may be left out of account.

In later documents we hear of Achaean attacks on Cyprus. Somewhat after 1250 B.C., during the reign of the Hittite King Dudchalia, a man with the name Attarissiyas [2] made repeated attacks on Caria but was driven back. Later, about 1225 B.C., the same king ravaged and plundered Cyprus. Forrer adds that, according to Egyptian information, Cyprus was definitely colonized by the Greeks thirty years later. This information also agrees with our other knowledge, the colonization of Cyprus by Arcadian-speaking Greeks, i.e. the Achaeans, in the Late Mycenaean period. It is, however, evident and only natural that the events referred to are not

---

[1] Cp. my *Mycenaean Origin of Greek Mythology*, p. 130.

[2] Forrer's identification of this name with Atreus disagrees admittedly with phonetics and is to be disregarded.

the very beginning of this colonization. The Greeks began their attacks on Cyprus at some time before the events mentioned in the Hittite documents and after the final sack of Cnossos. In one of the Tell-el-Amarna letters the king of Cyprus complains that the Lukki, i.e. the Lycians, had founded colonies on Cyprus. If these were, as some are inclined to think, the Greek invaders of the southern coast of Asia Minor, we have an early mention of Greeks colonizing on Cyprus, but this is uncertain. Lukki may also be the native inhabitants of Lycia. Archaeology proves early connections between Cyprus and southern Asia Minor.[1]

Other identifications are extremely doubtful and not of importance for our subject. A country with the name Assuva seems to have been situated in north-western Asia Minor. Here there was a city called Taroisa, and near it a city or a district called Lazpa. These are identified with the well-known names Asia, Troy, and Lesbos. King Antaravas of Ahhiyava ruled over Lazpa also. These identifications were contested on philological grounds.[2] To accept them I should like to hear of Mycenaean remains on Lesbos, but very little is forthcoming, and according to my views the Achaeans did not care much for these districts towards the north. Another identification has been proposed by other scholars.[3] Alakshandush, King of Vilusha in Arzawa, lived at the time of the Hittite King Mutallu with whom he made an agreement, c. 1300 B.C.; but the relations between this city and the Hittites go back to the times of King Labarnas in the early part of the second millennium. The name is said to correspond to Alexandros, and Vilusha is identified with Ilion (Ϝίλιος), or by others with Ialysos on Rhodes or Elaioussa in Cilicia. Thus Alexandros-Paris would be a historical personage. But Vilusa was situated in southern Asia Minor, so that mythology must have moved him to its north-western part [4] if the identification is to be trusted.

---

[1] See E. Gjerstad, "Studies on Prehistoric Cyprus," *Uppsala Universitets Årsskrift*, 1926.

[2] Friedrich, loc. cit., pp. 99.

[3] Luckenbill in *Classical Philology*, vi, 1911, pp. 85; P. Kretschmer in *Glotta*, xiii, 1924, pp. 205.

[4] Kretschmer refers further to the statement in *Stephanus Byz.* s.v. Σαμυλία, that this town in Asia was founded by Motylos, who received Helen and Paris, and thinks that Motylos is the Hittite King Mutallu.

We pass to the Egyptian inscriptions which allow us to follow the further progress of the Greek tribes.[1] In the Tell-el-Amarna letters it is mentioned that the tribe of the Danuna was settled on the coast of Palestine. If this tribe, as is probable, is to be identified with the Danaoi, part of a Greek tribe had reached Palestine and settled there in the early part of the fourteenth century B.C., not long after the sack of Cnossos. In the great battle which Ramses II fought at Kadesh with the Hittites in 1288 B.C., there appear, allied with the Hittites, tribes which certainly belong to Asia Minor, but no Greeks, Lukki, Pidasa, Kalakisha, Dardenui, Masa, and another tribe whose name is read variously.[2] The identifications proposed are uncertain except for the Lukki-Lycians.

In the close of the thirteenth and in the beginning of the twelfth centuries B.C. Egypt was vigorously attacked by coalitions of tribes. Egyptian inscriptions say that they came from all directions and from the islands in the wide, green sea, fighting daily in order to fill their stomachs. The Libyans came from the West; others came from the North. Some of these were accompanied by wives and children; these and other belongings they carried with them on huge waggons drawn by oxen. Evidently they went along the coast, and it was a real migration of people. Meneptah succeeded in beating them off in a combined battle at sea and on land in the Delta in 1221 B.C. The tribes mentioned here are Luka, i.e. the Lycians, again, Aqaiwasha, Turusha or Thuirsha, which are identified with the Tyrsenians, Shakalasha, and Shardina. The identifications of the three last-mentioned tribes are somewhat uncertain, but the identification of the Aqaiwasha with the Achaeans is generally accepted.[3] In the end of the thirteenth century B.C. the Greek migrating tribes battered at the gates of the richest and most civilized

---

[1] Concerning the tribes whose identity is uncertain see H. R. Hall, " Keftiu and the Peoples of the Sea," *Annual of the British School at Athens*, viii, 1901-2, pp. 157, and in the *Cambridge Ancient History*, ii, pp. 275.

[2] The identifications with the Ionians is to be discarded.

[3] The difficulty consisting in the ending -*sha* is well explained by Hall, *The Oldest Civilization of Greece*, p. 178, through a reference to the medium of a language in Asia Minor.

country of the world, following the old trade route along the coasts to the distant Delta of the Nile.

The Egyptians did as the Romans of the Late Empire ; they hired the barbarians as mercenaries. With the help of the Shardina and some Thuirsha Ramses III succeeded

FIG. 20.—THE BULL-CARS OF THE PHILISTINES, FROM MEDINET HABU

in 1190 B.C. in warding off another attack of the northern peoples. The following tribes are mentioned : Shardina, Pulusatha, Uashasha, Tshakaray, and Danau or Danauna. Again, identifications are uncertain in some measure. The Pulusatha are, however, identical with the Philistines, whom the

FIG. 21.—RAMSES III DEFEATS THE SEA-RAIDERS, FROM MEDINET HABU

Semites call Pelishtim. Biblical tradition says that they came from Caphtor, i.e. Crete.[1] Their peculiar head-dress, a feather crown, recurs on the Phaistos discus (fig. 49), and so does also the round shield which the Shardina wear. Driven back from Egypt the Pulusatha settled on the southern coast of Palestine,

---

[1] The identifications of the Biblical Caphtor with Crete and of the Keftiu with the Minoans are, however, contested ; see above, p. 97, n. 5.

and the archaeological corroboration of their Greek origin
is given by the Mycenaean pottery found in Philistia.[1] They
were, however, probably not of Greek stock, perhaps they
belonged to the indigenous population of Crete, perhaps they
were a tribe of a foreign race which had taken over the
Mycenaean civilization. Many other tribes as well as the
Greeks took part in these migrations. It is usual for such
a great unrest to draw tribes of different origin into its sphere.
So not only Teutonic tribes but Slavs and Mongols also took
part in the great migrations which put an end to the ancient
world. The Danauna are certainly to be identified with
the Danaoi. This is an old name of a Greek tribe which
Homer uses as a designation of the Greeks, but is already
obsolete in his time. In mythology the Danaoi are so closely
connected with Argolis that this province must have been
their habitat, and myths seem to preserve a reminiscence of
their Egyptian adventure, viz. the myth of the Danaan maidens
who killed their husbands, the sons of Aigyptos. I have
advanced the opinion that this story goes back to the Mycenaean
Age, and refers to some Danaan captive women who killed
their masters and escaped.[2]

This historical information is uncertain and disputed in
many details, but the outstanding and important main outlines are generally acknowledged, and they fall in exactly with
facts and inferences drawn from the history of language and
archaeology, and even with traces in mythology preserving
reminiscences of this age. The Achaeans were one of the
migratory tribes of the Late Mycenaean Age, and the most
important of them ; for the Greek Great Empire was theirs.
This empire was the organization which was at the back of
their great enterprises. The expeditions towards the south-
east began soon after the final sack of Cnossos, and this fact
corroborates the view that the Greeks were from the beginning
of the Late Mycenaean Age reinforced by fresh and strong
waves of immigrants. Enticed by the lure of wealth and
civilization the Greeks turned towards the east and south,
following the old highway along the southern coast of Asia
Minor and the eastern coast of Syria to the Delta of the Nile,

---

[1] Above, p. 102.
[2] See my *Mycenaean Origin of Greek Mythology*, pp. 64.

and this way is marked by secondary Mycenaean centres on Rhodes, on Cyprus, and in Philistia, by the Achaean colonization in Pamphylia, Cilicia, and on Cyprus, by finds in Syria and in Egypt, and even by myths localized in Lycia, Cilicia, and Egypt. The attacks on Pamphylia and on Cyprus preceded those on Egypt by about a century. The migrations went on, increasing in size until they reached Egypt. The attacks on this country were in some measure also due to the fact that Egypt at this time had lost its power ; formerly it had, owing to its domination in Syria, been able to prevent aggressions. The attacks on Egypt were the high-water mark ; after this the great migrations ebbed back. They lasted about two centuries, from c. 1400 B.C. until c. 1200 B.C., i.e. they cover the Late Mycenaean period.

8. The End of the Migrations. Troy. Mycenaean Greece

This was really the Heroic Age of the Greeks, no words will be needed to emphasize this fact, but a reference to the Heroic Age of the Teutons during their great migrations and of the Scandinavians in the Viking Age will be illuminating. The similarity with the latter age is especially striking and conspicuous, owing to the fact that the wanderings were sea expeditions. It is generally to be observed that when such migrations have commenced and go on briskly they are carried further by the spirit of the age, fostering the lust of adventures and the desire for plunder, until they are checked by exhaustion. So it was in Europe in the beginning of the Middle Ages, and in Scandinavia there is a very marked setback after the Viking Age. In Greece also the exhaustion caused by these great exertions is very visible in the poverty of the sub-Mycenaean period.

The debacle was accomplished by the immigration of a new Greek tribe, the west Greeks. They did not, as the earlier immigrants on the whole did, conquer land inhabited by the pre-Greek population. First the Dorians took possession of the provinces of the Peloponnese opening on the Aegean which from of old were the centres of civilization. Then, following in the footsteps of their predecessors, they went

over to the islands of the southern Aegean and colonized
them, and proceeded along the southern coast of Asia Minor
to Pamphylia where they mixed with the Achaean colonists.
There they stopped ; they did not reach Cyprus.   In the wake
of the Dorians came the north-west Greeks.   Other west Greek
tribes invaded Thessaly and Boeotia.   Thus the settlement
of the Greek tribes of the historical age was accomplished
except on the western coast of Asia Minor.

The wandering Greeks neglected the much nearer western
coast of Asia Minor, because they followed the beaten road
leading towards the riches of the Near East.   Thus Cilicia,
Pamphylia, and Cyprus are the earliest Greek colonies, whilst
Ionia has very few Mycenaean remains and very few myths
too.   Miletus was settled at the end of the Mycenaean Age.
Archaeological evidence from other places is insufficient, but
the statement is warranted that, generally speaking, the
colonization of Ionia took place at the very end of the
Mycenaean Age or after it, the Ionians being ousted from the
mainland by other tribes.[1]   This is implied in the foundation
myths of the cities which in their earliest parts go back into
the sixth century B.C., and apparently contain valuable information in mythological guise.[2]   The settlers in Ionia were a very
mixed lot.[3]   The Cretans are often mentioned among them,[4]
and even the Minyans, but the most conspicuous rôle is
attributed to the Pylians.   The Athenians were originally
little implicated, but later, when Athens attained a leading
position, they supported the claims of Athens to be the mother
city of the Ionian colonies by remodelling the foundation
legends, making the Pylians emigrate first to Athens and from
there to Ionia.   Nor had the Athenians so much reason to
emigrate as other peoples, who were ousted by invaders, the
Minyans by the Aeolians and the Cretans and Pylians by the
Dorians.   This follows from the time in which the colonization

---

[1] Cp. above, p. 99.

[2] Cp. my *Mycenaean Origin of Greek Mythology*, pp. 153.

[3] *Herodotus*, i, 146 ; Wilamowitz, " Die jonische Wanderung," *Sitzungsberichte der Akademie der Wissenschaften zu Berlin*, 1906, pp. 59.   Perhaps
he justly considers the emigration of the Ionians from Achaea as a late
invention.

[4] S. Casson, " Trojan and Cretan émigrés," *Classical Review*, xliv, 1930,
pp. 52.   He does not take the Ionian traditions into account, and seems not to
know Bethe's paper which treats the same subject.

of Ionia took place, being roughly contemporaneous with the
last waves of immigrants. As the Ionian dialect prevailed
the majority of the colonists must have been Ionic-speaking
people. That is the chief reason for my belief that the
Minyans were Ionians, and here, I would add, the Pylians too.
Granted the assumption that the Achaeans immigrated at
the beginning of Late Mycenaean, and that the Ionians were
the dominating people in the earlier Mycenaean Age, this
hypothesis finds a certain support in the fact that the vases
from the two towns which are claimed to be the Homeric
Pylos, Kakovatos and the Messenian Pylos, belong to the
second Mycenaean period ; [1] moreover, the same date is claimed
for some vases found west of the Pagasaean Gulf, a district
inhabited by the Minyans.[2] Thus the story of the colonization
of Ionia seems to be clear in its main outlines. The Dorians
colonized the south-western corner of the peninsula, probably
at the same time at which the Ionians emigrated to Ionia or
a little later, first having taken possession of the islands in
the southern Aegean. The Aeolian colonization of the north-
western corner is later and generally ascribed to the seventh
century B.C.

I have strictly avoided any use of arguments drawn from
Homer, because for my purpose that would have been to
argue in a circle. My aim was to draw up a picture of the
Mycenaean Age from contemporaneous evidence. We find
that this picture in the main refers to the Late Mycenaean
period, the period from c. 1400 to c. 1200 B.C., as far as
archaeological and historical sources are concerned. We
may justly call this the Heroic Age of Greece or the period of
Achaean prevalence, implying even an Achaean Great Empire.
I cannot, however, avoid the question of Troy which has been
so vigorously discussed. Most people admit that the historical
fact of a war waged by Greek tribes against Troy [3] in the

---

[1] K. Müller in *Mitteilungen des deutschen archäolog. Instituts zu Athen*,
xxxiv, 1909, pp. 320.

[2] Wace and Thompson, *Prehistoric Thessaly*, pp. 206.

[3] I am not ignorant of the recent discussion concerning the site of Troy
(I quote only Ch. Vellay, *Les noveaux aspects de la question de Troie*, 1930,
and G. Seure, "A la recherche d'Ithaque et de Troie," in the *Journal des Savants*,
1931, pp. 207, 337, 400), but I am of the opinion that it is of no importance
for our purpose. The Homeric songs are treated as if they were just as exact

Mycenaean Age is underlying the Trojan myth, even if this war cannot be connected with the Aeolian colonization which is much later. Here we have only to treat the reason of this war.

In these days, when we are wont to think in terms of commercial science and economics, commerce and trade routes are often invoked to explain even prehistoric civilizations and events. The second and the sixth cities of Troy (figs. 22-24) were prosperous and strong cities the like of which is not found anywhere near. The source of this wealth is said to be commerce or toll levied on throughgoing traffic. That is not unlikely, for Troy has a favourable situation at the mouth of the waterway from the Aegean to the Black Sea, and ships often were compelled to stay over because of winds and currents. At the same time it guarded the land route from Europe to Asia. In this respect Constantinople was its heir. But when the further assumption is added that the wars which caused the destruction of these cities were due to commercial reasons I am sceptical because I do not believe that peoples of the prehistoric age thought in commercial terms. A recent hypothesis attributes a great commercial importance to the second city of Troy; it is believed to have served as a barrier diverting commerce from the Cyclades and thus causing the set-back in the beginning of the Middle Helladic Age as com-

---

as the reports of the headquarters in the war. We ought to remember that the detailed descriptions are due to minstrels who composed them centuries after the Trojan war. We know how careless epics are, especially in regard to geography. At all events Homer presents not a description of the actual Trojan war—or it must have been fought in the ninth century at the earliest —but the products of poetic imagination, drawing on a few scanty facts preserved in the mythical tradition and very largely supplemented by minstrels, who though they may have seen the district and have had a perhaps vague impression of it, yet composed their songs far away from it. We should not expect geographical and strategic accuracy from them, and the conflicting results of the discussion prove that it is wanting. If the story of the Trojan war is based, as I think it is, on an historical event from the end of the Mycenaean Age, which may have been much less important than the skirmish at Roncevalles, I shall continue to believe that it was the siege of Hissarlik-Troy, until another site, larger and with more conspicuous Mycenaean remains, has been found in this district. The argument drawn from the smallness of the site is inconclusive. The areas of the Mycenaean castles of the Mainland are also small, the *Oberburg* of Tiryns even smaller than Hissarlik. I prefer not to speak of the curious archaeological hypotheses put forward in this connection.

pared with the Early Helladic Age.[1] Such a hypothesis is
a little hazardous.

The very sagacious and interesting hypothesis of Leaf,
attributing the destruction of the sixth city of Troy to a desire
of the Greeks to free Greek trade from Trojan control, was
criticized above.[2] I only repeat my statement that I think
that the war waged by the Greeks was an expedition seeking
plunder and booty of the same nature as the raids on Crete
and on Egypt. The wealth of Troy acquired by commerce
or tolls was, of course, the reason why the city was attacked.
The numerous Mycenaean vases found in this city prove that
the Greeks knew Troy and traded with it before they went to
war against it. Now the enterprise against Troy took another
direction than those which followed the highway towards
the south-east, and we are bound to find an explanation for
this difference. Mythology retained only scattered and dim
recollections of the war-like expeditions towards the south-east.[3]
The myth of Troy became the centre of Greek epics. Generally speaking, we are at a loss to know why a certain event
became the centre of an epic ; it was often in itself of little
significance.   In this case it may, perhaps, be said that the
expeditions towards the south-east sank into the background
because they belonged to earlier times, and that the Trojan
expedition survived because it was later in date. The same
seems to be true of the other famous mythical expedition,
that of the Argonauts, which also was directed towards the
north-east and penetrated into the Black Sea. It may be
imagined that the great expeditions towards Syria and Egypt
caused so great losses—probably very few returned home—
that the Greeks realized that they did not pay, and desisted
from them. On the other hand, the war-like spirit and the
desire for plunder did not cease immediately but sought another
outlet. The Greeks sought a nearer goal, and the one available was the wealthy town at the mouth of the Hellespont
which they knew by commercial relations. When it had been

[1] H. Frankfort, *Studies in Early Pottery of the Near East*, ii, " Asia, Europe
and the Ægean, and their Earliest Interrelations," *R. Anthropological Institute*,
Occasional Papers, No. 8, pp. 110 and 143.
[2] Cp. above, p. 26.
[3] In the myths whose stage is laid in Lycia and perhaps in the myth of
the Danaides ; cp. below, pp. 261.

destroyed the way to the Black Sea was opened and penetrated by some enterprising band.

Commercial reasons are also adduced in order to explain

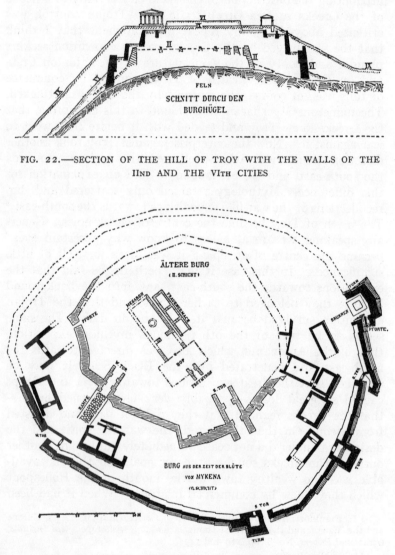

FIG. 22.—SECTION OF THE HILL OF TROY WITH THE WALLS OF THE
IIND AND THE VITH CITIES

FIG. 23.—PLAN OF THE WALLS OF THE IIND AND THE VITH
CITIES OF TROY

FIG. 24.—THE WALLS OF THE VITH CITY OF TROY

the wealth and dominant position of Mycenae ; they are justly criticized by Leaf.[1] The central situation of Mycenae is best attested by the paved and bridged roads radiating from

FIG. 25.—MAP OF THE MYCENAEAN ROADS IN
THE ARGOLIS

Mycenae,[2] not only towards the Corinthian Gulf but also towards the Argive Gulf past Midea and Tiryns (fig. 25). Asine and probably Nauplia also were harbour towns. The princes of

[1] See above, p. 27.
[2] Steffen, *Karten von Mykenai*, 1884, Text, p. 8.

the other fortresses, Midea and Tiryns, cannot have been independent rulers, at least in the time of the bloom of Mycenae,
for then the city would have been cut off from the southern
sea and the roads would have been useless. But it is far from
certain that this superior position lasted very long, we have
to reckon with changes in power and influence of the various
cities in an age so loosely organized and so turbulent as was
the Mycenaean Age. Disregarding the shaft-graves, the glory
of Mycenae belongs to the beginning of the Late Mycenaean
Age, which is the period of a great building activity. The
greatest power of Tiryns is later, and belongs to the middle or
end of the thirteenth century B.C.

The myth of the war of the Seven against Thebes which
admittedly has an historical background [1] proves that there
was internal strife and war in the Mycenaean world. It was
an attempt of an Argive prince to acquire the principality
of Thebes with the aid of chiefs and soldiers collected from
different parts of Greece. It may reasonably be surmised that
Thebes and the other Mycenaean centres were semi-independent,
ruling at least over the neighbouring districts.

Homer and the myths depict such a state of things. Leaf
has shown that the Homeric picture is consistent in regard to
the realm of Agamemnon, including Argolis ; the dominion
of Peleus, including southern Thessaly and the Spercheios
valley ; and that of Odysseus, including the Ionian islands. [2]
The latter is, perhaps, the kingdom of the Cephallenes. [3] To
these the dominion of Nestor is to be added ; for the Homeric
description of this corresponds exactly to the Mycenaean
remains on the western coast of the Peloponnese. [4] Its centre
was Pylos, be it the Messenian Pylos or more probably
Kakovatos-Pylos in Triphylia. The latter opinion, proposed
by Dörpfeld [5] and embraced by many others, fits in better
with the fact that the Pylians fought principally with the

---

[1] See my *Mycenaean Origin of Greek Mythology*, pp. 107.

[2] W. Leaf, *Homer and History*, chs. iv, v, and vi.

[3] I put forward this view with reservations in my *Mycenaean Origin of
Greek Mythology*, pp. 95. Wilamowitz, *Die Heimkehr des Odysseus*, p. 188,
says that the myths show that the Cephallenians were introduced instead of
the Taphians.

[4] See my *Mycenaean Origin of Greek Mythology*, pp. 79.

[5] W. Dörpfeld, " Alt-Pylos," *Mitteilungen des deutschen archäol. Instituts zu
Athen*, xxxviii, 1913, pp. 97.

Epeans or Eleans in the north and with the Arcadians in the east ; they had also friendly intercourse with the Eleans. The Messenian Pylos may have belonged to the dominion, but it seems too far removed towards the south, when we recall the lively relations with the Eleans and the Arcadians.

The western coast of the Peloponnese is the only district of the peninsula except Argolis and Laconia which has earlier and more important Mycenaean remains, especially the two sites claimed to be Nestor's Pylos. Both have bee-hive tombs with vases from the second Mycenaean period ; those at Kakovatos had been especially rich, and there are also the remains of a palace. Furthermore, a fairly important Late Mycenaean settlement has been discovered in the Sulima plain in eastern Triphylia which is reached by the valley of the river of Cyparissia.[1] The plain was settled from the west coast, for the Lower Messenian plain has very few, and the Upper plain no Mycenaean remains.[2] The dominion of Pylos is referred to in an epos of which fragments were incorporated into the Iliad in the tales of old Nestor.[3]

The Pylians are closely connected in mythology with southern Thessaly and Orchomenos in Boeotia, and these two districts, which have conspicuous Mycenaean remains, are again closely interconnected in myths and cults, especially those of Athamas. These relations show that the tribe of the Minyans, whose centre was inland Orchomenos, inhabited the seaboard also at the Euripus and of the Pagasaean Gulf.[4] Orchomenos is famous for its wealth in Homer, and it seems that the Minyans were a trading people, prominent towards the end of the Mycenaean Age. Their riches were also derived from the cultivation of the plains laid dry by the draining of the lake of Copais, the greatest peaceful work of the Mycenaean Age. The expedition of the Argonauts sailed from Iolcos, the northernmost Mycenaean site of importance ; it belonged to the district of the Minyans. Aulis was probably their harbour at the Euripus, and this is the reason why this place

[1] N. Valmin, "Two Tholos Tombs at Bodia in Eastern Triphylia," *Bulletin de la Société des Lettres de Lund*, 1926-27, pp. 53, and "Continued Explorations in Eastern Triphylia," *ibid.*, 1927-28, pp. 171.

[2] N. Valmin, *Études topographiques sur la Messénie ancienne*, Lund, 1930.

[3] See below, p. 260.

[4] See my *Mycenaean Origin of Greek Mythology*, pp. 133.

was chosen by the myth as rallying place of the fleet which sailed for Troy, with that disregard for history and geography which is peculiar to epic poetry.[1] The Minyans existed at an earlier date than that of the dominion of Peleus which covered part of their district.[2]

What is said here of the various dominions of the Mycenaean Age in Greece is, of course, of a somewhat hypothetical nature, being inferred from epics and mythology, even if the inferences are to a certain extent supported by archaeological facts. Here it was only possible to give brief outlines, hence I have referred to another book, in which I dwelt on the analysis of the myths and the corresponding archaeological facts. These are, however, minor details of secondary importance for our main purpose. This was to draw a picture of the immigration of the Greeks and of their wanderings during the Mycenaean and especially during the Late Mycenaean Age. The sources of our knowledge are such that this picture must always be in some measure uncertain and subject to doubts, but its main outlines are sure enough. The Mycenaean Age was a true Heroic Age, an age of wars and of strife, of extensive wanderings and oversea expeditions, the Heroic Age of the Greeks. This is the background of the Greek myths and of the Homeric poems.

[1] Loc. cit., p. 145.   [2] Cp. above, p. 96.

CHAPTER III

DATABLE ELEMENTS OF CIVILIZATION IN HOMER

IT is recognized both by separatists and by unitarians that the Homeric poems were composed in the beginning of the Historical Age, or, to take Lang's view, exactly on the earliest limit of its extent.   The dates or rather guesses offered by various scholars vary not a little, from the tenth to the sixth century B.C., but all these centuries fall within the limits of the beginning of the Historical Age or, to speak in archaeological terms, the Geometric and the Orientalizing periods of the Archaic Age.   In Lang's case it is the transitional period leading up to the Geometric Age.   Shortly after the discovery of the Mycenaean civilization it was realized that certain descriptions in Homer correspond closely to and are explained by objects and elements appearing in the Mycenaean civilization but not in the Archaic Age.   The recognition of this fact is, at least in some instances, universal.

Hereby a problem was put which proved to be very difficult and was judged very differently by various Homeric scholars. There were few who, on the strength of the Mycenaean elements, without question took Homer to be Mycenaean.   They were, of course, compelled completely to disregard other elements which clearly belong to the Archaic Age.   This mixed state of things is a stumbling-block to the unitarians.   Trying to preserve the unity of Homer at all costs they fell back on the hypothesis that the cultural background of Homer is an arbitrary creation of the poet himself, who mixed up modern elements of his own time with old, obsolete elements known to him by tradition.   Or they tried to place Homer at a time in which it could be imagined that the differing elements co-existed, viz. in the transitional period between the Mycenaean and the Geometric periods, a period of which we know next

to nothing.   So Scott says that the Homeric picture is of
the Mycenaean civilization near its collapse, *c.* 1100 B.C.[1] He
does not give voice to any definite opinion as to the time in
which Homer composed his poems, whether it was contemporary with the civilization he depicted or later, but from
his reasoning in regard to the time of the year in which the
Pleiades and Arcturus would be seen contemporaneously,[2]
he seems to think of the eighth or the ninth century B.C.
Though he does not enter closely into the problem, he is
apparently influenced by Lang, the stout defender of Homer's
unity in regard to composition as well as in regard to culture.
Lang's thesis is that Homer depicts a culture differing both
from the Mycenaean and from the Geometric civilization
and intervening between these two periods. Lang cannot
be acquitted of having passed over such instances as did not
fit in with his views. I shall have more to say later of
this and of his interpretation of the relevant archaeological
materials.

Separatists tried for some time enthusiastically to apply
archaeological criteria to the discerning of earlier and later
strata in the Homeric poems, but as the attempts ended in
failure, they settled down to neglecting them. And from their
point of view nothing else was possible, because the Mycenaean
elements were much earlier than the time which they were able
to reach by literary analysis. They admitted—that was, of
course, unavoidable—that certain survivals from the Mycenaean
Age were left like erratic blocks in the Homeric meadows.
I quote two characteristic dicta of Wilamowitz. In regard
to Nestor's cup he says [3] that it was a work of Minoan-
Mycenaean art. If this poem, i.e. the Pylian epos, he adds,
is descended from so early a time, all chronology of the epos
will be futile. This is not so, and our conclusion will be he
thinks, that old heirlooms, works of an art which could no
longer be produced, had been preserved down to the time of
the poet. In a later passage he gives voice to his opinion
from the point of view of principles.[4] The Minoan-Mycenaean
elements in domestic life and in art are on a par with the

---

[1] Scott, *The Unity of Homer*, p. 117.
[2] *Ibid.*, pp. 107, referring to *Od.*, v, v. 272.
[3] Wilamowitz, *Die Ilias und Homer*, p. 201.   [4] *Ibid.*, p. 360.

Aeolic and early Ionic elements in language.   Epics go back into a very early age ; when they still consisted of lays (*Lieder*) Minoan-Mycenaean art flourished, but what is preserved of this is but survivals mixed with recent and modern elements. That is true, but on the other hand, here is a problem which cannot be so lightly dealt with.

Only Evans attacked the problem seriously with archaeo-logical insight—the problem how the Mycenaean elements had been incorporated into the epics which took their definite shape in a much later age, emphasizing the influence which epical tradition has on the preservation of old, time-honoured elements which, at the date of the final composition of the poems, have long since vanished.[1] His paper was an essay, and he was no Homeric scholar. His words concerning the Homeric problem were little heeded, whilst his views on the nationality of the Mycenaeans, embodied in the same paper, were vigorously discussed. The problem remains unsettled.

Whenever datable elements in Homer, whether from the Mycenaean or from the historical epochs, were discussed, the opposing views, one of which strove to push Homer back into the Mycenaean Age, the other to push him forward as late as possible in the Historical Age, obscured the issue. Scholars divided themselves into two parties as if engaged in a tug of war. One party tries to put as much as possible in a time as late as possible, i.e. in the developed Geometric and the Orientaliz-ing periods and, where this is impossible, to treat the rest as irrelevant survivals. The other party takes Homer on the whole to be Mycenaean, and treats the elements which belong undoubtedly to a later age as irrelevant additions. In the very numerous cases which are open to discussion, and in which the reference to the one or the other period may be questioned, because of the scarcity or obscurity of the poet's words, both parties use all means of interpretation to enlist such on their own side. Reichel set the example in his book on Homeric armour and weapons and his opponents followed it.

It appears that neither of these two methods is the right one, or, more justly speaking, the method is one and the same, though applied for different ends. What we have to do, as

---

[1] Evans, " The Minoan and Mycenaean Element in Hellenic Life," *Journal of Hellenic Studies*, xxxii, 1912, pp. 277. Cp. above, pp. 28.

is our plain duty if we wish to proceed in the spirit of unbiassed science, is simply to try to discern and to state the
cases which can be dated unquestionably or with tolerable
certainty, to discuss uncertain cases as far as possible without
bias, and to leave in doubt such cases as are doubtful. The
result is certainly embarrassing, viz. that elements from widely
different ages appear together in Homer. If this result appears
soundly and surely founded, we have to accept it without
circumlocution and to try to comprehend this state of things
and to explain how it is possible and how it came about. We
should not try to obliterate it and to get rid of it by means of
artificial interpretations. Thus we shall be led to propose and to
consider earnestly a problem which was put on one side and
somewhat obscured by the general bias of Homeric research.

Consequently we are concerned not with erecting subtle
hypotheses but with finding out hard facts. To this end it
would of course be the simplest way to pick out and to state
such cases only as undoubtedly and admittedly refer to one
or the other age. They are, however, not so many ; the
cases which are open to discussion are much more numerous.
As the problems of Homeric archaeology are of great importance
for our understanding of the poems and have been much
discussed, we cannot avoid entering upon a discussion in
certain cases. But it will be limited by the scope of this book
and cannot give a survey of the whole field. Anyone who
undertook to write an archaeological commentary on Homer
in the light of modern research, as Helbig once did, would do
a real service to scholars, but that would be a very comprehensive work. Our survey will not be restricted to archaeology
alone, though it offers the most evident means of dating, but
it will comprehend other historical circumstances, too, which
can be dated—geographical and historical instances, elements
of state organization, customs, and religion. But the reader
ought to be warned at the outset that elements of the last-
mentioned kinds are much more difficult to date than others.

1. ELEMENTS DERIVING FROM THE GEOMETRIC AND ORIENTALIZING PERIODS

I commence with the instances referring to the early
historical age of the Geometric and the Orientalizing periods.

The use of fibulas for fastening together the garment is mentioned several times in Homer. The mantle which Hera put on when going to her rendezvous with Zeus was artfully woven by Athena, and it was pinned upon her breast with brooches of gold.[1] The peplos which Antinoos offers as a gift to Penelope, great and very fair, had brooches, twelve in all, fitted with well-bent clasps.[2] Among the handiwork of Hephaestus during his stay with the daughters of Oceanus were bent brooches.[3] The most graphic description is that of the brooch with which Odysseus pinned his mantle together ;[4] it is evidently planned with much care because it is contained in the answer to Penelope's request to the alleged foreigner, i.e. Odysseus himself, to describe Odysseus' attire in order to prove his trustworthiness. The thick two-fold purple mantle which Odysseus wore had a brooch fashioned in gold, with two sheathes (or tubes for the pins) and before them (or on their faces) was a work of art : a hound held in his forepaws a dappled fawn, seizing it whilst it writhed. All men marvelled to see how, wrought as they were in gold, the hound was seizing the fawn and strangling it and the fawn was writhing with his feet and striving to flee. Whilst Evans compares this animal scene with those frequent on Minoan gems and thinks that the description is derived from a work inspired by Minoan art,[5] Dr. Poulsen, who champions the late Orientalizing origin of the Homeric descriptions of works of art, finds that the subject suits excellently the seventh century B.C., comparing animal scenes from this time.[6]

The discussion of the spirit of art is highly subjective and uncertain ; we recur to the fibula or safety pin, for in this regard objective archaeological facts allow a dating within certain limits.[7] The fibula does not appear before the last period of the Mycenaean Age ; in the Late Mycenaean period it is still very simple resembling a modern safety pin (fig. 26).

[1] *Il.*, xiv, v. 180.
[2] *Od.*, xviii, vv. 292.
[3] πόρπαι γναμπταί, *Il.*, xviii, v. 401.
[4] *Od.*, xix, vv. 226.
[5] Evans, loc. cit., p. 292.
[6] F. Poulsen, *Der Orient und die frühgriechische Kunst*, 1912, p. 117. See especially the last chapter : " Die Denkmäler und die homerischen Gedichte."
[7] Chr. Blinkenberg has laid a solid foundation in his work, " Fibules grecques et orientales," *K. Danske Videnskabernes Selskab, Historisk-filologiske Meddelelser*, xiii, 1, 1926. Cp. above, p. 76.

A few examples having a flattened narrow bow with very plain ornaments of short zig-zag lines or points, belong to a late part of this period or to the sub-Mycenaean period, in so far as the circumstances of the discovery are known.   The fibula is evidently another of the special features of Mycenaean civilization, appearing only in its latest period in a most simple and unsophisticated form.   The fibula described by Odysseus in his invented narrative is on the contrary very complicated and is more justly called a brooch ; it has two sheaths or tubes (αὐλοί), evidently for fastening the pins, and before them the animal group was added as a decoration. Here the question is not of this group but of the elaborate form of the

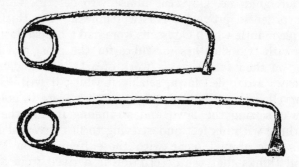

FIG. 26.—MYCENAEAN FIBULAE FROM MYCENAE

brooch. Studniczka tried to date it from the archaeological point of view.[1] He encountered some difficulty in showing up a form exactly corresponding to Homer's description (fig. 27), but stated as his opinion that the probable date was *c.* 700 B.C. Referring to Studniczka's discussion Blinkenberg found that the description reproduces a Peloponnesian kind of brooch, perhaps manufactured in Argolis or Corinth.[2] The actual examples [3] represent a lion without a base, beneath its forelegs are two perforated half-circular projections in which the pins were fastened with hinges, and beneath the hindpart of the lion is a simple or a double catch for the pin (*crochet*) (fig. 28). This type corresponds as well as possible to the double sheathes of

[1] In an appendix to Bethe's *Homer*, vol. ii, pp. 385.
[2] Blinkenberg, loc. cit., p. 35, n. 2.
[3] *Ibid.*, pp. 280 and fig. 319.

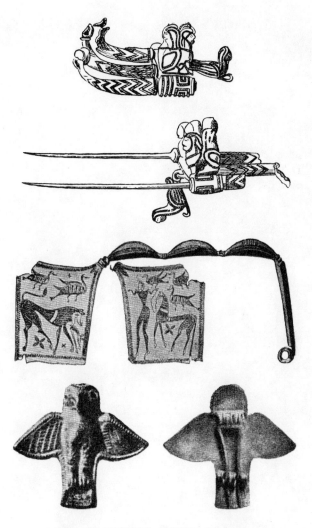

FIG. 27.—VARIOUS ARCHAIC FIBULAE

1. ETRUSCAN DOUBLE FIBULA
2. GEOMETRIC FIBULA FROM BOEOTIA
3. IONIAN FIBULA FROM THE ARTEMISION AT EPHESUS

the brooch of Odysseus. Two examples found at the temple of Artemis Orthia at Sparta go back well into the seventh century B.C., according to the stratification observed there ;[1] others are more recent and belong probably to the sixth century. In any case there can be no doubt that this complex form of brooch belongs to the seventh century B.C. at earliest. For the animal group a fairly numerous class of ivory carvings from Sparta may be compared which represent a beast of prey with its quarry (fig. 29).[2]

Another description which Poulsen, I think, has put beyond doubt as belonging to the archaic art is that of the cuirass given to Agamemnon by King Cinyras of Cyprus.[3] Therein were ten bands (οἶμοι) of dark cyanus and twelve of gold and twenty of tin ; and serpents of cyanus writhed up towards the neck like rainbows, etc. Poulsen's comparison with Phoenician and Orientalizing works of art is striking. A Phoenician silver plate (fig. 36) found at Praeneste shows the representations encircled by a huge snake. One of the Assyrian-izing shields from the cave of Zeus on Mount Ida (fig. 30) offers a still better analogy. A huge snake raises its body upright at either side of the figures. It is well known that snakes, painted or formed of clay, are common on Geometric vases.[4] Poulsen is right in stating that the snake was not used for decorative purposes in the Minoan-Mycenaean art. The snake goddesses and the cult vessels with snakes are very well known ; a snake is thrice recognizable among the Cretan conventionalized picto-graphs.[5] Otherwise the snake occurs rarely and only in repre-sentations of religious scenes.[6] This is decisive. The decoration

FIG. 28.—FIBULA FROM OLYMPIA

[1] " The Sanctuary of Artemis Orthia," Supplement to the *Journal of Hellenic Studies*, vol. iv, 1929, p. 200, and pl. lxxxvii *et seq.*

[2] Op. cit., pp. 233, and pl. cxlix *et seqq.*

[3] *Il.*, xi, vv. 20. Poulsen, loc. cit., p. 170.

[4] F. Küster, " Die Schlange in der griechischen Kunst und Religion," *Religionswissenschaftliche Versuche und Vorarbeiten*, xiii, 2, 1913.

[5] Evans, *Scripta Minoa*, p. 180.

[6] Cp. my *Minoan-Mycenaean Religion*, p. 276.

of the cuirass given to Agamemnon by King Cinyras is taken
from the archaic art.

It is likely but cannot be proved definitely that the decoration of the sword-strap of Heracles described in the Nekyia [1]
reflects the Orientalizing art. It runs : a baldric of gold on
which wondrous things were wrought, bears and wild boars
and lions with flashing eyes and strife and battles and slaughters
and murders of men. We find, of course, battles, lions, and
boars on Mycenaean monuments but no bears, nor are any
bears found in early Greek art. Miss Heinemann pointed to
the fact that bears are sometimes represented in Syrian art ; [2]

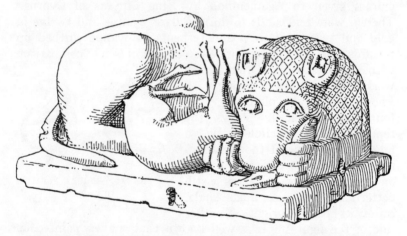

FIG. 29.—IVORY CARVING FROM SPARTA, REPRESENTING A BEAST OF
PREY WITH ITS QUARRY

on the other hand, Poulsen objects pertinently that this art
hardly knows the boar ; at least it does not use it for decorative
purposes as does Greek Orientalizing art, especially the
Corinthian vases.[3] The disconnected enumeration is thought
to show the description of the disconnected animal frieze of
this art, but this is an uncertain point of view ; the poet may
only have hinted at the representations in enumerating them
shortly.

[1] *Od.*, xi, vv. 610.
[2] Margaret Heinemann, *Landschaftliche Elemente in der griechischen
Kunst bis Polygnot*, Bonn, 1910.
[3] Poulsen, loc. cit., pp. 171.

FIG. 30.—ORIENTALIZING SHIELD FROM THE IDAEAN CAVE

FIG. 31.—"ETAGENPERÜCKE," LEAD RELIEF,
FROM SPARTA

FIG. 32.—"ETAGENPERÜCKE," JEWELLERY, FROM RHODES:
THE MISTRESS OF THE ANIMALS

Somewhat uncertain also are certain epithets referred to by Wilamowitz with just doubt.[1] A cauldron is twice said to be " flowered " (ἀνθεμόεις),[2] and Achilles' cuirass is said to be " starry " (ἀστερόεις).[3] One thinks of the flowers of Phoenician art and of the decorative rosettes of Orientalizing vases or, if the word " starry " is to be taken literally, of the stars of Babylonian monuments, but these are only vague probabilities.

In the description of the arrangement of the hair Poulsen believes he has found a means of dating the composition of the Homeric poems with great accuracy.   For the epithets applied to women, ἐυπλόκαμοι or καλλιπλόκαμοι, etc. " with beautiful plaits " are frequent.   Homer's ladies wore plaits and we are even allowed to assist at the toilet of Hera, when she combed her hair and with her hands plaited the bright tresses.[4]   The men, too, wore plaits, it seems, for it is said of Euphorbos that his plaits were bound tightly with gold and silver.[5]   Poulsen alleges that the wearing of plaits is not Mycenaean, contending that in this age the women arranged their hair in loose tresses or locks ; nor were plaits fashionable in the seventh century B.C., he says, for to this century belong the figures with that kind of hair-dress, which Poulsen styles " Etagenperücke " (figs. 31 and 32) and which for him is a very important chronological landmark in the history of early Greek art.   In the ninth and eighth centuries it was, according to certain monuments, fashionable all over Greece to wear long plaits ; this fashion, was, he says, originally Syrian, and he emphasizes very strongly that this hair-dress allows a more exact determination of the time of composition of the Homeric poems than any other criterion taken from the poems themselves or from the monuments.

I am sorry to be obliged to question this exact determination.   First, none of the works of art adduced of figures wearing plaits goes back into the ninth century B.C., but that is of minor importance.   More relevant is that both men and women wore plaits in the sixth century B.C.   Poulsen styles the hair-dress of the sixth century " Perlenperücke " because the plaits

---

[1] Wilamowitz, *Die Heimkehr des Odysseus*, p. 178, n. 1.
[2] *Il.*, xxiii, v. 885, and *Od.*, iii, v. 440.
[3] *Il.*, xvi, v. 134.   [4] *Il.*, xiv, vv. 175.
[5] *Il.*, xvii, v. 52 : πλοχμοί θ', οἳ χρυσῷ τε καὶ ἀργύρῳ ἐσφήκωντο.

resemble strings of pearls, which may be due to artistic conventionalism or, if it reproduces reality, to a fashion of binding
strings around the plaits ; the plaits are thin and numerous.
Thus the " *Etagenperücke* " of the seventh century intervenes
between two periods in which plaits were fashionable and
the question is to be considered what kind of hair-dress in
reality corresponded to this artistic representation.   It cannot
be a real wig such as the Egyptians wore, but it is an elaborate
hair-dress in which the dividing of the hair into horizontal
sections is prominent, the vertical division being only faintly
indicated or mostly neglected.   This horizontal division seems
to be afforded by means of bead strings or devices of some
similar kind such as the gold and silver ornaments tightly
bound around the tresses of Euphorbos.   But that cannot
possibly be made without dividing the hair into some kind of
plaits.   In other words, the " *Etagenperücke* " is only a certain
fashion of plaited hair in which, by fashion or by the artistic
representation, the strings encircling the plaits horizontally
are given the prominence ; artistic device probably exaggerated the reality.   The later limit given by Poulsen is not unquestionable.   Nor is the earlier limit unquestionable.   Women
of Cnossian wall paintings seem to have flying locks, in the
wall paintings from Tiryns the hair-dress seems to be somewhat different.   The hair of the famous Lady of Court carrying
a box (fig. 33) [1] is very neatly divided into three tresses on
either side and two shorter tresses before the ears.   The two
women driving in a chariot (fig. 5) [2] have a closely resembling
hair-dress with the same curling locks rising over the forehead.
If these tresses reproduce nature, they ought to be plaited, or
they could not be so neatly divided.   Such small and numerous
plaits are fashionable among certain peoples, and they were so
in Greece later, in the sixth century B.C.

It appears that even Mycenaean women wore some kind of
plaits with ornaments or strings containing them.   If we
consider the works of art which Poulsen adduces as examples
for the fashion of plaits in the seventh century, the small ivory
figure from the Artemisium at Ephesus (fig. 34) [3] wears a hair-

---

[1] *Tiryns*, vol. ii, pl. viii, restaured, fragments, figs. 27 and 28, p. 71.

[2] *Ibid.*, pl. xii, reconstruction, fragments, fig. 40, p. 98.

[3] *Excavations at Ephesus*, 1908, pl. xxii ; in Poulsen, figs. 113 and 114.

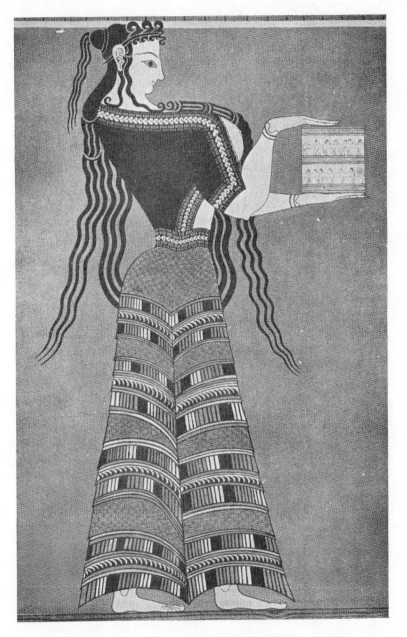

FIG. 33.—LADY OF THE COURT: FRESCO FROM TIRYNS

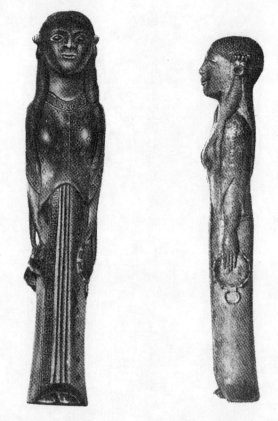

FIG. 34.—IVORY STATUETTE OF A PRIESTESS, FROM THE
ARTEMISION AT EPHESUS

dress which to me seems almost exactly similar to that of the women from the wall paintings of Tiryns, a plait hanging down at each ear and the rest of the hair hanging down in a great mass at the neck. Others have more or less roughly indicated plaits : in regard to an ivory figure from Sparta (fig. 35) [1] one would in fact doubt whether plaits or hair hanging down free is meant. This representation is much more dissimilar to plaits than that of the Tirynthian Lady of the Court. I have added these considerations in order to show that the distinction between plaited and unplaited hair is not quite easy, but is sometimes due to subjective interpretation of the artist's work. The conclusion is that Poulsen has not proved his point and that even Mycenaean ladies may have had plaited hair. Modes of dressing the hair give no clue to Homeric chronology. Only the plaited hair of Euphorbos points to the Archaic Age, for Mycenaean men did not wear plaits.

FIG. 35.—IVORY RELIEF
FROM SPARTA

The stephane, a kind of diadem, may correspond to the head-dress of the Lady of the Court and of the female charioteers from Tiryns as well as to the head-dress of certain archaic figures,[2] and is to be left out of account. The head-dress of Andromache is, however, still more elaborate, consisting of bright bands, a head-band, a net, a plaited band, and a veil.[3] The exact signification of the words is doubtful, but it must be conceded that this seems to be much more complex than any head-dress figured on Mycenaean monuments and to find better analogies in archaic art. A veil is never worn by Mycenaean ladies, it was probably borrowed from the

[1] *Excavations in the Sanctuary of Artemis Orthia*, pl. xci, 1, and xcii, 2 ; in Poulsen, figs. 119 and 120.

[2] E.g. ivory figures from Rhodes and Sparta, Poulsen, loc. cit., figs. 83 and 85.

[3] *Il.*, xxii, vv. 468 : τῆλε δ' ἀπὸ κρατὸς βάλε δέσματα σιγαλόεντα, ἄμπυκα κεκρύφαλόν τε ἰδὲ πλεκτὴν ἀναδέσμην, κρήδεμνον.

Oriental peoples. This passage describes a head-dress later than the Mycenaean Age, but an exact date cannot be given.

The outcome of our exposition may seem to be meagre. We have made out four passages only certainly referring to archaic times : the head-dress of Andromache, the plaits of Euphorbos, the cuirass given to Agamemnon by King Cinyras, and the brooch of Odysseus. Those who wish to do so, may of course, believe that these four passages are due to later remodelling or interpolation. The unitarians ought to do so, for a flat denial of the late age of these descriptions will not do.

2. THE PHOENICIANS

There is another condition of life, more frequently referred to in Homer, which can be dated with a fair certainty, the domination of the Phoenicians as sailors and traders and of Sidonian craftsmanship. An especially vivid story of their ways and manners is told by Eumaios to Odysseus.[1] He was a son of the king of the island of Syrie. Once there came deceitful Phoenicians bringing a number of pretty things in their ship. They remained a whole year exchanging their goods for the products of the country. At last when they were ready to leave a man went to the house of the king with a necklace of gold and amber. Whilst the queen and her servant maidens admired it, a Phoenician servant maid, born in Sidon but carried away to Syrie by Taphian pirates, who was in private understanding with her country folk, stole the small Eumaios and other costly objects and hurried to the ship which sailed away with them. With this description the invented story told by Odysseus[2] falls into line. He says that staying in Egypt during some years he collected many goods, in the eighth year he encountered a Phoenician who persuaded him to go with him to Phoenicia. There he stayed a year until his host put him on board a ship bound for Libya in order to sell him there. He was, however, shipwrecked near Crete and went ashore in Thesprotia.

It is a characteristic and well-known feature that the Phoenicians brought the costliest and most admired objects to the Greeks. It is said of the bowl which Achilles offers as

---

[1] *Od.*, xv, vv. 403.   [2] *Od.*, xiv, vv. 285.

a prize to the winner in the foot-race in the funeral games of
Patroclos, that it excelled all others on the whole earth in beauty
because skilled Sidonians had wrought it well. Phoenicians
had given it to King Thoas of Lemnos when they anchored in
his harbour.[1] Menelaos promises to give to Telemachos the
costliest object he possesses in his house, a bowl of silver with
a rim of gold, which he received as a gift of the king of the
Sidonians when he stayed in his house.[2] That it is said to be
a work of Hephaestus does not impair its Phoenician origin.
Hecabe chose one of her variegated robes, works of Sidonian
women, which Paris had carried home from Sidon, in order to
offer it to Athena.[3]   Sidonian craftsmanship was superior to
that of the Greeks at the time to which these passages belong,
and the Phoenicians appeared in the Greek Sea as unscrupulous
merchants and slave-traders.

It is, however, a fairly common opinion that the Phoenicians
of Homer are in reality the Minoans. Fick pointed to the
fact that the word Φοίνικες has a wide significance in Greek ; [4]
English scholars drew the inference that it applies to the dark-
skinned Minoans.[5] Attention was further called to the fact
that Homer uses the word Sidonian when speaking of craftsmanship and the city but the word Phoenician when speaking
of sailors and traders. The view that the traders and kid-
nappers whom Homer calls Phoenicians were really Minoans,
is said to be an accepted one.[6] This view originates, however,
in the desire to get rid of the late date of a series of Homeric
passages referring to the Phoenicians, and to push them back
into Mycenaean times. But Sidon and the Sidonians are
mentioned as often as the Phoenicians, and the reference of
the former passages to Phoenicia cannot be denied nor can
their late date be denied. The opinion above-mentioned is
based on the assumption that Minoan sea-raiders harried
Mycenaean Greece ; but those who conversely are of the

---

[1] *Il.*, xxiii, vv. 740.   [2] *Od.*, iv, vv. 614 ; repeated xv, vv. 114.
[3] *Il.*, vi, vv. 289.
[4] A. Fick, *Vorgriechische Ortsnamen*, 1905, pp. 123.
[5] R. Burrows, *The Discoveries in Crete*, 1907, p. 142 ; H. R. Hall, *Proceedings of the Society of Biblical Archaeology*, xxxi, 1909, p. 282, concerning
Cadmos ; Evans, *Scripta Minoa*, p. 80, and others, e.g. to quote a recent
paper, A. Shewan, " Ithakan Origins," *Classical Philology*, xxiv, 1929, pp. 343.
[6] Shewan, loc. cit., p. 344.

opinion that the Mycenaean Greeks raided Minoan Crete, cannot approve of this view. If we read the passages in question as they stand, without prejudice, we find that the Phoenicians of Phoenicia whose principal city Sidon was,[1] are meant in each case. Moreover, a Phoenician woman is expressly said to be from Sidon.[2] This is sufficient for my reasoning to whatever people the word Phoenicians may have referred originally.

That the importance of the Phoenicians belongs to post-Mycenaean times is acknowledged, and their appearance may be considered as the introduction of the Orientalizing period in Greece. It is necessary that we should try to determine the date at which the Phoenicians appeared in the Aegean as closely as possible. In regard to the later limit it has been remarked that only Sidon, not Tyre is mentioned in Homer. Sidon was completely overthrown by Esarhaddon in 677 B.C. and Tyre succeeded it as a trading centre. Homer refers consequently to conditions which terminated in 677 B.C.[3] For other reasons, this date falls in well with the date to which we shall come, but we need the warning that language may for long retain the memory of vanished conditions. The passages in question may be later than this year.

In regard to the earlier limit the received opinion that the Phoenicians did not appear in the Aegean during Mycenaean times, must be tested in the light of historical circumstances. No Phoenician objects from so early a time are found in Greece, but this is no certain proof, for the Phoenicians were at first traders who carried goods manufactured by others, Syrians and Egyptians, and only developed later an industry of their own.[4] In early times Phoenicia was no trading country, the Phoenician towns belonged to Egypt during the twelfth and eighteenth dynasties. Egypt ruled the sea and carried goods from Phoenicia to Egypt. The centre seems to have been Byblus.[5] The grip of Egypt relaxed during the troubles of the Amarna period and the wars with the Hittites ; Phoenician ships are mentioned in the Amarna letters for the first

---

[1] Especially *Il.*, xxiii, vv. 740 ; *Od.*, iv, v. 84 ; xiii, vv. 272.
[2] *Od.*, xv, vv. 415.   [3] Scott, *The Unity of Homer*, p. 9.
[4] Even this is denied by Blinkenberg, *Lindos*, i, 1931, pp. 42.
[5] See above, pp. 100.

time : Ramses II again asserted Egypt's power over the coast south of Berytus, whilst the northern part fell to the Hittites. The great migration of the peoples of the sea attacking Egypt, c. 1200 B.C., finally swept off the Egyptian dominion. What an Egyptian trying to trade in Phoenicia had to endure in the following century, is described graphically in the narration of Wen-Amon [1] which belongs to the end of the twelfth century. The tribe of the Zakaray, one of those who had attacked Egypt a century earlier, was settled at Dor and harried the coasts and their towns. The migrations of the foreign tribes and their settlement, e.g. on the coast, that of the Philistines, brought unrest and turmoil which hindered the development of a regular and lively trade. It seems even that people who were either Mycenaeans or closely related to them, in the end of the Mycenaean Age, played a very important rôle on the Syrian coast. The settlement at Minet-el-Beida is thought by the excavators to have been a Mycenaean trading station.[2] The island of Cyprus had very brisk trade with the East as well as with the West during late Cypriot I and II, but during Late Cypriot III, which corresponds to the sub-Mycenaean period, the island was cut off and became isolated.[3] The Phoenician colonization of this island is later than this time and belongs to the beginning of the historical age.[4]

The general opinion is well founded. There was no place for commercial activities of the Phoenicians before the end of the Mycenaean Age, and their time came when the unrest had settled down. The political circumstances of this time should be well observed. Egypt was of no account after c. 1200 B.C., being weak and confined to the Nile valley. Babylonia was decaying politically under the rule of the second dynasty of Isin. The Hittite empire was crushed and replaced by the domination of the Phrygians. Nor was Assyria to be reckoned with. After the exertions and conquests of Tiglath Pileser I in the end of the twelfth century it fell back into lethargy until it asserted itself again with Ashurnasirpal

---

[1] G. Maspéro, *Les contes populaires de l'Egypte ancienne*, 4th ed., pp. 214 ; cp. *Cambridge Ancient History*, ii, pp. 192. The story is dated to the reign of Ramses XI, 1118-1090 B.C.

[2] Cp. above, p. 101.

[3] E. Gjerstad, *Studies on Prehistoric Cyprus*, Upsala, 1926, p. 328.

[4] Cp. *Cambridge Ancient History*, iii, p. 640.

in the beginning of the ninth century. If we reasonably
discount the twelfth century as a time in which unrest pre-
venting the development of trade still lingered on, the eleventh
and the tenth centuries are found to present the most favourable conditions for the development of the Phoenician trade,
the Phoenician towns being free and independent and not

FIG. 36.—PHOENICIAN SILVER PLATE FROM PRAENESTE

threatened by any dominant power. It must have taken
some time, before the Phoenicians extended their voyages
to the Greek sea ; they may probably have entered it in the
tenth century.

It is impossible to determine the earlier limit of the presence
of the Phoenicians in Greece from archaeological evidence
because of the lack of objects produced by the Phoenicians

themselves. The objects ascribed to Phoenician industry show a soulless mixture of Egyptian and Assyrian elements and appear only in the very beginning of the Orientalizing period. But the Phoenicians traded also with Egyptian and Syrian products and their imitations. The earliest Orientalizing objects appear in late Geometric graves,[1] but these are perhaps more probably due to the mighty influence which penetrated Greece from Asia Minor. Egyptian finds occur in Geometric graves and in the lowest stratum at the sanctuary of Artemis Orthia ; we do not know for certain who imported them into Greece.

In regard to the lower limit it is generally stated that the advancing Greek colonization ousted the Phoenicians from the sea. This is a truth subject to some modification. For the well-known Phoenician silver vessels presenting a mixture of Assyrian and Egyptian elements (fig. 36), are found in Greece as well as in Italy, together with sub-Geometric proto-Corinthian lecythi of the end of the eighth century ; the Greek colonization began in the later half of this century.[2] We have to admit that the Phoenician trade ran parallel and competed with Greek trade for a certain time in the beginning of the Orientalizing period, until it was completely ousted. A sure sign of the victory of the Greeks is the foundation of their factory at Naucratis, which according to the finds took place c. 650 B.C.

On the whole, Homer's description of the vessels carried by the Phoenicians seems to be in conformity with the vessels dated in the later part of the eighth century, and does not seem to apply to the Egyptian objects from the Geometric period, which may have been carried by them also, scarabs and ivories and small faience figures. Or it must be assumed that the larger objects imported by the Phoenicians in the earlier period have been completely lost. In our present state of knowledge the Homeric passages referring to the Phoenicians fit in best with the eighth century, and this is in agreement with the fact that all these passages are found either in the

---

[1] E.g. the graves v and xii at the Dipylon in Athens, *Mitteilungen des deutschen archäol. Instituts zu Athen*, xviii, 1893, pp. 109 and 126.

[2] Concerning the chronology see the discussion in K. Friis Johansen, *Les vases sicyoniennes*, 1923, pp. 179.

Odyssey or in such parts of the Iliad as are recognized to
be late.

The same result is attained by a consideration of the ignorance of the Eastern Mediterranean shown in certain passages.
It has been pointed out pertinently [1] that the description
how Menelaos was driven off by wind and waves over a
sea so vast that even the birds cannot fly over it in a year,[2]
shows that the Greeks were unacquainted with this sea and
exaggerated the distances.   The same ignorance is revealed
when it is said that the island of Pharos is situated a day's
journey before Egypt or the Nile.[3] Such blunders would
hardly be thinkable at the time when the Mycenaean Greeks
harried the Delta of the Nile, and when, with the ascendancy
of the Saïte dynasty, Greek traders and soldiers regularly
visited Egypt.   But in the intermediate time when the Greeks
knew Egypt by hearsay only, they are quite comprehensible.
When the Greeks again commenced their sea voyages, they
were, of course, excluded from competing with the Phoenicians
in the eastern Mediterranean.   It is natural that they began
by going north-eastwards and westwards where they were less
hampered by their rivals.

The evidence adduced proves that there is in Homer
a considerable number of descriptions and references which
must belong in date to the beginning of the Orientalizing
period in the eighth and the commencement of the seventh
century B.C.   On the other hand, the imperfect notions of
Egypt in the lay of Telemachos goes far to prove that even
this part, admittedly one of the latest, can hardly have been
composed after the middle of the seventh century, for a minstrel
would not have received so inaccurate a description after the
Greeks began to visit Egypt and became better acquainted
with this country.

Before we leave this subject the marked difference between
the Iliad and the Odyssey ought to be insisted upon.   Most
of the evidence quoted for the Orientalizing period is taken
from the Odyssey and the less numerous passages adduced
from the Iliad are found in parts which for other reasons also
are considered to be late.   It is well known that a similar

---

[1] By Poulsen, *Der Orient und die frühgriechische Kunst*, p. 169.
[2] *Od.*, iii, vv. 318.   [3] *Od.*, iv, v. 356.

difference prevails between the two poems in other respects also. We shall see that the social organization has proceeded further towards the dissolution of the old kingship and the predominance of the nobility in the Odyssey than in the Iliad. The adventures at sea which take a prominent place, and according to some are the kernel of the poem, reflect the interests of the age of the beginning of sea voyages ; they are in marked contrast to the achievements of the heroes on the battle-field, which fill the Iliad. It has been said, not without reason, that the city of the Phaeacians on the island of Scheria is the model of a prosperous colony. The other chief part of the Odyssey, the very plot of the poem, the return and vengeance of Odysseus, is not a heroic legend but a novel. There is a great difference of interests and of taste between the two poems. A modern writer may perhaps compose one day a realistic story and the next a romantic one, but such premeditated versatility is scarcely credible in a naïve age when men lived in the present with their thoughts and feelings and took over the traditional lore as a part of their craftsmanship. The differences quoted above, prove to every one who weighs them without prejudice that the Iliad and the Odyssey, speaking of both as a whole, disregarding additions, cannot have been composed in the same generation of men.

3. ELEMENTS DERIVING FROM THE MYCENAEAN AGE

Turning to the elements which must be dated to the period of the Mycenaean civilization, we begin with the outstanding and well-known instances where reference to Mycenaean art is recognized by all,—Nestor's cup and the boars' tusks helmet. The cup which Nestor places on the table is described as studded with golden nails ; it had four handles, on either side of which fed two golden doves, while beneath were two stems ($\pi\upsilon\theta\mu\epsilon\nu\epsilon\varsigma$).[1] The form of this cup has been very sharply discussed since ancient times, but nobody was able to give a satisfactory explanation of what the stems were, until a golden cup was discovered in the IVth shaft-grave at Mycenae (fig. 37) which, disregarding only the number of handles and

[1] *Il.*, xi, vv. 632. The reference was made by Schliemann, *Mykenai*, p. 273, and supported in a thorough discussion by Helbig, *Das homerische Epos*, 2nd ed., pp. 371.

doves, exactly corresponds to Homer's description and at once explained the enigmatical stems beneath the handles, a really unique feature.[1] For no other example of the same rather odd shape has been forthcoming. This unique feature puts the matter beyond doubt.

The second instance is the helmet which Meriones lends to Odysseus in the Doloneia.[2] It is described thus : a helmet fashioned of leather, with many straps within it was tightened firmly, and outside white teeth of a boar with gleaming tusks were set firm and true, many on either side. Its Mycenaean origin was observed by Kluge,[3] but he did not find out any relevant archaeological matter, and its construction was not explained, until Reichel pointed to the pieces of boars' tusks, cut and perforated for attachment to some material (fig. 8),[4] which are found in several Mycenaean tombs, and to Mycenaean sculptures (fig. 7) showing that such pieces were arranged in concentric rows around a helmet or cap, probably of leather.[5] In this case, too, the correspondence between the Homeric description and the Mycenaean finds is beyond all possible doubt. It is, however, said that Nestor's cup was an heirloom which by chance had survived from olden times for centuries and which the poet chanced to describe. Such an opinion cannot possibly apply to the helmet, for the cap was of leather or some textile material and the tusks were fastened on to it with strings. Such an object, the containing parts of which were of perishable materials and which, moreover, was used in warfare, would not have survived the centuries separating the Mycenaean Age from the beginning of the historical period. There is no explanation left but the one that the description was preserved through the lapse of time by the epic tradition.

The third instance is perhaps not so striking, the cyanos frieze in the palace of Alkinoos.[6] The word κύανος signifies in later Greek lapis lazuli, or an imitation of it in blue glass paste. In fact there is no other instance by which a cyanus

---

[1] Often illustrated, e.g. in G. Karo, *Die Schachtgräber von Mykenai*, 1930, pl. cix.

[2] *Il.*, x, vv. 261.

[3] H. Kluge, " Vorhomerische Kampfschilderungen in der Ilias," *Fleck-eisen's Jahrbücher f. class Philologie*, cxlvii, 1893, pp. 81.

[4] W. Reichel, *Homerische Waffen*, 2nd ed., pp. 102.

[5] The finds are mentioned above, p. 77.   [6] *Od.*, vii, v. 87.

FIG. 37.—"NESTOR'S CUP," FROM THE IVTH SHAFT-GRAVE AT MYCENAE

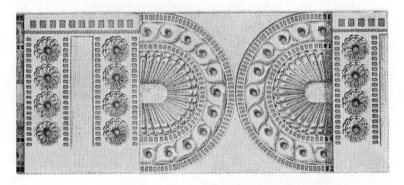

FIG. 38.—THE CYANUS FRIEZE FROM TIRYNS

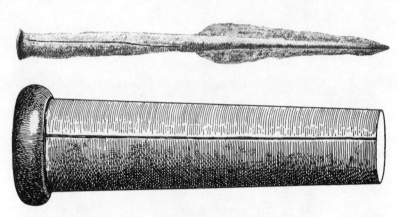

FIG. 39.—SPEAR-HEAD AND SOCKET OF SPEAR-HEAD WITH SLIT AND
RING, FROM THE VITH SHAFT-GRAVE AT MYCENAE

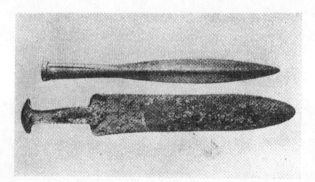

FIG. 40.—SPEAR-HEAD WITH SLIT AND RING, FROM A
CHAMBER TOMB AT DENDRA

FIG. 41.—DAGGER BLADE WITH LION HUNT, FROM THE IVTH SHAFT-
GRAVE AT MYCENAE

frieze can be illustrated than the gypsum frieze from the palace of Tiryns with rosettes and palmettes and encrusted with pieces of blue glass paste (fig. 38).[1]

Evans recently called attention to a fourth instance which seems to be very well founded.[2] In two passages it is said of Hector's spear that on its fore-end it had a head of bronze and that a golden ring encircled this.[3] No corresponding bronze spear-heads were known, until Evans pointed to some socketed bronze spear-heads from the shaft-graves at Mycenae, the sockets of which are not solid but formed of a tube of beaten metal showing a slit along the side and for that reason encircled by a ring of metal (fig. 39). Such spear-heads are also found in graves at Mochlos in Crete from the third Middle Minoan period and at Dendra (fig. 40). The spear-heads of the later Bronze Age and the early Iron Age are cast and solid and the circlet disappears as an organic feature. We must again state that the Homeric description is explained by Minoan-Mycenaean finds only.[4]

These are isolated things, mentioned once or twice in identical words. With the last instance, the descriptions of weapons and armour, we enter upon a topic which pervades all the Homeric poems. Nor has any subject been so much discussed as this in regard to Homer's connections with Mycenae. The vexed question of the use of bronze and iron in Homer has been treated so often that it may be dismissed very briefly.[5] Iron is mentioned fairly frequently in Homer,

---

[1] Schliemann, *Tiryns*, pl. iv ; the identification by Helbig, loc. cit., pp. 100.

[2] Evans, *The Shaft Graves and the Bee-hive Tombs at Mycenae*, 1929, pp. 39.

[3] *Il.*, vi, v. 320, and viii, v. 495.

[4] S. Marinatos, " Le Chernibon dans la civilisation créto-mycénienne," *Bulletin de correspondance hellénique*, liii, 1929, pp. 378, has drawn attention to the fact that a set of pitcher and basin used in Homer for washing the hands is depicted on Minoan clay tablets and that the corresponding vessels are found from the time of Middle Minoan III. This is true, but caution is necessary, for it is probable that the same custom and the necessary vessels existed even in post-Mycenaean times, although they may have been of more modest materials. The same set of a pitcher and basin is still used by the Greeks of Asia Minor ; it is called μαστραπᾶ.

[5] The fundamental paper is G. Beloch, " Bronzo e Ferro nei carmini Omerici," *Rivista di filologia ed istruzione classica*, ii, 1873, pp. 49 ; repeated with some modifications in his *Griechische Geschichte*, 2nd ed., i, 2, 1913, ch. x. The importance of the statistics given by Beloch is with some reason questioned by A. Lang, *Homer and his Age*, p. 176, n. 1, and by Jevons, " Iron in Homer," *Journal of Hellenic Studies*, xiii, 1893, pp. 25. Cp. Cauer, *Grundfragen der Homerkritik*, 3rd ed., pp. 311.

and many passages referring to it cannot be cut out as later additions. The use of the word in metaphors and in proverbs shows that the use of iron was current.[1] But it is used for tools only, never for weapons except in two special instances, the iron club of Areithoos and the iron arrow-head of Pandaros.[2] The last-mentioned passage has been much discussed, but it has hardly been noticed that it proves that iron was not only much used but also cheap. First the arrow-head is simply called " the iron," and secondly as arrow-heads were commonly lost when shot off, they were made of cheap material. During the Bronze Age arrow-heads were seldom made of the expensive bronze but generally of cheap obsidian flakes.

Such passages cannot belong to the beginning of the Iron Age ; they testify to a fairly advanced stage of it. This observation militates against Andrew Lang's well-known theory,[3] according to which the Homeric civilization belonged to an overlapping stage of the Bronze and the Iron Ages in which iron was used for tools and bronze for weapons, because the iron swords, being badly tempered, were unreliable in the battle, as were those of the Gauls which became bent by a stroke, so that the warriors must trample upon them in order to straighten them ; I do not object that the process of tempering iron is described in Homer [4]—it may still have been imperfect—and that iron is taken to be the hardest of metals in metaphors. We have to test the foundation of the hypothesis.

There has been an age in which both metals were used for weapons. In the proto-Geometric graves on the S.W. slope of the Acropolis at Athens all weapons were of bronze except one iron sword. In a grave at the Areopagus a spear-head of bronze was found together with a sword of iron. In the

---

[1] σιδήρειον ἦτορ, Il., xxiv, vv. 205 and 521 ; σοί γε σιδήρεα πάντα τέτυκται, Od., xii, v. 280 ; αὐτὸς γὰρ ἐφέλκεται ἄνδρα σίδηρος, Od., xvi, v. 294. This last-mentioned passage is remarkable for giving a reason why the weapons should be removed from Odysseus' hall, it proves that iron weapons were familiar to the man who conceived it.

[2] Il., vii, v. 141, and iv, v. 123, respectively. νευρὴν μὲν μαζῷ πέλασεν, τόξῳ δὲ σίδηρον. See Lang's discussion, Homer and his Age, ch. ix.

[3] Cp. above, pp. 22. He had predecessors : Helbig, loc. cit., p. 330 ; Jevons, loc. cit., pp. 25.

[4] Od., ix, vv. 392.

developed Geometric Age weapons are always of iron.[1] The
intermediate age between the downfall of the Mycenaean
civilization and the Geometric period is notoriously very poor,
too poor to correspond to the civilization described by Homer
if taken as a unity. Lang's view is indissolubly bound up with
his attempt to prove the unity of the Homeric civilization.
Recognizing elements on one hand from the shaft-grave period
and on the other from the beginning of the Orientalizing
period, we have seen that this unity is a phantom. Another
explanation must be found which takes the difference of age
between the different elements of the Homeric poems into due
account.

Less objection could be made against the bold supposition
of Ridgeway that in the Homeric Age the weapons in fact were
of iron, although they very often are said to be of bronze.[2]
Such ever-recurring phrases as e.g. " he wounded him with
the grim copper " and similar ones [3] may not be more than
old heirlooms just as the blacksmith always was called " copper
smith " ($\chi\alpha\lambda\kappa\epsilon\dot{\upsilon}s$). Even tools are sometimes said to be of
bronze, but such phrases seem to be old and misapplied.[4] We
find not only isolated words but also partly unintelligible
stock expressions with a fixed place in the verse. As the
word $\chi\alpha\lambda\kappa\acute{o}s$ has not remained in the language with the
significance of "weapon," as $\chi\alpha\lambda\kappa\epsilon\dot{\upsilon}s$ remained with the
significance of "blacksmith," we are bound to admit that
these phrases were coined at a time in which weapons and
tools really were of bronze, just as the Iron Age coined the
proverb saying that iron draws a man toward it by itself.
Preserved by the epic tradition they were used for centuries
even after they had ceased to correspond to the reality. But
they testify to the origin of epics in the Bronze Age, as Beloch
justly inferred, and as admitted even by those inclined to

---

[1] F. Poulsen, *Die Dipylongräber und die Dipylonvasen*, 1905, pp. 39.
[2] W. Ridgeway, *The Early Age of Greece*, i, pp. 294.
[3] E.g. οὔτασε νηλέι χαλκῷ, κατέκτανον ὀξέι χαλκῷ, νώροπα (ι) χαλκόν (ῷ), κτλ.
[4] Eleven examples ; see Beloch, *Griech. Gesch.*, loc. cit., p. 111. The
phrase ταναηκέι χαλκῷ concerning the axe used by wood-cutters for felling
trees, *Il.*, xxiii; v. 114, is misused, for the attribute is, as Lang pointed out,
loc. cit., p.' 183, inappropriate to a wood-cutter's axe. It is a nice instance
of the phenomenon discussed in the text.

share Ridgeway's view.[1] It is to be added that the Greeks in the beginning of the historical age knew of the existence of the Bronze Age.[2]

Next we come to the much-discussed problem of Homeric armour. A thorough treatment would require a book of its own, nor is it wanted here where the comparatively few undoubted testimonies are to be adduced, whilst a full discussion would include the bulk of more or less uncertain passages. Homer knows a shield which was big enough to cover the body from the chin to the feet. It was worn on a strap passing over the left shoulder,[3] and could be flung back and be left hanging on the back. It is said that when Hector went back from the battle the rim of the shield hurt his ankles and his neck.[4] Peripetes wore a shield which reached down to his feet and he stumbled over it.[5] It is said of Idomeneus that his whole body shrunk behind his shield.[6] Aias' shield is compared with a tower and is made by a leather-worker having seven layers of hide and an eighth layer of bronze.[7] The epithet ἀμφίβροτος seems to apply to this body-shield. Certain phrases and words used in describing the taking up of the shield are explained by reference to the body-shield, suspended on a strap passing over the left shoulder, whilst they do not fit in with the shield of the later age which was worn by an arm-loop and a hand-grip. The wording is : " he put the shield around his shoulder," [8] and the same words are used for " putting on " the shield as for putting on a piece of garment.[9] Further there is at least one passage in which a hero did not wear any corslet or cuirass. Hector hit Aias on the spot where two baldrics—that of the shield and that of the sword—were stretched over his breast and these protected

---

[1] E. Drerup, *Homerische Poetik*, i, p. 169 ; G. Finsler, *Homer*, 3rd ed., p. 130. Cauer, loc. cit., who has an illuminating discussion of the passages in question, sticks to the opinion that the occurrence of iron serves for discerning earlier and later layers in the poems, and there is undeniably some truth in this assertion, although it is of no great importance for our aim.

[2] Hesiod, *Opera*, vv. 150.   [3] *Il.*, xvi, v. 106.

[4] *Il.*, vi, vv. 117.   [5] ποδηνεκής, *Il.*, xv, v. 646.

[6] τῇ ὕπο πᾶς ἐάλη, *Il.*, xiii, v. 408.

[7] *Il.*, xi, v. 485 ; xvii, v. 128 ; vii, v. 219.

[8] *Il.*, iii, vv. 334 ; xvi, vv. 135 ; ἀμφὶ δ' ἄρ' ὤμοισιν βάλετο ξίφος ἀργυρόηλον χάλκεον, αὐτὰρ ἔπειτα σάκος μέγα τε στιβαρόν τε.

[9] ἐσσάμενοι, *Il.*, xiv, v. 372 ; δύω, *Il.*, xiii, v. 377 ; cp. xviii, v. 192 ; passages collected by Robert, *Studien zur Ilias*, p. 19.

his skin.[1] If Aias had had any corslet or cuirass it would not have been possible to leave it unmentioned in this connection.

On the other hand, a small shield is to be recognized in other passages. For example, when it is said that Aeneas shrank and held up his shield before himself,[2] this is only understandable if the shield was of small size. The epithets παντόσ' ἐίση and εὔκυκλος must needs be referred to the round shield. When γύαλα are mentioned it cannot be denied that they are the breast and the back pieces of the bronze cuirass, which always were called by this word.

It has already been observed by Helbig that the big shield described by Homer is illustrated by Mycenaean monuments, e.g. the inlaid dagger with the lion hunt from the fourth shaft-grave at Mycenae (fig. 41) and a sardonyx from the third shaft-grave (fig. 42).[3] The big Mycenaean body-shield reaching from the chin to the feet has two forms, a form with straight sides conventionally called the tower shield, and another with incurved sides, called the figure-8 shield. The latter form is evidently Minoan, for it is very often used for decorative purposes in the Minoan as well as in the Mycenaean art.[4] Kluge made the acute observation that Homeric heroes who wore the body-shield had the upper part of the body unprotected,[5] but his paper was overlooked because of Reichel's comprehensive work, in which this scholar took up the question of Homeric armour and weapons with much ability and energy and which is the starting-point for the vast amount of later discussion.[6]

Reichel described the construction and the use of the body-shield very well ; his errors were that he pushed the discovery too far and tried to show that on the whole Homer referred to the Mycenaean equipment but that his descriptions had been blurred by later changes and interpolations only. He applied this view especially to the corslet or cuirass, which, according to him was inconsistent with the body-shield and

[1] *Il.*, xiv, vv. 402.

[2] *Il.*, xx, v. 278 ; the decisive word is the preposition in ἀνέσχεν.

[3] Enumeration in H. L. Lorimer, " Defensive Armour in Homer," *Liverpool Annals of Archaeology*, xv, 1928, pp. 91.

[4] Cp. my *Minoan-Mycenaean Religion*, pp. 349, and Evans, *Palace of Minos*, ii. pp. 52.

[5] Kluge in the paper quoted, p. 138, n. 3.

[6] W. Reichel, *Homerische Waffen*, 1st ed., 1894 ; 2nd ed. posthumous, 1901.

had been introduced into the poems later. The subject was skilfully reworked by Robert ; [1] correcting Reichel's conclusions he acknowledged the frequent occurrence of Ionian panoply, i.e. the bronze cuirass and the round shield ; he used the difference between the Mycenaean and the Ionian equipment in order to distinguish between earlier and later layers in the Iliad, and this resulted in a failure.[2]

The discussion which admits the difference of armour may be passed over lightly, because fundamentally it agrees with the view here proposed. In contrast to this opinion others have tried to obliterate the difference, and their reasons for so doing must be tested. Lang did the same with much energy owing to his conviction of the unity of the Homeric civilization.[3] The result is a harmonizing of the apparently

FIG. 42.—GOLD BEAD-SEAL FROM THE IVTH, AND SARDONYX
FROM THE IIIRD SHAFT-GRAVE AT MYCENAE

conflicting descriptions in Homer. Lang denies that small circular shields or bucklers worn on the left arm are ever mentioned in Homer. On the other hand, the Homeric armour is said to be later than that of the early Mycenaean Age, in which, according to the monuments, only huge leather shields were used. Homer lived in an intermediate age, in which both huge shields and light corslets were used. The type of shield was intermediate, as large as the Mycenaean but plated with bronze ; it was suspended on a baldric. Its size depended on the fact that it served as protection against showers of arrows. Lang admits its shape to be varying, oblong or circular.[4]

---

[1] C. Robert, *Studien zur Ilias*, 1901.   [2] Cp. above, p. 20.

[3] A. Lang, *Homer and his Age*, chs. vii and viii.

[4] The huge circular shield, *c.* 4½ feet in diameter, is impossible, not so much because of its weight as because of its breadth which would be a great hindrance and is absolutely unnecessary. Huge shields are by necessity

Lang's view amounts to this : that the small shield and the metal cuirass are wanting in Homer. But the word which always signifies the two halves of the metal cuirass, γύαλα, is not to be misunderstood, and there seems to be evidence for the small shield too and the panoply of the historical age. Lang's opinion of the exclusive use of the huge shield in the intermediate age is in conflict with the monuments, according to which the huge body shield belongs to the Early Mycenaean Age and the small shield appeared in the Late Mycenaean period.[1] It is generally admitted that Lang has not succeeded in obliterating the difference.

Another attempt in quite another manner was made by Lippold in a comprehensive treatment of Greek shields.[2] He calls attention to a type well known from vase paintings and called the Boeotian shield. It is oval and seems to be cut out on both sides. On the Dipylon vases a somewhat similar type occurs ; it has strongly incurving sides being of " hour-glass " form (fig. 45). Lippold thinks it to be identical with the Boeotian shield. He supposes, however, that the cuttings are not real but due to a conventionalized representation : the shield consisted of hide stretched out between an upper and a lower horizontal staff, joined by a vertical cross staff in the middle ; the free sides of the hide would consequently shrink inwards. He thinks that this type of shield developed parallel with the Mycenaean body-shield from a common origin. Lippold identifies the Homeric body-shield with the Dipylon shield which he even styles a tower shield.[3] He acknowledges that the round shield also occurs in Homer and explains the fact that Homer mentions both the tower shield and the round shield by the composition of the Iliad in the eighth century B.C. For in this century the round shield had just appeared, he says, and the tower shield was still in use. The fatal objection to Lippold's attempt of harmonizing is that the **Dipylon**

oblong. This is the reason why with Helbig, loc. cit., p. 313, I distrust the Aristonothos vase (fig. 43) which Lang produces as a testimony to the huge circular shield. It is most probable that the painter has pictured the shields of the men on the ship to the right too large. He has no sense of proportion ; cp. the small man on the top of the mast whose lower part apparently is wanting.

[1] Cp. below, p. 147.

[2] G. Lippold, " Griechische Schilde," in *Münchener archäologische Studien dem Andenken A. Furtwänglers gewidmet*, 1909, pp. 399.

[3] In his chapter on the shields in the epos, loc. cit., pp. 460.

shield was no tower shield corresponding to the Homeric description of the body-shield. It is represented so often that there cannot be any doubt that it did not reach from the chin to the feet. In spite of Lippold's assertion it is not ποδηνεκής and hardly longer than the common round shield.

FIG. 44.—SHIELDS ON A DIPYLON VASE

FIG. 45.—"HOUR-GLASS" SHIELDS ON A DIPYLON VASE

Owing to the evident objections, the attempts to obliterate the existing differences in the Homeric descriptions of armour, and to harmonize them, have not met with approval, but a more penetrating research into the extant monuments has

FIG. 43.—THE ARISTONOTHOS VASE

FIG. 46.—MIRROR HANDLE FROM ENKOMI IN CYPRUS:
WARRIOR COMBATING A GRIFFIN

shown that the archaeological evidence from the Mycenaean Age is more complicated than was formerly believed.[1] The monuments which show the body-shield in actual use come all from the shaft-graves at Mycenae; there are objects of art found in them and a stele which was erected on the fifth grave. Late Mycenaean monuments show the figure-8 shield, but only used for decorative purposes, e.g. on the well-known fresco from Tiryns. Small shields are on the contrary represented on monuments from the end of the Mycenaean Age. The men on the Warriors' vase (fig. 47) wear a small shield of a roughly circular shape with a segment cut out of the lower edge, and a corslet. The form of the shields on the back side of the vase is not clear, but the shields are relatively small and have a hand-grip suggesting that the shield was carried by this and an arm-loop.[2] The equipment of the warriors on a stele found covering a pit in a chamber tomb at Mycenae (fig. 4) [3] is quite similar. Probably of a later date is a vase fragment showing two warriors with small shields in a chariot [4] and a fragment from Tiryns showing warriors with small round shields in an altogether barbarous sub-Mycenaean style (fig. 48).[5] An ivory handle from a tomb at Enkomi on Cyprus showing a warrior combating a griffin (fig. 46), is important because the round shield is slung on a baldric.[6]

The small, and even the small round, shield appears in the Late Mycenaean Age, and we are probably able to say whence it came. The Phaistos discus (fig. 49), which was found in Middle Minoan III layers, has among its signs the round shield and a head with a feather crown. According to Egyptian monuments the crown is found also on the heads of the Pulusatha which attacked Egypt in the reign of Ramses III, 1190 B.C., and the round shield is worn by them and by the

[1] Last treatment in the paper by Miss Lorimer, quoted above, p. 143, n. 3; cp. " Homer's Use of the Past," *Journal of Hellenic Studies*, xlix, 1929, pp. 145.

[2] Often illustrated; originally in Furtwängler und Löschcke, *Myke-nische Vasen*, pls. xlii and xliii.

[3] *Ephemeris archaiologike*, 1896, Pl. i.

[4] Lorimer, loc. cit., pl. xlviii, 5, from Furtwängler und Löschcke, op. cit., pl. xli, 427.

[5] Lorimer, loc. cit., pl. xlix, 1, from Schliemann, *Tiryns*, pl. xiv.

[6] *Excavations in Cyprus*, pl. ii; H. R. Hall, *Aegean Archaeology*, p. 202; the style is of that kind which is influenced by Oriental art.

FIG. 47.—THE WARRIORS' VASE FROM MYCENAE

FIG. 48.—VASE FRAGMENT FROM TIRYNS, SHOWING WARRIORS
WITH ROUND SHIELDS

FIG. 49.—THE PHAISTOS DISCUS

Shardina together with a corsleti (fig. 50). The latter appear also as mercenaries in the army of Ramses II in 1288 B.C. The Greeks had evidently learnt to know this equipment during their expeditions towards the East and had taken it over because the body-shield was too heavy and too cumbrous.

Consequently the two kinds of equipment refer to much earlier ages than was supposed by the scholars who recognized the Ionian panoply in every case where a small shield is mentioned. Only the metal halves of the cuirass, the γύαλα, can with certainty be referred to the Ionian equipment. It is no wonder that the old descriptions, stock expressions, and epithets, coined in the early Mycenaean Age and repeated by tradition by the minstrels, were misunderstood and mixed up with later descriptions, phrases, and epithets in the lapse of centuries.

FIG. 50.—A SHARDINA

There is, however, a serious objection to this opinion, for it is assumed by some scholars that the body-shield survived down into the beginning of the historical age.[1] Miss Lorimer refers to the Assyrian reliefs of the time of Sennacherib representing Ionian or Carian mercenaries carrying tower shields slung on their backs, and also to other reliefs of Ashurbanipal's guards, Assyrian in type and carrying huge shields.[2] The evidence is not convincing for the Assyrians knew all kinds of shields, even one so large as to cover three men with a hand-grip and a foot-support. They were very effective in military organization and inventions and may have given their mercenaries the equipment which seemed good to them for some special purpose. Much more important are the verses in Tyrtaeus : " covering the thighs and the legs (κνήμας)

---

[1] Reichel's statement, op. cit., p. 75, is hardly worth mentioning. Other alleged instances justly rejected, *ibid.*, p. 50. *Herodotus*, i, 171, is of no value in this connection; nothing is said of the size of the shield, and small shields also were suspended at a baldric.

[2] Lorimer, loc. cit., pl. xlix, 6.

beneath and the breast and the shoulders with a wide hollow of the shield." [1] Such a covering can in fact be effected with the body-shield only, so that it seems that Tyrtaeus testifies to its use among the Spartans of the second Messenian war. This is, however, absolutely contradicted by the archaeological evidence, the finds from the excavations at Sparta. Woodward states that not a single shield of the figure-8 type is forthcoming on the Geometric or archaic works of art found at Sparta. In these periods the Spartan shield was essentially the round one, the Boeotian being relatively rare. He adds that it is not to be believed that the countless lead figurines of soldiers would all have the round shield, if this was not the normal type and that the collective evidence may be regarded as convincing against the figure-8 shield having been in use in Sparta in post-Mycenaean times. [2] There is no other course left but to regard Tyrtaeus' words as a literary cliché not corresponding to the actual custom of the time.

4. CONTROVERSIAL POINTS. BURIAL CUSTOMS. POLITICAL GEOGRAPHY

If any one would render valuable service to Homeric scholarship in compiling a book on Homeric archaeology as illustrated by the monuments according to our present knowledge, a book which is very much needed, he would have to treat the much discussed questions of domestic architecture and of dress in detail. As our aim is different, namely, to single out elements which can be dated with certainty, these questions must be passed over in a very few words. For the Mycenaean house, the megaron which was the kernel even of the extensive Mycenaean palaces, [3] was the ordinary type of house even in the Geometric and the following Ages.

---

[1] *Tyrtaeus*, fragment 11 Bergk., vv. 23 *et seq.*

μηρούς τε κνήμας τε κάτω καὶ στέρνα καὶ ὤμους
ἀσπίδος εὐρείης γαστρὶ καλυψάμενος.

[2] Cp. my paper " Die Hoplitentaktik und das Staatswesen " in the periodical *Klio*, xxii, 1928, pp. 241. Woodward's statement may now be checked by the great publication of the excavations in the sanctuary of Artemis Orthia.

[3] F. Noack, *Homerische Paläste*, 1903 ; A. Lang, *Homer and his Age*, ch. x. Cp. above, pp. 72.

Although the remains are of the scantiest,[1] the fact is certain, for the megaron survived until the beginning of the Hellenistic Age.[2] The change of dress had already taken place in Late Mycenaean times, when the men wore a short chiton (fig. 51) and the women a much simpler garment than the elaborate Minoan costume, although the small monuments representing the new dress do not allow us to make out its shape exactly.[3] Domestic architecture and dress allow no certain dating.

Descriptions of works of art are often said to refer to the Minoan art. It would not be astonishing if they did, as Nestor's cup certainly does, and I am quite willing to believe that some of them go back into this Age. But the question being so controversial they cannot be adduced as reliable evidence. The same controversy exists in regard to the similes, of which something will be said in another place.[4] Much has been written on Achilles' shield in which were wrought the sea and the heavens with the sun and the moon and the stars ; a wedding scene, and another of siege and war, scenes of harvest, of grape collecting, herds of cattle, and a dancing party.[5] Parallels were eagerly sought for in the Minoan-Mycenaean art on the one side, and in the archaic art on the other. Here it is of no interest to review the discussion, I only quote briefly two adherents of the opposite views.

Evans[6] compares the siege scene of the shield with the siege and battle scenes on a fragment of a silver vase from Mycenae (fig. 11),[7] and finds a still nearer parallel in the Shield of Heracles described by Hesiod. Here the coincidences, he says, extend even to particular details and the dramatic moment. He compares, furthermore, the town mosaic in faience plaques from Cnossos, part of which represents glimpses of civic life within the walls, of goats and oxen without, of fruit trees

---

[1] Most remarkable are those at Thermos, Rhomaios, *Deltion archaiologikon,* i, 1915, pp. 242.

[2] This is well known from Priene. Most interesting is the palace on Vouni, near Soloi, on Cyprus (fig. 52). It is built in the end of the sixth, and remodelled in the fifth century B.C. The plan of the later palace is quite Mycenaean. For references see above, p. 82, n. 1.

[3] See above, p. 75.　　　　　　　　　[4] Below, p. 275.

[5] *Il.,* xviii, vv. 478.

[6] *Journal of Hellenic Studies,* xxxii, 1912, pp. 288.

[7] G. Karo, *Die Schachtgräber von Mykenai,* pl. cxxii.

and running water.¹ Poulsen embraces the opinion that the description fits in better with archaic art.² He denies, perhaps a little incautiously, that agricultural scenes occur in Minoan art and points to such scenes in the Phoenician and the Geometric art ; in the latter they are, however, rare. Others have contended that the disconnected enumeration of different scenes testifies to a device, well known in archaic art, e.g. on the famous chest of Cypselus, of putting together a series of different scenes without any internal connection between them.

We ought to recognize the different conditions of expression in art and in words. Both the artist and the poet may have keen eyes, but the artist may be hampered by his formal manner and his want of technical skill, the poet may master a rich language and be able to express in words what he sees and to interpret the works of art according to his imagination which supplies what is wanting in the design he actually sees. Among the treasures of language which the minstrels had at their disposal there were certainly descriptions of works of art and similes derived even from Mycenaean times. They took them over and adapted them to their purposes.

In regard to burial customs there seems to be a sharp contrast between the Mycenaean Age and Homer. In the Mycenaean Age the corpses were laid down with valuable objects in a shaft-grave, a bee-hive tomb, or a chamber tomb. Homer mentions cremation only, not inhumation, and the gifts to the dead, weapons, clothes, and other valuable objects, are burned together with the corpse. The bones and ashes are placed in a box or urn, a mound heaped over it, and a stele erected on its top. This picture is consistent, and has been utilized by Lang in order to prove that Homer differs from the burial customs of the foregoing age as well as from those of the following age.³

---

¹ Cp. Evans, *Palace of Minos*, i, pp. 301. If Miss Lorimer, *Journal of Hellenic Studies*, xlix, 1929, pp. 146, were right in her assertion that the technique of Achilles' shield is the same as that of the inlaid dagger blades from Mycenae, this would be decisive, but the poet's words give hardly any certainty in this respect.

² F. Poulsen, *Der Orient und die frühgriechische Kunst*, pp. 172.

³ Even the word ταρχύειν, which according to its etymology may have signified some kind of embalming, has lost its meaning and is applied to the ordinary burial customs ; *Il.*, xvi, vv. 456 and vv. 674 ; cp. vii, vv. 85.   For another hazardous etymology see R. Blümel, in the periodical *Glotta*, xv, 1927, p. 78.

FIG. 51.—HUNTING SCENE, MAN DRESSED IN SHORT CHITON:
FRESCO FROM TIRYNS

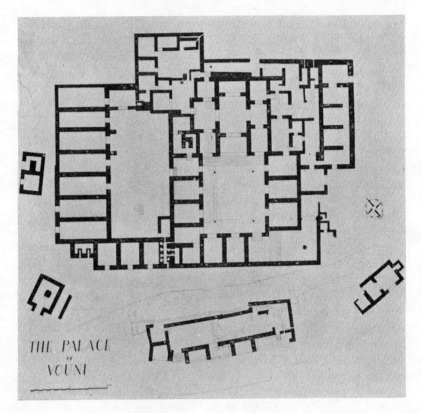

FIG. 52.—PLAN OF THE PALACE AT VOUNI IN CYPRUS

Before this distinction is admitted some facts are to be considered. The mound is said to be uńknown to the Mycenaean Age, in which the dead were buried in bee-hive and chamber tombs. The shaft-graves at Mycenae were not covered by a mound, but above them was an area on which the stelai were erected.[1] But caution is necessary. There are mounds from pre-Mycenaean times, e.g. at Aphidna in Attica, and others from post-Geometric times, e.g. at Velanideza, Petreza, and Marathon also in Attica. The mounds were not always big and conspicuous; small mounds, which are often depicted on the white lecythi, were, of course, levelled down. It is a curious fact and an objection of some weight to Lang's view, that mounds are not known precisely from the time in which the Homeric poems were composed according to him, i.e. the intermediate and the Geometric periods; it may, however, be accidental. But even in the Mycenaean Age mounds are not absent. The room excavated in the rock for a bee-hive tomb is often not deep enough, so that the top of the cupola projected above the ground; it was, of course, covered by a mound, even if the earth has been carried away and left no traces of the mound.[2] Sometimes the tholos tombs were built on flat ground and covered with earth so that they present the appearance of a mound. This is the case with some tholos tombs in Messenia (figs. 53 and 54) and with three recently discovered tombs near Patras.[3] It may perhaps be suggested that the cupola of the tholos tomb represents the interior of a mound in a monumental shape. There is, furthermore, some evidence pointing to the fact that a stele was erected above the tholos tomb.[4]

In the Mycenaean Age inhumation only is known. In the Geometric,[5] as well as in the whole historical age of Greece,

[1] *Annual of the British School at Athens*, xxv, 1921-23, pp. 103.

[2] Cp. *American Journal of Archaeology*, v, 1901, pp. 266 and 270.

[3] N. Valmin, "Two Tholos Tombs at Bodia," *Bulletin de la Société des lettres de Lund*, 1926-27, pp. 53, pls. vi and vii, and "Continued Explorations," etc., *ibid.*, 1927-28, pp. 201, pl. xii. The tholos tombs near Patras, *Archäologischer Anzeiger*, 1930, p. 120.

[4] This subject has been exhaustively treated by N. Valmin, "Tholos Tombs and Tumuli," in the "Corolla archaeologica," *Acta Instituti Romani regni Sueciae*, vol. ii, pp. 216.

[5] There are local differences. In Attica inhumation was more common than cremation, see F. Poulsen, *Die Dipylongräber und die Dipylonvasen*, pp. 10. Cremation is the rule in the early tombs on the S. slope of Acropolis and on Thera.

inhumation was in use together with cremation. Cremation appears, however, as the distinguishing feature of Greek burial customs and may as a broad statement be said to be the Greek custom of burial.[1] Likewise Homer mentions as normal the most sumptuous and honorific mode of burial which was the only one convenient for warriors and heroes, passing over the more modest inhumation. It was certainly not unknown at the time of the composition of the Homeric poems, whenever this may have been.[2]

The contrast between the burial customs and those of the Mycenaean Age seems, however, to be very marked ; with regard to cremation Homer does not, of course, reproduce Mycenaean customs but those of a later age. In order to bridge over the apparent gap in respect to burial customs, Dörpfeld imagined his curious hypothesis that the corpses of the dead were dried or roasted by fire before the burial, and tried to demonstrate this from the Mycenaean Age by certain traces of fire in the tombs and from Homer by an interpretation of his descriptions.[3] This hypothesis is very improbable. Traces of fire are very frequent in Minoan and Mycenaean tombs, but they are to be explained in other ways, either for burning sacrifices or, according to Evans, for purificatory purposes.[4]

That the former explanation is the right one as regards the Mycenaean Age is proved by a recent find, and this find gives, moreover, the means of connecting with Mycenaean burial customs a survival very frequently cited of more sumptuous and crude burial customs in Homer, the funeral of Patroclos.

[1] E.g. Lucian, De luctu, 21 ; cp. Herodotus, iii, 38.

[2] It existed in the intermediate period. Inhumation in the sub-Mycenaean necropolis on Salamis, Mitteilungen des deutschen archäolog. Instituts zu Athen, xxxv, 1910, p. 17.

[3] W. Dörpfeld, " Verbrennung und Bestattung der Toten im alten Griechenland," in Mélanges Nicole, Geneva, 1905, pp. 95 ; for references to other papers on this subject see Pernice in Gercke-Norden, Einleitung in die klassische Altertumswissenschaft, ii, 1, 4th ed., 1930, pp. 66.

[4] See my Minoan-Mycenaean Religion, p. 523. A recent curious find from Karteros in Crete is related by S. Marinatos, Archaiologikon Deltion, xi, 1927-28, p. 70. Six sarcophagi from L.M. III were found in a chamber tomb, and beneath three of them charcoal stored in vessels ; in one of the sarcophaguses also there was charcoal. Marinatos suggests forms of some purification, but charcoal seems hardly suitable for this purpose ; it seems more probable to me that the charcoal was collected and stored because it came from some funereal ceremony, just as the ashes from the pyre in the Historical Age.

FIG. 53.—MOUND COVERING THE EASTERN THOLOS TOMB AT
KOPANAKI IN EASTERN TRIPHYLIA

FIG. 54.—MOUND COVERING THE WESTERN THOLOS TOMB AT
KOPANAKI IN EASTERN TRIPHYLIA

Achilles slaughters four horses, nine dogs, and twelve Trojan captives, and flings their corpses on the pyre on which Patroclos' body is burned, together with sheep and oxen. The poet is unable to conceal his disapproval of this cruelty. Though this description cannot possibly be referred to the Geometric or to the period immediately preceding it, hitherto it has not been possible to connect it with Mycenaean customs because Patroclos, and with him the corpses of the slaughtered men and animals are burned. On the other hand, it has been contended that men were slaughtered at funerals in the Mycenaean Age, but there was no certain evidence for this supposition : the human bones found in the earth above the shaft-graves at Mycenae came with the filling from earlier tombs, and it cannot be demonstrated that skeletons found in the passage-ways of Mycenaean tholos tombs belong to men sacrificed at the funeral. At last, however, through the brilliant discovery of an

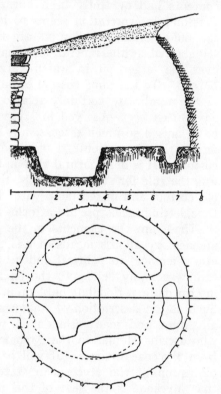

FIG. 55.—SECTION AND PLAN OF THE THOLOS TOMB AT DENDRA

(The dromos is cut away in this reproduction)

untouched kingly tomb, that of the prince of Midea near Dendra, we have learnt to know something about the ceremonies at the funeral of a Mycenaean king and are able to find a connection with Homer's description of Patroclos' funeral.[1] The dead were buried in two shaft-graves within

[1] Axel W. Persson, *The Royal Tombs at Dendra near Midea*, pp. 12 and 69 *et seq.*

the tholos and besides these there were two shallower pits. The smaller one contained human and animals' bones, among which was the skull of a dog. The larger one was filled with earth mixed with charcoal containing minute fragments of bronze and ivory, glass paste and semi-precious stones. The contents had evidently been burned on the spot. Professor Persson's interpretation seems to be fully justified, viz. that the bones in the smaller pit are those of men and animals slaughtered at the funeral, and that a pyre had been erected over the larger pit in which various precious objects were burned. To the same custom of burning offerings to the dead in the tomb, are certainly related the traces of fire, which have often been observed in Mycenaean chamber tombs and have caused so much discussion. I have no hesitation in referring the description of Patroclos' funeral to this Mycenaean custom. It is only natural that in an age in which cremation was the rule for stately funerals, the poet misunderstood the old custom and mixed it up with those prevailing at his own time, letting the corpse of Patroclos also be burned on the pyre.

These are the elements in the Homeric poems for which archaeology affords means of assigning a date, but there are also references to political and geographical conditions which cannot possibly belong to the Archaic Age of Greece or the intermediate period but only fit in with the Mycenaean Age. Such is the description of Agamemnon as a king ruling over all Argos and many islands, in which even those scholars who ascribe Homer to the Archaic Age recognize a survival from Mycenaean times. It will be the starting-point for our discussion of the Mycenaean state organization.[1] The fact that Mycenae is the seat of this mighty king must likewise be a reminiscence of the wealth and power of this town in that age. For why should a poet of the Archaic Age have lighted upon just that decaying place—for such it was since the end of the Mycenaean Age—as the seat of the Great King, and have described it as rich in gold ? [2] The same is true of the importance of Troy which after its destruction at the end of the Mycenaean Age was occupied by unimportant settlements only.[3]

---

[1] See below, ch. vi.   [2] Cp. above, p. 49.   [3] Cp. above, p. 45.

I pass over political geography [1] except for the dominion of Nestor, for his kingdom covering the western coast of the Peloponnese corresponds to an archaeological fact, the flourishing Mycenaean settlements on this coast and cannot be explained under later conditions.[2] Lastly, the well-known fact must be emphasized strongly, that the Dorians are not mentioned in Homer except once in passing, in the passage concerning the many peoples inhabiting Crete,[3] and that the Achaeans appear as the ruling people. But the Dorians had invaded the Peloponnese and conquered Argolis and other provinces already before the Geometric period. It is a common saying that Homer pictures a pre-Dorian Greece, but it should also be fully realized that this picture refers to a time at least three centuries earlier than that in which the bulk of the extant poems was composed, according to the references to the Geometric and Orientalizing periods embodied in them.[4] This simple fact has been too much forgotten, whilst the race of the Achaeans and the true bearing of their name has been much discussed.

The whole background of the Homeric poems in regard to political geography and state organization is not that of the time in which they were moulded into their ultimate form but many centuries earlier, going back into the Mycenaean Age.

Finally, there is a curious detail to which Miss Lorimer has called attention.[5] The old capital of Egypt, Thebes, is mentioned in two identical passages : " the Egyptian Thebes where most wealth is amassed in the houses." [6] This mention has always been considered as a sign of a late date. Miss Lorimer pointed, however, to the fact that Thebes was abandoned as a capital by Echenaton and finally by Ramses II, and thinks that the Northerners who raided Egypt after 1200 B.C. would not have been able to penetrate as far as to Thebes. Consequently it looks as if the reference to Thebes were derived from the fifteenth century B.C. The argument can be considerably strengthened. Thebes was sacked very

---

[1] Cp. above, pp. 114.   [2] Cp. above, pp. 116.   [3] *Od.*, xix, v. 177.
[4] The attempt to evade this conclusion by identifying Achaeans and Dorians is most unfortunate, see above, pp. 91.
[5] *Journal of Hellenic Studies*, xlix, 1929, pp. 153.
[6] *Il.*, ix, vv. 381 ; *Od.*, iv, v. 126.

thoroughly by Ashurbanipal in 663 B.C.,[1] before the reign
of the Saïte kings opened the doors of Egypt to the Greek
soldiers and merchants. When these came to Egypt in the
next few years they saw a ruined city. In the centuries before
the sack of the city, the period to which the reign of the
Theban priest kings belongs and which corresponds to the
intermediate and the Geometric periods, the Greeks did not
visit Egypt. The finds show that even commercial relations
were but slight after the end of the XVIIIth dynasty, i.e.
the fourteenth century B.C.[2] In view of these circumstances
there is hardly any course left but to acknowledge that the
reference to the wealth of Thebes goes back to the fourteenth
century B.C.

5. SUMMARY

To sum up. There is considerable evidence in Homer
which without any doubt refers to the Mycenaean Age. Some
descriptions are illustrated by and must be referred to Mycenaean
finds, and it is a remarkable and hitherto overlooked fact that
some of these finds, especially the body-shield and Nestor's
cup, even belong to the Early Mycenaean Age, the period of
the shaft-graves. The background of the Iliad, the absence
of the Dorians, the wealth of Mycenae and its position as
the kingly seat of the leader of the Greeks, belong to the
same age.

On the other hand, other and not less conspicuous elements
in Homer refer certainly to the Archaic Age, the Geometric,
and the beginning of the Orientalizing periods. So do certain
descriptions of works of art and the presence of the Phoenicians
as traders and sea-farers and the prevalence of their craftsmanship. Such elements give a *terminus post quem* for the
composition of the parts which are connected with them
organically, and they are so extensive that a large part of the
extant poems must have been composed in this age. It is
very unwise to treat Homer as chiefly a product of the Mycenaean Age, and to consider the elements from this age as

---

[1] See *Cambridge Ancient History*, iii, p. 285.
[2] Cp. J. D. S. Pendlebury, *Aegyptiaca*, "A Catalogue of Egyptian Objects
in the Aegean Area," 1930.

survivals which may be put on one side is as unwise as to consider the passages referring to the Archaic Age as irrelevant additions. In both cases the instances to the contrary will remain as stumbling-blocks which cause such one-sided hypotheses to break down.

The Homeric poems contain elements from widely differing ages. The most bewildering fact is, however, that the Mycenaean elements are not distributed according to the age of the strata in the poems. The graphic description of Hector's body-shield is found in the sixth book of the Iliad and that of Nestor's cup in the eleventh and that of Hector's spear in the sixth and eighth ; all these books are reasonably thought to be late. And the description of the boars' tusks helmet is found in the Doloneia which is a notorious addition.

The Mycenaean and the Orientalizing elements differ in age by more than half a millennium. They are inextricably blended. How is it credible that the former elements were preserved through the centuries and incorporated in poems whose composition may be about half a millennium later? Our best method will be to acknowledge the full importance of these facts and to try to find an answer to the proposed question. But before we do so we will turn to the questions of language and style in which we shall find similar facts.

CHAPTER IV

HOMERIC LANGUAGE AND STYLE

THOSE philologists who have tried to solve the Homeric question have proffered their opinions on archaeological and historical matters with much confidence, but one who is not a philologist himself is bound to approach questions of language and style with the utmost caution. In this survey of the epic problem, however, the subject cannot be entirely neglected. It is the more necessary because philological research in the last two decades has attained important results, the bearing of which on the epic problem has hardly been fully appreciated as yet.

There are, of course, still unsolved riddles and unsettled questions in which the opinions of experts are at variance ; in all such cases the decision must be submitted to the philologists, and it is to be hoped that the progress of research will contribute largely to a decisive solution of controversial points. The progress is, however, remarkable and a common trend is distinctly visible. Whilst scholars some time ago devoted their attention chiefly to old sounds, forms, and formations, and tried to explain these by the regular phonetic changes, research of late years took up ideas which before had only been cursorily set forth, working out fully the influence of the verse and the epical diction on Homer's language. Thus the paramount importance of the epical technique was revealed. The philological arguments used by separatists as well as by unitarians are placed in a new light.

1. THE DIALECT MIXTURE OF THE HOMERIC LANGUAGE

Homer's language is a mixed dialect, Ionic, but to a fairly large extent interspersed with elements of other dialects. His style is especially remarkable for obsolete words and frequently repeated phrases and stock expressions, in the latter respect differing even from the style of epic authors of a later age. In this connection the relevant question is— What bearing on the problem of the origin and development of Greek epics have the mixture of various dialects and the use of stock expressions ?

The most conspicuous of the elements mingled with the Ionic dialect of Homer is Aeolic. Further definite traces of the Attic dialect have been recognized, and lastly there are a few traces of the Arcado-Cypriot dialect. It will be convenient to begin with that dialect which is the latest in regard both to the development of language and the history of Homeric epics, the Attic dialect. On this subject we are fortunate enough to possess the masterly treatment by Professor Wackernagel,[1] whose results afford a solid foundation, and in a few details only have been modified or doubted by subsequent research.[2]

Wackernagel divides his main subject into two sections, of which one treats the Attic redaction of Homer's text and the other the atticisms of the Homeric poets. To the first class such atticisms belong which could be introduced without altering the text, e.g. certain Attic peculiarities of sounds. One of these is the *spiritus asper* which was absent from the Ionic dialect and which has been introduced into our texts only in words occurring in the Attic dialect ; it is consequently absent in words which ought to have it for etymological reasons, but which are wanting in the Attic dialect.[3] Attic forms of flexion are rare and for a great part uncertain.

The cases treated in the second section are of more importance because the forms in question are bound up with the metre. As non-Attic forms cannot be substituted for them, they must have been introduced by the poets who

---

[1] J. Wackernagel, *Sprachliche Untersuchungen zu Homer*, 1916; pp. 1-159, were also printed in *Glotta*, vii, 1916, pp. 161-339.

[2] More especially by K. Meister, "Die homerische Kunstsprache," *Preisschriften der Jablonowskischen Gesellschaft zu Leipzig*, xlviii, 1921.

[3] This explanation seems to agree strikingly with the facts, but has been contradicted by K. Meister, op. cit., pp. 209 ; his opinion is, however, rejected by most scholars ; cp. Kretschmer in *Glotta*, xiii, 1924, p. 249. I abstain from the vexed question of the "Zerdehnung" (forms of the type ὁρόωντες instead of ὁράοντες, ὁρῶντες ; see Wackernagel, pp. 66 ; cp. Meister, pp. 61).

composed the verse or verses in which they occur. Wackernagel counts as such κεῖντο, *Il.*, xxi, 426, *Od.*, vi, 19; ἦντο, *Il.*, iii, 153; ἑωσφόρος, *Il.*, xxiii, 226; the neglect of F in μήδ' οἱ, *Od.*, xi, 442; δένδρῳ,[1] *Il.*, iii, 152; ἐνεγκέμεν, *Il.*, xix, 194; βεβῶσα, *Od.*, xx, 14, and finally certain atticisms of quantity.

I have enumerated these cases in order to show how few the passages are in which Attic forms are connected organically with the verse. There is only one case in which Wackernagel gives voice to the opinion that a passage of some extension is due to an Attic poet, the Teichoscopia in the third book of the Ilias, because of the Attic forms ἦντο and δένδρῳ, to which he adds the mention of Theseus' mother, Aithra. Some of the instances adduced by Wackernagel have, however, been doubted or explained otherwise.[2]

Wackernagel's work was the outcome of a question asked by Bethe, who wanted philological proofs for his opinion that our Homer was put together and completed in Athens. Even granting that Wackernagel is right in all cases which have been doubted or explained otherwise by other scholars, the passages in which Attic forms are inherent are too few and too insignificant to prove that the Homeric epics were composed in Athens. They can very well have been introduced by way of recitation of the epics by Attic minstrels; for every recital gives rise to slight variations. The instances treated in the first section are but a very thin and translucent Attic varnish, which at most proves that the manuscripts from which our texts are derived were produced in Athens, and that is almost self-evident in view of the dominating position of that city in letters. The conscientious work of Wackernagel has shown that the Homeric epics were finished when they came to Athens, and that only few and slight alterations and additions were made in Athens.

The admixture of Aeolic elements is much more conspicuous and extensive, and the problem is at the same time

---

[1] Wackernagel recognized the Attic form δένδρον in the phrase δενδρέῳ ἐφεζόμενοι, but according to information in a letter he does not now attribute importance to this instance. The same shortening occurs in χρυσέῳ ἀνὰ σκήπτρῳ, *Il.*, i, v. 15, but here he thinks Lehrs' correction ἀν σκήπτρῳ to be almost certain.

[2] Wilamowitz, *Die Ilias und Homer*, pp. 506, thinks most of these forms to be corrupt. He reads, e.g. κέατο and ἔατο with synizesis, δένδρει, etc.. Concerning ἑωσφόρος see Meister, pp. 190.

more complicated and important. Whilst in the case of the in-fluence of the Attic dialect on the Homeric language we argue from a well-known dialect and a fairly late date, the Aeolic dialect is too little known, and the time in which it influenced the Homeric language is much earlier than any written documents. The sources for our knowledge of the Aeolic dialect are all later, some very much later than Homer, the fragments of literature, chiefly Lesbian lyrics, and inscriptions, chiefly Thessalian. We know only two Aeolic dialects and these imperfectly. The age in which the Aeolic dialect contributed to the formation of the Homeric language is subject to dispute, but it cannot possibly be later than the composition of the earliest extant poems. Generally it is supposed to be earlier and even very much earlier. The Aeolic dialect which is the linguistic foundation of Homer is another, at all events it is earlier, than the Aeolic dialects known through written documents. It is a great difficulty that we have to argue concerning a time much earlier than that represented by our sources for the Aeolic and even for the Ionic dialect. In the space of time intervening between the creation of the Homeric language by mixing Ionic with Aeolic elements and the written documents through which these dialects are known, extensive changes had certainly taken place in both dialects. They may have deviated from a common origin. Consequently the chief difficulty lies in the uncertainty whether a form differing from the known Ionic dialect is Aeolic or an old form once common to the Aeolic and the Ionic dialects. It is not always possible to decide the question and opinions differ in certain cases. We turn to the principal Aeolic elements of Homeric language.[1]

Aeolic forms are rather rare in such cases where an Ionic form of the same metrical value exists, and their preservation is generally explained by special reasons. While Homer has the form $\theta\acute{\eta}\rho$ elsewhere, he uses the form $\phi\acute{\eta}\rho$, which is

---

[1] I quote only surveys in which references to the extensive literature may be found : A. Meillet, *Aperçu d'une histoire de la langue grecque*, 2nd ed., 1920, ch. vi ; P. Cauer, *Grundfragen der Homerkritik*, 3rd ed., 1923, pp. 148 ; K. Witte in Pauly-Wissowa's *Realencyklopädie der classischen Altertumswissenschaft*, viii, pp. 2214 (s.v. Homer). I add a few very important old works : Ph. Buttmann, *Lexilogus*, 1818-25, 4th ed. 1860-65; I. Bekker, *Homerische Blätter*, 1863 ; Gu. Schulze, *Quaestiones epicae*, 1892.

known from the Thessalian dialect, when speaking of the centaurs, *Il.*, i, 268, and ii, 743. The Aeolic form πόρδαλις occurs thrice as a variant in Ven. A., whilst all other manuscripts have the common form πάρδαλις. The perfect participle κεκλήγοντες, which is an Aeolic formation in analogy with the present participle, occurs four times in the end of the verse. In the following more numerous cases, the reason for the preservation of the Aeolic forms is evidently the absence of the word in the Ionic dialect : ἀργεννός and ἐρεβεννός keep their Aeolic form, whilst φαεινός appears in the Ionic form. The Ionic prefix ἀρι- corresponds to the Aeolic ἐρι-, but the two prefixes are distributed among different words, never occurring in the same word, and the words with ἐρι- occur very often in stock expressions, filling the last part of the verse.[1]

Except the last-mentioned compound words, the instances belonging to this class are rare, almost exceptional ; much more numerous and important are the cases in which the Aeolic forms differ from the Ionic forms in their metrical value, e.g. πίσυρες as compared with τέσσαρες, ἄλλυδις, ἄμυδις, πολυπάμ(μ)ονος instead of πολυκτήμονος, *Il.*, iv, 433, υἱός Ἀφείδαντος Πολυπαμονίδαο.[2] Aeolic forms are especially frequent in proper nouns, e.g. Αἰνείας,[3] etc. Patronymica with the ending -ιος, which so far as we know are peculiar to the Thessalian dialect, appear in Homer in the end of the verse before or after the bucolic diaeresis in stock expressions, e.g. Τελαμώνιος Αἴας. Other well-known examples are the plural forms of the personal pronouns ἄμμες, ὔμμες, etc.,[4] the aorists with double σ,[5] the datives in -εσσι, e.g. κύνεσσι, which are an extended formation not original and peculiar to the Aeolic dialect. The infinitive in -μεναι is found in the Lesbian dialect only and appears in Homer generally before the bucolic diaeresis.

The particle μάν appears in the Ionic dialect as μέν and in the Attic as μήν. In Homer, μάν occurs in almost every

---

[1] E.g. ἐρίγδουπος πόσις Ἥρης, ἐρίηρες ἑταῖροι ; see Witte, loc. cit., p. 2216.
[2] *Od.*, xxiv, v. 305. This restoration by Cobet of the Πολυπημονίδαο of the manuscripts is evident because of the name of the man Ἀφείδας.
[3] Wackernagel, op. cit., p. 2.
[4] Concerning ἀμός and ὑμός see Wackernagel, op. cit., pp. 51.
[5] Meillet, op. cit., p. 125.

case only where a long vowel is needed, the following word commencing with a vowel. It is a most striking proof of the opinion that aeolisms were preserved, generally speaking, only if no Ionic word which was metrically equivalent existed.[1] The particle κε(ν) is Aeolic and has in the Doric dialect the form κα, the Ionic dialect has ἄν. That Homer has κε as well as ἄν, an evident mixture of dialects, is also due to the facility it offered to the versification.

With the infinitive in -μεν we come to forms which the Aeolic dialect has in common with other dialects, but in view of the apparent Aeolic influence on the Homeric language there is evidently an assumption that such forms have been taken over from the Aeolic dialect. Nobody has supposed that the Doric dialects have contributed to forming Homer's language. The apocope of the prepositions is most probably of Aeolic origin, although it is found even in other dialects, and was preserved because the double forms, with and without apocope, facilitated the versification, e.g. κάββαλε instead of κατέβαλε, which does not fit in with the metre, etc.

To the aeolisms belongs certainly even ā in such cases in which the Ionic dialect has η. Wackernagel states it to be a well-known fact that α, in so far as it does not appear in the Ionic dialect also, e.g. καλός, πᾶς, ἄτη, is Aeolic.[2] The subject comprises, however, certain difficulties, e.g. why Homer always has on one hand λαός but on the other νηός.[3] The duals in -α, e.g. Ἀτρείδα, are perhaps Attic.[4] The genitive singular in -αο becomes in the Ionic dialect through metathesis -εω ; Homer has Ἀτρείδαο as well as Ἀτρείδεω ; the forms in -āο were preserved, being especially convenient for the end of the verse. Likewise Homer has two forms, differing in metrical value, in the genitive plural, the older -άων and the Ionic -έων. Whether the older forms were borrowed from the Aeolic dialect, is a question which could only be answered with absolute certainty if we knew the date when the forms in -αο, -άων vanished in the Ionic dialect. The most probable opinion is that they belong to the Aeolic elements, The parallel forms of the genitive singular in -οιο and -ου.

---

[1] Wackernagel, op. cit., p. 19.   [2] *Ibid.*, p. 1.
[3] Cp. Meister, op. cit., pp. 168.   [4] Wackernagel, op. cit., pp. 56.

to which the philologists with reason have added a third intermediate form in -oo, abstracted from certain phenomena in our texts,[1] present a similar difficulty. For it is probable that -ου is derived from -oo, -οιο (from -οσιο) ; in the Thessalian dialect forms in -οι and -οιο appear. The question is whether the ι vanished in the Ionic dialect before or after the creation of the Homeric language. Most scholars embrace the former opinion.[2] The forms in -φι are most prominent archaisms, -φι being related to the ending –bhis in Sanskrit and -biš in old Persian. Ancient grammarians state that these forms are Aeolic, and there are slight traces of them in the Cypriot and Boeotian dialects.[3]

At last we come to the most persistent and complicated phenomenon of all, the digamma, ϝ, which was discovered by Bentley.[4] It is well known that very many verses, which are vitiated by a hiatus or a short syllable in the arsis, become correct if ϝ is introduced.[5] Some editors have printed ϝ in their texts. But there are also cases in which ϝ is neglected.[6] The attempt to prove the transition of ϝ into a vowel in the Ionic dialects has not been successful.[7] Certain cases, in which ϝ became υ after a vowel, agree with Aeolic forms.[8] The question is, as Cauer says,[9] whether ϝ was a vanishing element of the Ionic dialect or was borrowed from another

---

[1] E.g. Od., xiv, 239, δήμου φῆμις ; x, 60, Αἰόλου κλυτὰ δώματα, are metrically false, and will be corrected by the insertion of the forms δήμοο and Αἰόλοο respectively.

[2] These forms are much discussed : see Witte, loc. cit., p. 2219 and pp. 2233 especially ; Cauer, op. cit., pp. 146.

[3] Meister, op. cit., p. 142.

[4] The last comprehensive discussion, ibid., pp. 196.

[5] E.g. Il., xxiv, 152 et seqq. :

μηδέ τί ϝοι θάνατος μελέτω φρεσὶ μηδέ τι τάρβος ·
τοῖον γάρ ϝοι πομπὸν ὀπάσσομεν Ἀργειφόντην,
ὅς ϝ’ ἄξει

as compared with Il., xxiv, 181 et seqq. :

μηδέ τί τοι θάνατος μελέτω φρεσὶ μηδέ τι τάρβος ·
τοῖον γάρ τοι πομπὸς ἅμ’ ἔψεται Ἀργειφόντης
ὅς σ’ ἄξει

[6] E.g. Il., xv, 35, ("Ηρη) καί μιν φωνήσασ’ ἔπεα κτλ. ; cp. Il., i, 201, (Ἀχιλλεύς) καί μιν φωνήσας ἔπεα πτερόεντα προσηύδα.

[7] Meister, op. cit., pp. 196.

[8] E.g. ταλαύρινος, ἀπούρας, εὔαδε, αὐέρυσαν, etc.

[9] Cauer, op. cit., p. 151.

dialect and misunderstood.   Opinions are at variance, although that ascribing an Aeolic origin to the Homeric F is prevalent.

2. ORIGIN OF THE DIALECT MIXTURE

Even if those cases are discounted, the Aeolic origin of which is subject to doubt or disputed, enough remain to prove a deep-seated Aeolic contribution to the creation of the Homeric language.   It· is consequently a mixed dialect, chiefly Ionic, but interspersed with extensive Aeolic elements, and the question important for our purpose is precisely how this mixture came about.

Different explanations have been proposed.[1]   One opinion is that the Homeric language originated in a speech older than the Ionic and Aeolic dialects, from which these were later evolved into separate dialects.   It is maintained that these two dialects were separated in Asia Minor after its colonization only.[2]   This is evidently much too late a date for the origin of the dialects.   The emigrants certainly brought their dialects with them.   In the Peloponnese, the Doric dialect was superimposed upon the Arcadian dialect by the Dorian immigration at the end of the second millennium B.C. The difference of these two dialects must have been established before that time.   The difference between the Ionic and the Aeolic dialects cannot reasonably be supposed to be later.

Another opinion is that the Aeolians and the Ionians who emigrated to Asia Minor became mixed together, and that consequently their dialects too were mixed, and some colour is lent to this view by the fact that several Aeolian places were conquered by the Ionians, e.g. Smyrna, which is said to be the birth-place of Homer, in the end of the eighth century B.C., and that the Ionic dialects of Erythrae and Chios show Aeolic traces.[3]   According to this view the Homeric dialect would be a mixed dialect of daily life of a

[1] Cp. Cauer, op. cit., pp. 173.

[2] Ed. Meyer, *Forschungen zur alten Geschichte*, i, 1892, pp. 132 ; *Geschichte des Altertums*, ii, pp. 75 ; cp. Wilamowitz, *Herakles*, 1st ed., 1889, i, p. 66, n. 31.

[3] Cp. Wilamowitz, " Über die ionische Wanderung," *Sitzungsberichte der preussischen Akademie der Wissenschaften*, 1906, pp. 61.

fairly late date, which with the victory of the Ionic element was more and more Ionicized. This view is contradicted by the fact that the Aeolic elements evidently are archaisms, and to-day it is held by very few.[1]

The archaic appearance of the Aeolic elements is very well explained by another hypothesis which for a long time played a prominent part in the discussion of the Homeric question, viz. that the Homeric poems were originally composed in the Aeolic dialect and afterwards word by word translated into Ionic, and that in this translation Aeolic words and forms, to which metrical equivalents were wanting in Ionic, were simply allowed to remain. To prove their thesis Fick and Bechtel undertook to retranslate the old parts of the Iliad into the Aeolic dialect.[2] For they were of the opinion that the old parts were originally composed in the Aeolic dialect and that the later parts were composed by Ionic minstrels in the mixed dialect, which was the result of the translation.

The issue was a failure, but the work was very illuminating concerning the problem of the Homeric language. It was proved that there were on one hand " superfluous aeolisms," i.e. aeolisms to which metrically equivalent Ionic words correspond and which very well might have been exchanged for the Ionic forms,[3] and on the other hand, that there were " fixed ionicisms " even in the parts considered to be old, i.e. Ionic forms which have no Aeolic equivalent and consequently cannot be replaced.[4] It was only possible to get rid of them by the assumption of interpolations and other violent means which discredited the hypothesis. Finally, speaking of the frequently occurring Ionic form $\tilde{\eta}\epsilon\nu$, Bechtel himself conceded

---

[1] Wackernagel remarks that this explanation is contradicted by the fact that certain peculiarities of the Aeolic dialect of Asia Minor, which are not found in the Thessalian dialect but appear in certain Ionic dialects, neighbouring to the Aeolic area, e.g. on Chios, are precisely absent from Homer, e.g. -αισ-, -οισ-, -ωισ-, instead of -ανσ-, -ονσ, -ωνσ-, the flexion of the cardinal numbers from five on, e.g. πέμπων (cp. Jacobsohn in *Philologus*, lxvii, 1908, pp. 360 *et seq.*, n. 51, and in *Hermes*, xlv, 1910, p. 95, n. 1). If the Homeric dialect were a mixed dialect from the borderland between Aeolians and Ionians in Asia Minor, it would certainly be astonishing that aeolisms appearing on Chios were absent from Homeric speech.

[2] See above, p. 9.   [3] E.g. ἴμεναι—ἰέναι ; cp. pp. 163.

[4] E.g. μέν before a vowel ; see pp. 164.

that even the earliest parts of the Iliad were influenced by the Ionic dialect.[1] The process by which the Aeolic forms were introduced into Homer was evidently more complicated than a mechanical translation from the Aeolic dialect into the Ionic.

It is well known since the statistical work of Hartel [2] that ϝ has not always the same force as other consonants have. On one hand it prevents with few exceptions elision of a short and shortening of a long preceding vowel or diphthong, on the other hand a preceding syllable consisting of a short vowel and a consonant is treated as long in the arsis only, in the thesis generally as short, e.g. κρήγυον εἶπας, Il., i, 106. The right explanation is given by Danielsson.[3] Pointing to the fact that ϝ generally prevents elision, he explains the difference in the force of ϝ by the assumption that the Ionian minstrels did not pronounce ϝ themselves but had learnt by tradition that certain words were treated as if they began with a consonant before the vowel. They followed this tradition, as e.g. Nicander does, admitting the hiatus ἀλώϊα ἔργα after the pattern of the Homeric πολεμήϊα ἔργα, etc. As hiatus occurred in other cases also in Homer, especially in certain places of the verse, and even in daily language, it is no wonder that there was not much difficulty in keeping the traditional hiatus caused by the vanishing of an old ϝ. It was much more difficult to keep as long, syllables which had become short through the vanishing of ϝ, for there were few examples of the lengthening of such a short syllable and these occur especially before the caesurae. ϝ was an inheritance from an earlier form of language whose results only were preserved embodied in the epical technique. It had vanished from the spoken language of the Ionian minstrels, and sometimes they forgot the tradition and elided or shortened a vowel before ϝ according to their own pronunciation.

Striving after a more high-sounding and more exquisite mode of expression every higher style preserves words and

---

[1] F. Bechtel, Die Vokalkontraktion bei Homer, 1908, p. xi.

[2] W. Hartel, " Homerische Studien," iii, Sitzungsberichte der Akademie der Wissenschaften zu Wien, lxxviii, 1874, pp. 60.

[3] Indogermanische Forschungen, xxv, 1909, pp. 264.

forms which have vanished from the speech of daily life and from literature of more humble aims ; so does, for example, the English religious literature. The same striving has contributed not a little to preserving the archaic and Aeolic forms in epic poetry for, being handed down by tradition, they were felt as appropriate to the epic style.

It has been often observed that the preservation of old forms is due to the facilities of versification.[1] This does not mean that the old forms occur only in crystallized contexts which were as such taken over from earlier poems, i.e. that they were archaisms in the ordinary sense. They were part of the epic technique, and were used by the poets in new connections also where they were appropriate to the metre. Consequently F prevented hiatus even after it ceased to be pronounced, the genitives in -οιο are not in all cases older than those in -ου, and the like is true in regard to other parallel forms. The epic technique permitted the poets to use both forms at their discretion and convenience. The forms differ in age, but because of the tradition they could be used contemporaneously. This characteristic feature of the Homeric language is the reason why it is justly called an artificial language or still better, to use the German word, a "Kunstsprache." The use of the old forms was thus in a certain measure extended, e.g. that of the infinitives in -μεναι, and as the sense of their significance had become somewhat obliterated, they were liable to be used not always appropriately.

A very neat example is the old case in -φι which is almost obsolete except in Homer. It occurs in singular as well as in plural, and its sphere of significance is unusually varying. Meister [2] seems to have proved that the plural forms are old, the singular forms later, and that there is a special significance of the ending for every word to which it is attached, determined, of course, by the connection it had had from the first in the epic language. The forms were convenient for the verse in certain respects.[3] Hence the ending was

---

[1] Its influence on the Homeric language has been brought forward in recent works, especially by Witte and Meister, op. cit. The principle is unquestionable and sound but should not be exaggerated.

[2] Meister, op. cit., pp. 135.

[3] E.g. ἐσχαρόφι instead of ἐσχάρης, which does not fit in the hexameter.

used continually, but having vanished from the spoken language it was not always used correctly and its sphere of significance was extended. Such is often the case with archaic forms and words.

The case of the dual is analogous but more difficult. The dual does not exist in the Ionic dialect, in Homer the plural is freely used for two, often alternating with the dual ; the dual is even sporadically misused for the plural, evidently because the dual had gone out of use in the spoken language, so that the poets had lost the sense of its significance and used it promiscuously instead of the plural, when it was convenient for the verse.[1]

Other forms are parallel in the exact sense of the word, i.e. they differ in form only, not in significance. The forms which are supposed to be of Aeolic origin are morphologically earlier, except the perfect participle κεκλήγοντες and the dative plural in -εσσι. The use of parallel forms of which one is evolved from another is foreign to a language which is developed naturally and continually. It came about when the Ionian minstrels adapted the Aeolic epics to their own dialect, and it was preserved because it was felt as peculiar and appropriate to the epic style and facilitated the versification. That the epic technique played a great part is proved by the fact that several of these forms occur in preference to others in certain places of the verse. Many archaisms are especially found in the end of the verse.

The metre contributed to the preservation of old forms but caused some new formations also. There is a tendency, which has been especially emphasized by Witte, to keep the same metrical scheme for all forms of a word. Hence, e.g. the accusative ἡνιοχῆα was put at the side of the genitive ἡνιόχοιο. In a separate volume [2] he tried to prove that the use of the number in certain cases is determined by the

---

[1] E.g. Σειρήνοιιν in the end of the verse, *Od.*, xii, 52 ; elsewhere Σειρήνων. Boll seems to have shown very nicely that the much-discussed duals in the Embassy to Achilles, *Il.*, ix, have simply been taken over from the first book, a thoughtlessness which would hardly have been committed by a poet who had not lost the sense of the dual ; *Zeitschrift für österreichische Gymnasien*, lxviii, 1917, pp. 1, and lxix, 1919-20, pp. 414.

[2] K. Witte, " Singular und Plural," *Forschungen über Form und Geschichte der griechischen Poesie*, 1907.

metre, e.g. in the plural of abstract nouns, e.g. ὁμοφροσύνῃσιν, ἀιδρείῃσι, etc.

We have to consider the bearing of these results on the Homeric question. The separatists started from the very natural assumption that the language of the Homeric minstrels was subject to the normal evolution of language. Consequently the later parts of the poems should differ from the earlier by a consistent vanishing of old forms and words and an increased percentage of new forms and words. Statistics were made in order to prove the later date of certain parts by this method, e.g. in regard to the use of patronymics, abstract nouns, ὁ as definite article, the short forms of the dative plurals in -οις, etc., the perfect in -κα, not to speak of those mentioned above. But the statistics have been proved to be erroneous or fallacious.[1] There is no doubt that older and more recent forms occur in Homer. What was wrong is evidently the assumed principle of their distribution. The development of language in Homer is not normal in the sense that the earlier forms and words are ousted by those which are more recent in regular sequence. Such a development was thwarted by a strongly conservative element, the epic technique, through which a particular language was created, a store of forms, words, and stock expressions bound up with the metre. This style differing from everyday speech seemed the only one appropriate to epic poetry which strove after an elevated style. Wackernagel observed very pertinently that epic poetry avoids indecent and mean things.[2] Another very strong reason for keeping old elements was the metre ; for as they were bound up with the metre, often occurring at certain places of the verse, they facilitated the versification. The Homeric language is thus an artificial language, a " Kunstsprache," a catch-word which Meister took for the title of his book. The poets used the traditional forms at their pleasure without caring for their origin. They even combined Aeolic and Ionic elements in the same word, e.g. νέεσσι with the Ionic

---

[1] Especially by J. A. Scott in several papers quoted and summarized in his book, *The Unity of Homer*, ch. iii.
[2] Wackernagel, op. cit., pp. 224.

form of the stem and the Aeolic ending, to which, moreover, the Ionic ν ἐφελκυστικόν may be added.

The epic technique was learnt and inherited by the minstrels with all its paraphernalia, and they drew on the amassed store of centuries in composing their songs. In this way the old elements were incorporated indissolubly even into the most recent songs. In regard to language the same comparison is appropriate which was used in regard to the archaeological elements. The Homeric poems are not to be compared with a site of excavation in which more recent strata, characterized by more recent objects, are distinguished from earlier strata, characterized by earlier objects, but they are to be compared with a dough which has been rehandled and rekneaded constantly, not without adding new elements.[1] The oldest elements may in this way have been incorporated into the latest songs. This is the more true in regard to language, because the epic technique formed a peculiar language which the minstrels used constantly.

This applies especially to the only period of epic poetry in Greece which we know directly, the period in which the minstrels were Ionians, for epic language differed from their ordinary speech by its Aeolic and archaic forms. Unhappily we do not know the stage of development reached by the Ionic dialect at this time. This is a source of uncertainty in details, but it cannot interfere with the main issue. The minstrels were, of course, influenced by their ordinary dialect, which caused them to introduce elements from it, and to deviate on account of it from the epic dialect. It would be hard to deny that this may have increased with time and that in this respect there may be differences between earlier and later songs,[2] but as the language is so complicated, this difference evades such statistics as have been made. It is a fallacious method to count the occurrences of single phenomena.

---

[1] Below, p. 212.

[2] At the time when the songs of the Odyssey were composed the epic tradition was not so strong as at the time from which the Iliad is derived. Wackernagel remarks in a letter that it cannot be regarded as fortuitous that τύνη is absent in the Odyssey, that new formations, e.g. ποστός and ἐντεῦθεν appear, that a patronymicon Ὀδυσσείδης for Telemachos is wanting, and that words as Ὀρέσταο and Γιγάντεσσι occur with ictus on the second and the fourth syllable. Concerning the more recent date of the Odyssey, cp. above, pp. 136.

The greatest change came probably about the time when the Aeolic epic poetry was taken over by Ionic minstrels For stock expressions with Aeolic forms show that a traditional epic language must have existed in the Aeolic dialect already. We have seen that this taking over cannot have been a mechanical translation of some of the now extant Homeric songs into the Ionic dialect ; the Aeolic elements are much more intimately blended with a fundamentally Ionic language. We do not know how the process came about. We may surmise that the first Ionic minstrels took over Aeolic epics—but not the songs which we read to-day —perhaps rather mechanically substituting their own dialect and admitting chiefly such Aeolic stock expressions, words, and forms, for which metrically equivalent Ionic forms were wanting. As the songs were constantly rehandled and even new songs composed, the close fusion of Aeolic words and forms with an Ionic basis was the ultimate result.

It is impossible to guess how long a time such a process may have taken. We can only be certain that it must have been long, because the evolving of such an artificial language is a slow process. We have further to admit that this formation of a traditional epic language took place twice, first in the Aeolic dialect and for a second time in the Ionic dialect, the creation of the fundamentally Ionic language of Homer with an Aeolic admixture. Although the transitional period must have caused confusion, even this language was moulded in fixed forms, and it was used so long that even Ionic stock expressions were created, e.g. Κρόνου πάις ἀγκυλομήτεω, etc. When the epic language had reached its fixed form it may have persisted for a very long time. Wackernagel says very justly that the archaic appearance of the Homeric language is not so much dependent on the date of the extant poems as on the continuance of a tradition which goes back to the beginnings of epic poetry and consequently almost into the oldest period of the Greek people.[1]

---

[1] Wackernagel, op. cit., p. 201. Wackernagel remarks in a letter that the use of the article is very illuminating. On one hand there are many instances of its most developed use, on the other for its entire absence, such as never is found in Greek prose ; even this fact carries us back into the beginnings of Greek language.

3. ARCADO-CYPRIOT ELEMENTS AND THEIR IMPORTANCE

The pedigree of the Homeric language may be carried still further backwards. It has long been known that certain Homeric words recur in the Arcadian and the closely kindred Cypriot dialects. They are so few and also so important that they may be enumerated.[1] A very rare word, δέατο, "seemed," occurs once in Homer, *Od.*, vi, 242, and recurs in other forms in Arcadian inscriptions. A few of these words occur even in other dialects, αἶσα, "share," is found in the Arcadian, Cypriot, and even the Argive dialects; νυ occurs in the two dialects first mentioned and in Boeotian, but differing in use.[2] Some words, common to Homer and the Arcadian inscriptions, are found in later literary language, which of course is due to Homer's mighty influence on the literature : ἠπύω, "cry out," in Homer, Pindar, and the tragedians, and "speak," "address," in Homer and Arcadian ; κέλευθος, "road," λεύσσω, "see," ἆμαρ, βόλομαι, οἶος, "alone," δῶμα, εὐχωλά, "prayer," "imprecation," are found both in Arcadian and Cypriot. In Cypriot only occur Ϝάναξ, in the significance of "king," ἀνώγω, αὐτάρ, ἕλος, "meadow," ἰατήρ, χραύομαι, "border on " (Homer, χραύω, "graze,"), ἰδέ.

Because of the nature of the inscriptions in which these words occur it is highly improbable that they should be borrowed from the language of poetry, nor is such a view shared by any philologist. Fick tried to show that certain additions in Books IV, V, VII and XI of the Iliad are due to a Cypriot minstrel,[3] but in this connection he does not adduce the Cypriot words, but treats them in a separate place. It would be impossible to ascribe these words, some of which are found frequently in Homer, to the influence of late Cypriot minstrels, whose existence is extremely hypothetical, even if

---

[1] Lists in O. Hoffmann, *Die griechischen Dialekte*, i, 1891, pp. 276 ; C. D. Buck, *Introduction to the Study of the Greek Dialects*, 2nd ed., 1928, p. 132 ; cp. A. Fick, *Die homerische Ilias*, 1886, p. 548 ; last discussion by C. M. Bowra, "Homeric Words in Arcadian Inscriptions," *Classical Quarterly*, xx, 1926, pp. 168 ; cp. P. Wahrmann, *Glotta*, xvii, 1929, p. 207.

[2] νυ serves in Arcadian and Cypriot for the formation of the demonstrative pronoun ; it refers to the whole sentence in Cypriot and Boeotian as in Homer. F. Bechtel, *Die griechischen Dialekte*, i, 1921, pp. 293, 358, 429, 439.

[3] A. Fick, *Die homerische Ilias*, 1886, pp. 253 and 394.

the post-Homeric epos Cypria is said to have been composed
by the Cypriot poet, Stasinos. Nor are we able to imagine
that Arcadians and Cypriots contributed to the formation
of the Ionic epics in the beginning of the historical age. Consequently the problem becomes very far-reaching and important. For we must needs go back to the Aeolic period
of epic poetry. We remember that the form of the Aeolic
dialect which was incorporated into the epic language is not
identical with and must be earlier than the historically known
subdivisions of that dialect, the Lesbian and the Thessalian.
In fact, we do not know exactly what it was like, for we have
only detached fragments. From the facts before us we can
only conclude that the Arcadian and Cypriot words in Homer
must have been inherited from the language of the Aeolic
epics. Then we have to assume either that the Arcado-
Cypriot dialect has influenced the Aeolic epics or that the
words in question were once common to the Aeolic dialect
which has been incorporated into the epic language and the
Arcado-Cypriot dialect. The latter alternative comes very
near to saying that the Arcado-Cypriot dialect and the
historically known Aeolic dialects are derived from a common
origin from which they were later developed separately, so
that the words in question vanished in Thessalian and Lesbian.
At all events in these early days there must have been a
much closer connection than in the historical age between
the tribes which spoke Aeolic and those which spoke the
Arcado-Cypriot dialect.

Some philologists include the Aeolic and the Arcado-
Cypriot dialects in one group, the "Achaean" dialects, whilst
others prefer to take them as two separate groups. The
geographical separation of the areas covered by these dialects
may seem to corroborate the latter view. But if we take
into account the restriction of this area caused by the Dorian
invasion, it appears that they once covered a coterminous
area, the whole eastern part of the mainland except Attica.[1]
It seems that hardly any other explanation of the above-
mentioned coincidences between the Homeric and the Arcado-
Cypriot vocabulary is possible than this, that they are handed

[1] See above, p. 90.

down by the epic tradition from a time in which the Aeolic and the Arcado-Cypriot dialects were much nearer to each other, both in regard to geography and to language. If this conclusion is right the results are important. For the beginnings of epic poetry must be earlier than the Dorian invasion, i.e. they must belong to the end of the Mycenaean Age. They must further belong to the mainland where the geographical contiguity of the " Achaean " dialects was found. They can hardly belong to Thessaly which is situated at the extreme confines of the area of the Achaean dialects. When they are thrown back to the Mycenaean Age, why should we not dare to think of the centre of Mycenaean power and civilization, Argolis, where in that age certainly an Achaean dialect was spoken, or maybe of Boeotia also, which has such important Mycenaean remains ?

Those philologists are right who assume a closer connection between the Aeolic and the Arcado-Cypriot speeches, placing them together into the Achaean group. There were, of course, differences from the start,[1] and it is easy to understand that they deviated more considerably from each other after their geographical separation. The Arcadian dialect was, moreover, perhaps subject to Ionic influence.[2] Some scholars suppose it to be a mixed dialect which incorporated Ionic elements. This is very natural, because Argolis once seems to have been inhabited by Ionians, who were subjugated and ousted by the Achaeans.

After the Dorians had broken up the Achaeans and driven them out from the coastal provinces of the Peloponnese, the epic poetry was preserved by the northern branch of the Achaeans, the Aeolians. Although we do not know anything for certain, we must assume that in lapse of time, as their language underwent changes, the language of their epics underwent some changes accordingly, but preserved some traces of the old vocabulary.[3] Finally, when emigrating to

---

[1] Cp. above, p. 86.   [2] Cp. above, p. 89.

[3] In regard to flexion the dual forms τοῖς κράναιυν, τοῖς Διδύμοιυν in an inscription from Orchomenos in Arcadia, *Bull. de correspondence hellénique*, xxxix, 1915, pp. 53, ll. 8 and 25, must be noticed. I can only quote the judgment of Kretschmer, *Glotta*, x, 1920, p. 216, that by their appearance the origin of the duals in -οιυν is placed in a new light, but that the solution of the problem is difficult.

Asia Minor, they brought their epics with them and trans-mitted them to the Ionians.

This conclusion—that there are words in the Homeric poems which go back to the Mycenaean Age—may seem hazardous to many who are accustomed to erect a screen between the Mycenaean Age and the beginning of the His-torical Age. This screen is in reality only our ignorance of what happened in the intervening centuries. There must be a continuity between the Mycenaean and the Historical Ages ; the population remained essentially the same, although it was dislocated by the supervening of the Dorians. The separation of the two ages is absolutely unhistorical ; instead of erecting a screen between them we ought to try to find the connecting links and to recognize such as are probable.

Those who question the results stated above [1] will es-pecially base their case on the long lapse of time which is presupposed for the evolution of Greek epics ; they must have begun at least in the thirteenth or twelfth centuries B.C. before the Achaeans were broken up by the Dorian im-migration, and they took their ultimate shape in the Homeric poems in the ninth or eighth centuries B.C. at earliest. We shall treat this question below. In the preceding pages we have seen that the peculiarities of the Homeric language can be explained only by a long-continuing epic technique,

---

[1] I do not overlook the fact that there are certain difficulties. For such I quote from a letter of Wackernagel's : " Would it not be possible that words such as, e.g. ἰδέ, ' and,' once were common to all pre-Doric dialects, and that they went out of use in the Lesbian-Thessalian dialect before the date of our written documents ? If the epos originated in the Peloponnese it ought to be explained why such typical aeolisms as the dative in -εσσι are absent precisely in the Arcado-Cypriot dialect and occur only sporadically in the dialects of the Peloponnese. Does ἄν instead of κε in Homer belong to the Ionic elements or is it connected with the fact that it occurs in the Arcadian dialect, whilst κε is common in the Cypriot ? " On the other hand, he adduces the following fact in support of my thesis : " Latte remarks in *Gnomon*, vii, 1931, pp. 115, that there existed in the Historical Age at Epidauros two phylae, Azantioi and Hysminatai, in addition to two of the Doric phylae, Dymanes and Hylleis, but that at the time of the colonization of Cos and Calymnos the regular Doric phylae must have existed. The two new phylae have names derived from the pre-Doric speech; cp. the Azanes in Arcadia and the word ὑσμίνη, which only occurs in epics. It is a word inherited from of old, and has no related words in Greek except, perhaps, the proper noun ῾Υσμων. The names of the new phylae seem consequently to be derived from the earlier population which was subjugated by the Dorians."

a tradition which was formed long ago and handed down through generations. Next we have to observe that the same is true of the epic style.

4. THE HOMERIC STYLE

Concerning the most prominent peculiarity of the Homeric style, the ornamental epithet, we are able to form a solidly founded opinion, thanks to the able and sagacious work of Parry,[1] who took up and worked out consciously some ideas which Düntzer had put forth formerly without much effect.[2] These epithets have long been called ornamental, because people had the impression that they are of no importance to the thought of the sentence. They are fixed epithets, used repeatedly in conjunction with a certain noun, and because they do not refer to the thought of the sentence in which they appear, they are ornamental. The use of such epithets in conjunction with proper nouns has very marked and curious characteristics.

This may be illustrated by a few selected examples. The two most frequently mentioned heroes are Achilles and Odysseus. For Achilles, we have forty-six noun-epithet formulae, but no one with the same metrical value as any other, for Odysseus forty-five, but here two have the same metrical value. Certain epithets are special, i.e. always applied to one personage, others are generic, i.e. applied to two or more personages. If we take the commonest of the latter, δῖος, this epithet appears in 164 formulae, but these have 127 different metrical values; metrically equivalent formulae are relatively rare even in this case. Generally speaking, the generic epithets occur only with names of the same metrical value, e.g. the nominative δῖος with a word of the measure ⌣–– beginning with a vowel (e.g. δῖος ὑφορβός, etc. ; 183 instances with five exceptions). ἵππστα only with a word of the measure –– beginning with one consonant, ξανθός only with a word of the measure ⌣⌣–– beginning with one consonant, κρείων only with a word with the same measure but beginning with

---

[1] Milman Parry, *L'épithète traditionelle chez Homère*, Paris, 1928; cp. his "Studies in the Epic Technique of Oral Versemaking: i, Homer and Homeric Style," *Harvard Studies in Classical Philology*, xli, 1930, pp. 73.

[2] H. Düntzer, *Homerische Abhandlungen*, 1872, pp. 508.

a vowel, etc. Every statement is valid for a single case of the noun only, for a certain epithet occurs only or chiefly in a certain case, e.g. πολύμητις, πολύτλας, πόδας ὠκύς, in the nominative, ταλασίφρονος, θείου, ποδώκεος, in the genitive, πολυμήχανε, in the vocative, etc. An epithet rarely occurs in different cases except for such forms as have the same metrical value. It happens that if a formula is transposed into another case, the rules of versification are infringed, e.g. μέροπες ἄνθρωποι, *Il.*, xviii, 288, cp. μερόπων ἀνθρώπων ; οὖλε Ὄνειρε, *Il.*, ii, 8, cp. οὖλος ὄνειρος.

Thus the epithet is combined with the noun to form a noun-epithet formula of a certain metrical value. In order to create a language which fitted in with the needs of versification, the poets invented and kept such formulae, which have a definite place in the verse. The most usual of these stock expressions fill the space between the bucolic diaeresis, the feminine caesura, the hepthemimeris, the penthemimeris and the end of the verse, between the beginning of the verse and the said caesurae, and finally a whole verse. Where the combinations are more numerous, the system is, to use Parry's expression, characterized by a great complexity and a strict economy. E.g. in the case of the thirty-seven most important characters of the Iliad and the Odyssey, we find that each has a noun-epithet formula which fills the hexameter exactly between the feminine caesura and the verse end : in the number of such formulae lies the complexity of the system. On the other hand, we find for these thirty-seven characters only forty different formulae of the measure in question ; that is to say, in the case of thirty-three of them, no matter how often they may be mentioned, the poet uses only one formula which fills the verse between the feminine caesura and the verse end : in this lack of formulae which could replace one another lies the economy of the system.[1]

The use of the fixed epithet depends evidently on its convenience for the versification. There are such stock expressions not only for gods and heroes but also for peoples,

---

[1] These words are quoted from Parry's paper, " The Homeric Gloss, A Study in Word-Sense," *Transactions of the American Philological Association*, lix, 1928, p. 242.

things, places, situations, actions, etc. Through the repeated use of the formulae the epithet lost its connection with the sentence ; it became an ornamental epithet which the minstrel pronounced without thinking on it and which offered to him a welcome point of rest, whilst he formed the varied parts of the tale in his mind. The case is similar in regard to the audience ; the ornamental epithet is not absolutely over-heard but appears as a characteristic, not of the special noun, but of the epic style in general. It is often noticed that the epithets sometimes contradict the sense of the sentence, e.g. the swineherd is called " divine," because people did not consider whether this usual epithet was appropriate to a swineherd, it was appropriate to the epic style. The heavens are star-spangled even in day-time. The epithets are used still more thoughtlessly, when e.g. the mother of the beggar Iros is called " mighty " (πότνια, Od., xviii, 5).

The epithet had, of course, a special sense when it was first invented ; it became ornamental through repeated use in a certain case and at a certain place of the verse. There are other epithets which have a definite reference to the meaning of the sentence. Formulae were invented during the whole course of epic poetry ; e.g. Κρόνου πάις ἀγκυλομήτεω belongs to its Ionic period. But many more of them, e.g. ἵππota Νέστωρ, εὐρύοπα Ζεύς, etc., are by their forms proved to be inherited from its Aeolic period. We must suppose that most of them are so.

The existence of this system is the final refutation of the view that the poets composed their epics with the pen in the hand ; it is inconceivable, except in oral tradition, where it was a great boon to the minstrel offering him welcome facilities and rest points in his recital. Nor can it possibly be the work of a single poet ; it must needs be founded on a tradition of centuries, and it represents the work of genera-tions of minstrels who sought and kept the convenient ex-pressions generally to the exclusion of other formulae which could replace them.

The ornamental epithets are commonly " glosses," i.e. words that occur in Homer only and where they are borrowed from him, otherwise they are obsolete and their significance is forgotten. As they are not referred to and explained by the context, we are very often unable to understand them. Nor did ancient philologists have any more exact knowledge of their significance.

There are, however, many other glosses in Homer, but as they are referred to the thought of the sentence, their meaning is generally explained by this connection, e.g. δαήρ "brother-in-law"; ἔστωρ, "yokepin"; but the exact significance may remain uncertain, e.g. of the word ἐμμαπέως, which occurs twice in apparent stock expressions : ὁ δ' ἀρ' ἐμμαπέως ἀπόρουσεν and ὑπάκουσε, Il., v, 836 and Od., xiv, 485, respectively, or the phrase νυκτὸς ἀμολγῷ, which occurs five times.[1] Very seldom is such a gloss impossible to interpret, e.g. the adverb ἐντυπάς, Il., xxiv, 163.

The glosses are old, obsolete words which long ago passed out of spoken language and were preserved by the traditional language of epics only. So their significance was forgotten, and neither we nor the ancient philologists knew anything more of them than what can be inferred from the context. The question is, when did they pass out from the spoken language, for the epic language must once have taken them from the spoken. Some say that this happened first in the interval between the composition of the Homeric poems and the rise of written literature, but Parry seems to be right in rejecting this view.[2] It would presume an unbelievably rapid change of the Ionic dialect.

Such an explanation, moreover, would not apply to the glosses of Aeolic origin, which the Ionic epics took over from their Aeolic predecessors. It is very likely and understandable that precisely this process of taking over gave rise to many glosses ; words which were wanting in the Ionic dialect were preserved by the epic technique, though only half understood. It is probable that we have to go still farther back, viz. that there were glosses even in the Aeolic epics.

Anyhow, the existence of glosses is a proof of a high antiquity of language and a long-enduring development, in fact so long that certain words had been embodied in the traditional language as crystallizations, their significance having

[1] Concerning the probable significance of the phrase, see my *Primitive Time-reckoning*, pp. 35.
[2] See Parry's paper quoted, p. 180, n. 1.

been forgotten. The important result of this discussion is the apparent parallelism between language and style. Both were moulded in fixed forms by the epic technique and the same technique preserved them by continued use side by side, even if they had vanished from the current language and their significance had been forgotten. Thus the epic style was created, a conventionalized outcome of a long evolution of epic tradition which lasted for centuries.

But stock expressions and the like make up only a part of the epic songs ; they were rest-points in the recital. We should not forget that the other part of our Homer does not consist of such. Thus the reproach that the view taken up here does not do justice to Homer's genius is undeserved, but this genius was displayed in other forms than those which we are wont to take as natural for poetical work. The current language influenced the minstrels, sometimes its traces may be observed, but it was treated so as to conform with the epic style.

Homer's language goes far back into very old times, and the important thing is rightly to realize how his archaisms were preserved, viz. through an epic technique which constantly drew on a stock inherited from of old and embodied its elements even in its most recent products.

CHAPTER V

THE ORIGIN AND TRANSMISSION OF
EPIC POETRY

THE aim of the foregoing chapters was to show that in Homer there are elements which go back into much earlier times, both in respect of language and of civilization. In the latter case it can be definitely proved that some elements are Mycenaean. In another chapter we gave a survey of the Mycenaean Age in order to bring to the fore the fact that this was an age of great and valorous deeds and of mighty princes and warriors, a really Heroic Age, such as is a suitable background for epic poetry.

In order to explain how the transmission of epic poetry through many centuries, which its origin in the Mycenaean Age presupposes, was possible, it is necessary to see how epic poetry is made and preserved through the lapse of time. For this purpose a knowledge of the epic poetry of other peoples will be most useful. This comparative method was inaugurated long ago by Professor Steinthal,[1] but owing to the romantic prejudice which held epics to be a collective creation of the popular mind, it failed to produce substantial results. Professor Pöhlmann urged a more realistic and empirical conception of facts,[2] but Professor Drerup, who recently gave a useful survey of the extant materials, did not make much use of them for the understanding of Greek epics.[3] The brief but very substantial sketch of Professor John Meier [4] was very little noticed by classical philologists.

[1] H. Steinthal, "Das Epos," *Zeitschrift für Völkerpsychologie und Sprachwissenschaft*, v, 1868, pp. 1.

[2] R. v. Pöhlmann, "Zur geschichtlichen Beurteilung Homers," *Sybel's Historische Zeitschrift*, lxxiii, 1894, pp. 385; reprinted in the volume *Aus Altertum und Gegenwart*, i, 2nd ed., 1911, pp. 77.

[3] See above, p. 31 and n. 1.

[4] John Meier, *Werden und Leben des Volksepos*, 1909.

For my own part I am firmly convinced that a comparative and empirical study of all existing epics is the only method for attaining a better understanding of the origin and development of Greek epics, and especially a solution of the problems put forward in the foregoing chapters. But in such a study we must be well aware that we are working by way of analogies, and analogies are most useful tools for widening and bettering our explanation of difficult problems which cannot be attacked directly; but in certain circumstances they are apt to be misleading. In picking out one analogy of many, and following this one solely, one is liable to be led astray.

This one-sidedness is my objection against the comparison of the Homeric poems with French epics, the *chansons de geste*, instituted by Andrew Lang,[1] and the same objection is valid against the close comparison between Greek and Teutonic epics drawn up by Professor Chadwick in a very learned and stimulating book.[2] The right method is to try to get a survey of all extant epics, as far as possible in a necessarily brief compass, and through an analysis of these to try to discern what is applicable in our special case, viz. Greek epic poetry.

1. Epics of other Peoples

Unfortunately the Teutonic epics do not offer the most illuminating analogies; so many peoples are concerned in their development. Moreover, there are so many blank periods in our information—both before the earliest preserved epic and intervening between the different examples which we have —that, instead of offering us the help we seek, these epics raise many more problems than they can solve.

The oldest stage is testified by the information in Tacitus concerning the songs sung in honour of Arminius, the vanquisher of the Romans.[3] It is idle to discuss whether these songs were epics or romances; their subject was truly epic, and another piece of information in Tacitus [4] proves that there existed elaborate epics dealing with the origin of the Teutonic tribes in a mythological fashion, for Tacitus adds that these songs were their only kind of chronicles and annals.

[1] See above, pp. 22.
[2] H. M. Chadwick, *The Heroic Age*, 1912, 2nd impression, 1926.
[3] Tacitus, *Annals*, ii, 88.　　　　[4] Tacitus, *Germania*, 2.

Whatsoever the form of these oldest songs may have been, they were completely ousted by new songs dealing with the heroes of the stormy age of the Great Migrations, and their deeds. We have a vivid picture of bards singing at the evidently Germanized court of Attila,[1] and Teutonic poems and poets praising great men and deeds are not seldom mentioned by Latin authors of this age.[2] This was really the Heroic Age of the Teutons. The persons celebrated in their extant epics all belong to this age. Although Gothic songs mentioned Hermanaric's great-great-grandfather, King Ostrogotha, the persons belong, generally speaking, to a period from the Gothic King Hermanaric who died A.D. 375 to the king of the Lombards, Albion, who died in 572. The Beowulf epos refers to Scandinavian kings from the fifth and sixth centuries A.D.

The personages of the epics are throughout historical persons, but history is mixed up with mythical elements, dragon fights, etc., and persons living at different ages are brought together, e.g. Attila and Theodoric of Verona. Originally there seem to have been a great number of subjects, but in course of time a few only became prominent and were fused with others.[3]

A salient feature of these narratives is their dispersion among foreign countries, they are, so to speak, international, common to all Teutonic tribes. The Anglo-Saxon epos mentions no English king, for Offa I lived before the Angles had left their original home on the Continent, but only fights and deeds of Danish and Swedish princes.[4] The catastrophe of the Burgundians is celebrated in the songs of the elder Edda which were composed in Iceland and Greenland, and in the late epos of the Nibelungen, composed in Austria. Theodoric of Verona is the hero of Bavarian songs and of a Norwegian saga. This certainly came about not only through a wandering of the stories from country to country but was for a great part the work of travelling minstrels who visited different countries. Widsith, the English poem enumerating the famous

---

[1] *Fragmenta Historicorum graecorum*, ed. Müller, iv, p. 92 ; often quoted, e.g. by Chadwick, op. cit., p. 84, n. 2.

[2] See Chadwick, op. cit. pp. 84, or R. W. Chambers, *Widsith*, pp. 1.

[3] In regard of the development of the story of the Nibelungen, see A. Heusler, *Nibelungensage und Nibelungenlied*, 2nd ed., 1922.

[4] R. W. Chambers, *Beowulf*, 1921.

peoples and kings whom the bard visited, is the proof.[1] Widsith may be an imaginary person, at all events the poem is much later than the kings mentioned, but the underlying idea of the wide travels of the minstrels must be founded upon reality.

Chadwick justly describes the epics of the age of the Great Migrations as the first stage—though in fact not the very first —praising living men and contemporaneous events and distinguishes from this a second stage, epics founded on the first dealing with a not very remote past.[2] When he terms his third stage, continuing but remodelling epics of the second stage, popular epics, the distinction seems to me to be too sharp. There was a time in which both the noblemen and the people shared the interest in epics. We know from the seventh to the ninth centuries A.D. that epics were chanted in England in the streets and on the bridges, at meals and in the cloisters,[3] but that they were also enjoyed by kings. Alfred the Great was educated upon the English poems and recommended others to learn them by heart.[4] Einhard, in his *Life of Charlemagne* states that the emperor collected native and very ancient poems in which the deeds and battles of olden times were related.[5] Minstrelsy was a recognized profession in the eighth century A.D. according to the laws of the Frisians. Up to the ninth, and even the tenth century, epics were certainly favoured by the ruling classes too, not only the kings but also the many feudal lords residing in their castles everywhere in the country.

A change was, however, brought about by the introduction of Christianity, the Church was hostile to the essentially heathen songs. But curiously enough this hostility affected the early generations of Christianized Teutons but slightly. They kept their old modes and views of life, especially in regard to epic poetry, in spite of sometimes being devout Christians. The most outstanding example is Icelandic literature. The Christian veneer of Beowulf is but thin. In the early centuries of the Middle Ages Christianity was very superficial among the Teutonic peoples, epic poetry was honoured and common

[1] R. W. Chambers, *Widsith*, 1912. [2] Chadwick, op. cit., pp. 93.
[3] *Ibid.*, p. 79. [4] Chambers, *Widsith*, p. 2.
[5] Ch. 29 ; see Chadwick, op. cit., p. 5.

to them all.   For it is much more likely that the stories told in different Teutonic countries were told in verse than in prose.

As time went on the influence of Christianity became stronger and the modes of life and thought originating in southern Europe spread northwards, this had a profound effect on their epics.   At this time epics may have been less favoured by the upper classes, but they were still loved and preserved by the people.   The change affected also the form of epics : instead of the old Teutonic alliterative verse the rhymed verse was introduced.   Epics had a renascence in southern Germany when the famous " Nibelungenlied " and other epics were composed in the twelfth century.   This is Chadwick's fourth stage which he calls a kind of learned revival.

In the most distant of the Teutonic countries, Scandinavia, the old modes of life and thought lingered on longer.   Moreover, Scandinavia had a Heroic Age of its own, the Viking Age.   This brought about a rejuvenation of epics.   Whilst the old stories were chanted on the Continent, the praise of living men and their deeds was added at the courts of the Scandinavian kings.   The poetic art was especially developed in Iceland, and Icelandic minstrels visited regularly the courts of the Scandinavian kings and sang their praise.   But this poetry cannot have been truly popular, because the languages already markedly differed in the different Scandinavian countries.

The subject is in fact too complicated to be treated in a brief survey, and I wish especially to emphasize this complexity.   First there is the complexity of peoples, for the Teutons were divided into a great number of peoples who hardly understood each other's language.   The epics or stories had to be translated from one language into the other.   There are different styles of epic poetry, and it is only natural that such differences are found among the Teutonic peoples who lived under very different conditions in widely separated countries.   The concentrated and pathetic speed of the Edda songs differs markedly, for example from Beowulf.   In spite of this there are signs of similarity in the modes of expression, but in view of the scattered conditions of the remnants of

Teutonic poetry it is only natural that they are few and slight.[1]
There are resemblances not only in the subjects treated, but
also in the language, e.g. in the hortatory addresses and the
accounts of the dragon fights. The fact that these resemblances sometimes occur in stories relating to entirely different characters need not prevent us from believing that they
spring ultimately from a common origin. English and German
poetry are based on a common system of metre, a kind of
alliterative verse, down to the ninth century ; the usual
metre of the Edda songs differs but little from this type.
There is a sufficient amount of resemblance between English
and German poetry, not merely in the general metrical scheme
but also in the construction of individual verses. Chadwick
proves this by quoting parallel passages from Beowulf and
the "Hildebrandslied." The subjects show a great unity.
The same is true of the life depicted ; mean and gross things
are avoided ; the epics are courtly.

Secondly, there was a growing complexity of civilization.
There was the Church which was opposed to the old Teutonic
modes of life and thought and their expression in the epics,
and behind the Church there was the ancient Latin Literature
which was considered to be the unsurpassed model. It is
even asserted by certain scholars that the impulse to the
composition of the great epics, Beowulf and the *chansons
de geste*, came from Vergil's "Aeneid" and maybe Statius,
but definite proofs are wanting. The "Nibelungenlied" was,
however, certainly composed under the influence of the French
epics.

Thus, in regard to the transmission of the form of epics
we learn very little. What we see is the transmission of
subjects, which wandered from one country to another, and
the changes they underwent. We see how a new Heroic Age
arose and introduced new subjects.

There cannot be any doubt that the Franks who invaded
France cultivated Teutonic epics, but these fell into oblivion
because of the change of life and language. In France
brilliant new epics arose, the *chansons de geste*. It seems,
however, that all connections with the old Teutonic epics
were not cut off, for Gaston Paris and Pio Rajna have shown

[1] The following statements are taken from Chadwick, op. cit., pp. 77.

that there are considerable Teutonic elements in motifs and form.

Opinions concerning the origin of the *chansons de geste* vary considerably. The most recent hypothesis put forward by Professor Bédier would have it that they were composed by priests, monks, or indeed any *clericus* in certain places in southern France visited by pilgrims on their way to Spain, arising from almost nothing a few years before the date of the most famous of them, the epos of Roland, which is dated about A.D. 1120. Bédier's criticism of earlier theories may in many respects be just, but his hypothesis is exaggerated. Certainly clerics took part in composing the songs, but if they did cultivate this essentially secular kind of poetry, it was because the people wanted to hear it. They tried to make the best of the case by clothing the subjects in a pious garb. The language of Roland is a literary language which must have needed a long time for its development ; it is not of a southern but of a northern type. Besides elements derived from the twelfth century there are others showing a more archaic aspect of life. This presupposes an analogous earlier poetry in northern France dealing with other subjects.[1]

Further there are remains of earlier poetry, a Latin translation by Hildegaire, who died about 875, of a ballad praising a war carried on by King Clothar against the Saxons about 620. It was sung by women at their dance ; we know how fond people were of dancing in the beginning of the Middle Ages. Such ballads have in a certain stage of civilization an epic character. From the commencement of the eleventh century there is the Hague fragment, a Latin translation relating the siege of Narbonne by Charlemagne. Consequently intermediate links are not wanting, even if time and education have swept off most of them.

On the other hand, it is certain that the rise of French epics was due to a new impetus, the rise of chivalry with pious aims and the beginning of the crusades against the infidels who lived on the other side of the Pyrenees ; this may perhaps

---

[1] There is a vast literature on the *chansons de geste* which may be found in a history of French literature. I quote only a recent paper which I have used much for this paragraph : H. Schück, " La nouvelle théorie des origines des chansons de geste," *Neuphilogische Mitteilungen*, xvii, 1915, pp. 1.

explain why there came into the foreground the insignificant battle at Roncevalles, in which the enemies are made Saracens instead of Basques. Even an influence of Latin book epics has been assumed. This is possible in view of the fact that certain poets were clerics but it seems not to be proved conclusively.

Early in the development of French epics an important change of form took place : instead of assonance, rhymed verse was introduced. The *chansons de geste* offer a very rich and varied epic poetry praising various heroes, but Roland and the battle at Roncevalles are most prominent and Charlemagne is the central figure. The subjects are primarily historical, but they were remodelled, enlarged, and fused, and mythical elements were received. Social conditions were feudal, the poets who were called *jongleurs* and who accompanied their recitation on the fiddle, were court minstrels ; noblemen appear seldom, priests more often, as poets. Later the *jongleurs* sung also to the people in streets and market places ; and as civilization progressed, the *jongleurs* sometimes used text-books.

Teutonic and French epics have been almost the only parallels used for an elaborate comparison with Greek epics in order to elucidate their origin and development, and conversely the various hypotheses concerning the Homeric question have exercised a great influence on the conceptions of the problem offered by the former. The real reason for this is that these epics have captured the interest of scholars, for they are of outstanding importance in the history of the literature of the European nations. But if we are trying to find illuminating analogies we ought not voluntarily to restrict the search to western Europe but to make full use of other epics too. Generally they are mentioned only in passing. In view of the complexity of the Teutonic epic development and of the progressive culture of the age to which French epics belong they do not offer the clearest analogies. We ought to consider the epics of other peoples as closely as those of the Teutons and the French and to try and see what they may teach us.

Teutonic epics are probably at the bottom of the French epics. They have certainly other off-shoots. In this connection mention must be made of Sweden. We can infer that epic poetry existed in Sweden not only from the mention of Swedish kings in Beowulf but also at a later age from a runic monument in Södermanland illustrating the tale of Sigurd, and still more explicitly from the most remarkable of all runic monuments, the famous Rök stone in Ostrogothia, which has a couple of abridged and enigmatical verses probably referring to Theodoric.

Special note should be taken of this because Swedish epic poetry has a far-away off-shoot, the Russian bylinas,[1] which were written down from the people's mouths in the last centuries in northernmost Russia on the shores of the White Sea and of the lake of Onega. The bylinas belong originally to the old kingdom of Kieff which was founded by Swedish Vikings, the Varägs, and their central figure is King Vladimir the Great, who lived about A.D. 1100 and was a great-grandson of the founder of the Swedish empire in Russia, Rurik. Some of the heroes of the bylinas are mentioned in old Russian chronicles. The scene of their activities comprises the sea between Sweden and S.W. Finland, Ålandssea, Novgorod, Kieff, Constantinople ; the heroes go on pilgrimages to the Holy Land and they come to the Land of the Saracens and to southern Italy where the Varägs warred in the service of the Byzantine emperor ; this is the way of the Swedish Varägs. The bylinas contain enigmatical words and forms which cannot be explained from the Russian ; the attempts to explain certain of them from the Swedish seem to have been successful. There are many traits reminiscent of the life and manners of the Vikings, their chieftains and kings. The description of a ship shows, e.g. that the prototype was a Viking ship. But during the long lapse of time and the far-away wanderings of the poems the descriptions have been blurred and mixed up with things which are partly of quite recent origin, e.g. the use of guns and of charta sigillata. The ship becomes fabulous and the hero is made a merchant instead of a warrior. It is only to be wondered at that the old background has not quite

---

[1] Concerning the bylinas there is an old work of W. Wollner, *Untersuchungen über die Volksepik der Grossrussen*, 1879. The modern and for our purpose important work is written in Danish : St. Rozniecki, *Varægiske Minder i den russiske Heltedigtning*, 1914. Cp. also S. Agrell, " Fornnordiska element i den ryska folkpoesien," *Yearbook of the New Society of Letters at Lund*, 1922, pp. 65.

disappeared, but it remained owing to the low cultural stage and the static conditions of life of the backward people who kept the memory of these epics. It is significant that songs which were written down in the sixteenth to the eighteenth century do not essentially show an earlier standpoint than those written down in the nineteenth century, although they contain certain old features and word forms.

Swedish epic poetry has perhaps still another off-shoot, Finnish-Esthonian epics. In the last century a great and varying but kindred mass of songs was written down, partly in Esthonia, partly in the borderland between Finland and Russia ; of the former Kreuzwald composed the epos " Kalevipoeg," the latter were pieced together by Dr. Lönnroth to make the well-known Finnish epos " Kalevala ".[1] Kreuzwald destroyed his materials, Lönnroth's are preserved, and by those and the numerous songs written down later we are able to see how he worked. The result is most discouraging for those who think they are able through literary analysis to discern the earlier songs of which a great epos is composed.[2] Recent research [3] tends to show that the songs did not originate in the districts where they were written down but in S.W. Finland, i.e. the coast-land nearest to Sweden, and that the heroes originally were Viking chieftains. The heroes are tall and blond men with blue eyes, clad in red, blue and gaily-coloured mantles. There are traces reminiscent of the life and the manners of the Vikings, e.g. when the hero, Ahti, finds his ship weeping because for so many years it must rot on land. But these epics have been thoroughly remodelled, especially by the intrusion of magic elements which are now very conspicuous. The Middle Ages have left their traces : the Holy Virgin and the Saints are mentioned in prayers used for the purpose of sorcery. The setting has been moved from the sea between Gotland, Åland, and S.W. Finland to Lapponia ;

[1] The best-known earlier work on " Kalevala " is that of D. Comparetti, *Der Kalewala* (German translation), 1892.

[2] To take an example : the tenth song of the " Kalevala " has 510 verses. Of these only 130 belong to the original form in which it was recited by the singers ; Lönnroth has added the others from other passages of the "Kalevala " or from other songs.

[3] As represented by K. Krohn ; see his " Kalevalastudien, Einleitung," *FF Communications*, vol. xvi, No. 53, 1924.

the heroes have become great sorcerers. Even quite modern things, e.g. coffee-drinking and a telescope, are mentioned occasionally.

These are, perhaps, the most striking examples of the varying life and transference, the long continuance of the core and the slow transmutation of epic tradition, but there are many other important examples of epics, of which some are the more remarkable because they permit us to obtain a knowledge of living epic poetry.

Best known are Serbian epics.[1] According to some hints in Byzantine writers there must have been epic songs among the Serbians before the great national tragedy, the battle at Kossovo in 1389, which ended the freedom of the Serbian kingdom and around which centre the epic songs which have been written down in the last centuries. In this cycle the most prominent figures are the last king of the Serbians, zar Lazar, the traitor Vuk Brancovitch, and the Turkish sultan Murad, who was killed by a Serbian. Other poems deal with the nuptial journey of Maxim Tshernovitch who lived in the fifteenth century—in this cycle historical elements are very scarce—and still others with Marko Kraljevitch, a Turkish vassal who fell in 1392 and is described as another Hercules in strength and appetite. Heroes from different centuries are brought together ; e.g. Marko Kraljevitch is coupled with Vuk Despota who lived a century later, also with Ivo from Zengg who lived three centuries later.

In Bosnia and Herzegovina, however, epic poetry has survived to our own days.[2] Subjects have changed, they are here the incessant feuds in the borderland between Mahometans and Christians in the sixteenth and seventeenth centuries. The central figure is a certain Mustaj Bey from Lika, of whom very little is known. The feudal organization and backward conditions of the land have preserved the epics. The rich beys, Mahometan landed proprietors, had minstrels among their retinue, and some of them could sing themselves, and

[1] See especially works by V. Jagic and others in the *Archiv für slavische Philologie*.

[2] See the illuminating article by M. Murko, " Neues über südslavische Volksepik," in *Neue Jahrbücher für das klassische Altertum*, xliii, 1919, pp. 273, and the work of the same author, *La poésie populaire épique en Yougoslavie au début du XXe siécle*, 1929.

poetical ability was widespread among the people. Chants were intoned at festivals and weddings, at fairs and in coffee-houses, etc. There seems to be a more democratic trend among the Christians than among the Mahometans. The chants of the former depend nowadays partly on printed sources, and they have taken up such modern subjects as the Russo-Turkish and Russo-Japanese wars and the Balkan war. It appears that epic poetry, though living, is declining, and is soon to be ousted by printed books and newspapers. We note here, too, how living epic poetry is bound up with certain social and cultural conditions and incessant warfare, and how it changes its subjects whilst still living. So it came about that epic poetry lived and developed in Bosnia and Herzegovina, where the cycle of Kossovo is almost unknown, but the old epics of this and kindred cycles were preserved in Serbia.

A very remarkable epic poetry is recorded from the Kara-Kirgizes, a Turkish tribe in Central Asia.[1] The central figures are prince Manas and his heathen adversary Joloi, but in addition to these two there are several other heroes. The tribe is a nomadic one, rich in cattle, and there are wealthy and mighty men, some are even called sultans, who like to have minstrels among their retainers. The gift of singing is very widespread and the minstrels sing to the people also. They vary their songs according to their audience, inserting the praise of their families when singing before the wealthy ones, and bitter reproof of their arrogance when singing to the people.

A very marked contrast is offered by the epic poetry of the Abakan-Tartars,[2] a kindred tribe which was separated from the Kara-Kirgizes in the tenth century A.D. remaining at the river of Jenisei. Their conditions are poor, agriculture undeveloped, and they live chiefly by hunting. In the long evenings after the hunting the chants are intoned. They are of a fantastic character approaching to the folk-tale describing the wonderful life of a hero who ascends high mountains and even the heavens and descends below the earth to struggle with monsters. It may be surmised that, owing to the conditions under which the people have lived for a long time, the

---

[1] W. Radloff, " Proben der Volksliteratur der nördlichen türkischen Stämme," V, *Der Dialekt der Kara-kirgisen*, 1885.

[2] Radloff, op. cit., pp. v.

heroic background has been quite overlaid by elements deriving from the folk-tale.

I pass over the mediaeval Greek epic of Digenis Akritas because its historical setting is too little known,[1] and the modern Greek epics dealing with Ali Pasha's Suliot campaigns because they are inaccessible to me,[2] but it will not be out of place to say a few words on an epic cycle in prose, the cycle of the Nartes, which is current among the Ossetes and certain other tribes of the northern Caucasus.[3] The principal figure is Uryzmag, who is sometimes described as an aged and despised man, and his wife and sister Satana, and some others. The Nartes go on far-away expeditions and between the expeditions spend their time drinking ; the horse is essential to them. The cycle is crowded with supernatural elements and folk-tale motifs and shows the features of decadent epics. This is also true of the form, for all published versions are told in prose, but we know that minstrels once existed among the Ossetes, as they did among the eastern Tsherkesses ; the last one died about 1850.

Lastly, I would mention the epics of the Atchinese in Sumatra,[4] which are remarkable through the fact that epic poets are known by name ; it is to be regretted that the available information is scantier than seems to have been necessary. Three poems are mentioned. The first refers to

[1] Cp. a series of articles by H. Grégoire the latest of which is : "Autour de Digénis Akritas," *Byzantion*, viii, 1932, pp. 287.

[2] Mr. A. J. B. Wace kindly draws my attention to this epic giving the following valuable information. Leake, *Travels in Northern Greece*, I, pp. 463, gives an account of it. He had a manuscript as far as it had gone in his time ; it was then 4500 lines long, but unfortunately Leake's manuscript cannot now be traced. The only known manuscript is in the National Library at Athens which contains 10,000 lines, and this shows how the author added to his poem. He could not write but presumably composed his poem for recitation, and it was subsequently written down. K. Sathas, Ἱστορικαὶ διατριβαί, pp. 123, has an account of the epic and publishes a section of it. It does not deal with the Suliot war alone but with the whole history and exploits of Ali Pasha. Professor Marshall of King's College, London, is going to prepare an edition of it. I have not been able to take cognizance of these epics which seem to be very interesting, and this the more because there also is an independent collection of Greek ballads dealing with the Suliot wars ; they have been collected by Aravantinos.

[3] G. Dumézil, *Légendes sur les Nartes*, 1930.

[4] C. Snouck Hurgronje, *De Atjehers*, 1893-95 ; English translation : *The Achehnese*, 1906.

a naval expedition to Malacca in the first part of the seventeenth century, which is described in a fabulous manner ; the
adversaries are said to be Dutch, though according to the
historical circumstances they must have been Portuguese.
The second, called " Prince Mahomet," refers also to historical
events, but occurring in the middle of the eighteenth century,
it is much mixed up with miracles and dreams. The author
gives his name in the end of the poem. The third, " The
War with the Company," describes the feuds between the
Atchinese and the Dutch in modern times. It was made by
a poet Dokarim, who spent five years in composing it after
the model of the second poem and kept it in his memory,
for he did not know how to write or to read, and it was written
down after his recital. I shall later on return to what is said
about the composition of this poem which is illuminating in
regard to certain questions concerning the Homeric poems.

2. THE DEVELOPMENT OF EPIC POETRY. THE EPIC TECHNIQUE

From this condensed survey of existing epics we may
proceed to pick out some common traits and important details.
Before the appearance of epics, there certainly existed some
kind of poetry, but this is wholly unknown and research would
have to deal chiefly with primitive peoples. The form of early
epics has been much discussed, and it is a commonly received
opinion that the great epics of the European peoples have been
made up of short lays. It is not unlikely that the first songs
were short ; I agree with the opinion that the great epics are
developed out of the lays, not by a process of fitting together,
but rather by a retelling the story in a more leisurely manner.[1]
This view is consistent with what we know of the art of minstrelsy and of living epics.

The examples adduced above prove that epic poetry originally always deals with historical persons and events, and it
may be inferred that its origin is to be found in the praise of
living men and the description of contemporary events. But

---

[1] This is the view of Ker and Heusler. The above words are quoted from
R. W. Chambers, *Beowulf*, p. 116 ; cp. p. 115.

here it ought well to be observed that mythical traits and elements of the folk-tale can be applied to a living man ; [1] examples from our own days show that a man may become a myth during his lifetime.   The exaggerated praise of heroes and the still undeveloped intellectualism open the doors for supernatural elements from the beginning.

This kind of epic poetry is said to be court poetry, and such is the case, though with certain restrictions.   In this cultural stage there is no intellectual cleavage between people of a higher and a lower standing ; they all share the warlike spirit and the admiration of valorous deeds.   Our meagre information speaks of court minstrels only, but I cannot see any reason why minstrels should not have intoned their chants before the people also—at all events there were the retainers of the prince—or why everybody who had some ability in this respect should not occasionally have tried to sing of famous deeds.

These epics are truly the poetry of a Heroic Age.   But such a period of great exertions is generally short.   Circumstances change, exhaustion supervenes, the great deeds and adventures cease and people settle down to a more peaceful and uneventful life.   Tribes and kingdoms split up and small chieftains and barons attain to a more independent position, if there was formerly an overlord in war.   But the warlike spirit and the interest in great deeds do not die out immediately, they preserve epic poetry and are at the same time fostered by it, but it sings now of the deeds of a past age because there are no contemporary events to celebrate.   Of course certain cultural and social conditions are presumed.   The art of reading and of writing must not be in general use or must be altogether absent, even among those who possess political power.   Social organization must be in a certain sense aristocratic or feudal, viz. certain persons may be prominent through wealth and power and able to surround themselves with retainers, among whom often a minstrel is found.   Epic poetry is still more widespread among the common people, minstrels sing regularly in streets and at festivals and every one who has a certain ability may emulate them with more or less success.   Epic poetry may in this manner become the most favoured pastime

---

[1] A very illuminating example in Chadwick, *The Heroic Age*, pp. 97.

even of the common people and still be cultivated by the upper classes.

This state of things may be interrupted by a new Heroic Age and new epics dealing with contemporary men and events, but it may also continue until epics are abandoned or obliterated by a higher culture, first, of course, among the upper classes, whilst the unlettered people may preserve them for a long time. The epic poems may also wander far abroad, they may be received by people who lead a monotonous and uneventful life on a low cultural plane, but who may, in spite of this, love and preserve epic poetry.

It is needless to say that under such varying conditions epic poetry will undergo many and varied changes; I shall presently return to this topic. Here I wish to point to the fact that epic poetry is bound up with a certain cultural stage, and in its origin and first development, with certain social conditions. I wish to lay stress on the fact that the most important distinction is that between epics dealing with contemporary men and events, and epics dealing with men and events of bygone days. The former belong to an eventful age and in this case the old subjects are ousted by new ones. In the latter case, when the age of great deeds is past, and there are no new subjects to be chanted, the old ones are preserved, and are on the one hand enlarged and remodelled through the influence of new conditions and the embodying of elements from myths and folk-tales, and on the other are simplified and fused, for there is a tendency to fix the circle of subjects from which the poets choose their themes and to group them around a certain outstanding person and event. But this tendency seldom leads to a complete issue; epic poetry remains a fluctuating mass restricted within certain limits.

In order to attain an understanding of the changes which epic poetry undergoes during the sometimes lengthy course of a protracted life, it is essential to get a substantial idea of the art of singing or what is called the epic technique, and here there are what seem to be certain common features.

In their early days epics seem always to have been recited to the accompaniment of some instrument. This is recorded of the Greeks, the Teutons, the French *jongleurs*, the

Serbians, the Finns, and the Kara-Kirgizes.   In a later age
the accompaniment was felt as unnecessary and abandoned,
e.g. by the Greek rhapsodists ; nor did the singers of the bylinas
use any instrument.   There would be only one or at most
two melodies, e.g. among the Kara-Kirgizes a faster one for
the narratives and a more solemn for the speeches.   The
metre is always the same, and this is conditioned by the
technique being an improvisation.   On the other hand, the
melody serves to fix the metre.

These facts concern in a certain degree a topic which was
much discussed by students of the history of literature, the
difference between epics and ballads, especially dancing songs.
I cannot see that there is any very essential difference in the
age of minstrelsy.   We know, e.g. from Homer, that the
Greek minstrels were fetched to sing at the dance and to sing
dirges at the bier.[1]   The bards of the Ossetes were present
at all assemblies, dances, funerals, and in the battles.   They
performed especially at the funerals, the families communicat-
ing to them the memories of the dead ; in the battle they
improvised chants of praise in a protected place.[2]   Whatever
the occasion was, the minstrels were called upon to assist ;
their technique was, of course, one and the same, although
their chants varied accordingly.   The differences were certainly less than is imagined in our age of sharply distinguished
classification of different classes of literature.   We know
that songs of epic character accompanied the dance.[3]   The
cessation of the accompaniment of an instrument certainly
enlarged the difference between epics and dancing songs
considerably.   This we see in Greece, but on the other hand,
the fact that the main subjects even of choric lyrics are myths,
is certainly a heritage from the time in which minstrels chanted
epic songs at the dance.   When epics abandoned the accompaniment by an instrument or altogether vanished, the style of
the dancing songs was liberated and attained a character of
its own ; as long as they were sung by minstrels they must
have been closely akin to epics.

Epic poetry has been called sometimes court poetry,
sometimes popular poetry.   Both descriptions are in a certain

---

[1] *Il.*, xviii, v. 604, and xxiv, v. 720, respectively.
[2] G. Dumézil, op. cit., pp. 10.   [3] Cp. above, p. 190.

measure justified. It appears that we must take as a court the retinue of every small chieftain or baron, however small it may be in numbers; in this there may be a permanent or temporary place for a minstrel. It appears that the minstrels are favoured by and sing for not only the chieftains but also the people. Hence it may come about that epic poetry may survive under very simple conditions, where there is nothing whatever which can be called a court or a retinue and nobody is prominent in wealth and power.

Much has been said of the minstrels, but it ought to be carefully observed that they are only the most prominent of a multitude who know and use epics in a greater or less degree, and this circle may be widened so as to comprise a large part of the people. It is recorded from Bosnia that children begin to learn epic poetry from a very early age, eight years onwards; the interest ceases in many at an adult age when the needs and sorrows of life overtake them. A natural selection of the fittest takes place. It is often noted that epic poetry is in the hands of persons who are distinguished by excellent memory and certain poetical or linguistic abilities. Those who have such faculties and with them the love of poetry become famous and honoured singers and, if the social conditions are such, court minstrels. Others exercise their art in more modest circles, as is expressly stated concerning the Kara-Kirgizes. It is well known that minstrels are frequently represented as blind, and in fact they often are such, e.g. in Greece and elsewhere. A certain Slavonic tribe calls all singers " the blind ones " even if they have their eyesight. For while blind men are shut off from exercising other professions, their memory is often excellently developed. A man of higher standing may have the same faculties; he becomes a special protector of epic poetry and may occasionally rival the minstrels, as it is told of Achilles and of the Vandal King Gelimer, of King Hrothgar in Beowulf and of a Bosnian bey.

Every one learns through hearing and there is ample opportunity of hearing. But as on such a cultural stage traditions and knowledge are often accumulated within the family, it is only natural that we hear about the art of singing as attached to certain families; hereditary disposition may even contribute to this result. A son may learn from his father, but a young man interested in poetry may also attach himself to a famous minstrel and learn from him. Among the eastern Tsherkesses gifted children were entrusted to the minstrels for some years to be educated. This is the origin of singers' schools, a very late phenomenon which is only recorded from Bosnia and ancient Greece. I mean the Homeridae. The poet's art has become a profession, and the poets are at least within reach of forming a kind of guild. The minstrels may often travel far around as is recorded of Teuton and Scandinavian minstrels.

Thus epic poetry is in a certain sense popular poetry because the people take an interest in it and even exercise it, but gifted individuals take up the most prominent position ; they are especially honoured and admired, and they may, at least in certain cases, gain their livelihood from their art, becoming court minstrels of the great or receiving gifts from the people. Their influence in forming the epics should be judged accordingly.

We have heard that epic poetry is learnt. In proceeding to the question how it is learnt, we enter upon the all-important problem of the nature of epic tradition. We may put it thus that not the poems but the poetical art is learnt. Already the overwhelming mass of variants, e.g. of the Serbian, the Russian, the Finnish, and the Esthonian epics, proves that a chant is not learnt by heart, in spite of the fact that the Russian singers are said to consider it as a matter of honour to render the traditional matter just as they have received it. It is expressly stated that the Serbians and Kara-Kirgizes never repeat a chant in the same words but that the variants are as many as the recitations. Even Dokarim, who had made a poem of his own, varied it, and Professor Snouck Hurgronje who wrote it down gives voice to the opinion that the poem without difficulty may have been transferred from the praise of the Atchinese to the praise of their foes, the Dutch. Every poem, every recital is consequently more or less an improvisation.

The singer is able to improvise because he has learnt the epic technique or, to quote Goethe : *eine Sprache, die für dich dichtet und denkt*. In the epics of all languages there is a store of stock expressions, constantly recurring phrases, half and whole verses, and even verse-complexes. Standing epithets are added, even if in the special case they are out of place, e.g. in the bylinas, etc. Moreover, repetitions are characteristic of the epic style. For example, when a message is delivered it is repeated word for word. In the " Kalevala " the very conspicuous repetitions are due to the peculiar art of the recital, a second singer taking up and slightly varying the verse recited by the first one. The *recommencements* of the *chansons de geste* repeat the end of the preceding strophe in a slightly varied form. There are similar repetitions of four to eight verses in the bylinas. These stock expressions, phrases, and repetitions are a great aid for the singer, for whilst reciting them mechanically he is subconsciously forming the next verse which may be new.

Very important also are the typical descriptions. Though they are not repeated word for word but may be abridged or enlarged they are always substantially the same. In the Russian bylinas a difference is noted between the typical parts, viz. speeches and descriptions which are learnt by heart, including a number of incomprehensible terms, and the varying parts, especially the course of the action, in which a certain liberty of improvisation is permissible in regard to expressions and position of verses. And the bylinas are the most stagnant of all epics. The same facts are recorded of the old Serbian epics. There are, for example, different variants of the poem on the nuptial journey of Maxim Tshernovitch, but the course of events is always identical and so are all chief parts repeated in the same words, e.g. the description of the golden shirt on account of which the fight arises.

These are epics concerned with a cycle of events from a distant past, but the typical descriptions play as great a part in epics referring to contemporary events, and they are a most useful aid to the improvisator. Even in the modern Serbian epic poetry there are typical descriptions, e.g. of a maiden, of a hero, or of a horse. It is said of the Atchinese [1] " that some one man who like most of his fellow-countrymen knows by heart the classic descriptions of certain events and situations as expressed in verse by the people of olden times, but whose knowledge, owing to his training and environment, is somewhat greater than that of others, one who is endowed,

[1] Snouck Hurgronje, op. cit., pp. 100.

besides, with a good memory and enthusiasm for the poesy
of his country, puts his powers to the test by celebrating in
verses the great events of more recent times."

The epics of the Kara-Kirgizes are interesting, because
in a certain measure they take up an intermediate position.
They refer to past events, but so much is left of the older stage
that the poets often insert praise of the men before whom they
are singing and of their family. The minstrel who sang to
Radloff spoke of Manas as a friend of " the white czar," and
represented him and the Russians as everywhere taking part
in the course of events. It is recorded of them thus : [1] Through
a comprehensive practice the singer has a large series of poetical
parts ready which he composes according to the course of
events : descriptions of certain events and situations, e.g.
the birth of a hero, his growing up, the praise of weapons,
the preparations for a fight, the noise of the fight, the colloquy
of the heroes before the fight, the praise of the beauty of the
bride, descriptions of persons and horses, of houses and tents,
of banquets, invitations to a meal, the death of a hero, dirges,
the descriptions of a landscape, of the coming of night or
daylight, etc. The art of the poet consists in co-ordinating
these ready-made parts according to the course of events and
connecting them by new-made verses. These parts are,
however, treated in a varying manner, enlarged or abridged.
A skilled poet is able to improvise a poem on every subject
and every tale if only the course of events is clear to him.

This seems to be a remarkable description of living epical
practice. It agrees with those quoted formerly ; it may only
be noted that there are differences in regard to the liberty
of the singers, but that the typical descriptions are a most
prominent feature of epic art. If the choice of subjects is
limited to a certain cycle of events belonging to the past,
the background also becomes typical in a certain sense, at
least different from everyday life, for example, the heathen
elements in Beowulf, King Vladimir and his men in the bylinas,
the feuds between Joloi and Manas, etc.

Evidently all these circumstances, the stock expressions,
the typical descriptions, the background of olden days, tend
to preserve relics of the past ; though, during a long lapse of

[1] Radloff, op. cit., p. xvi.

time, owing to the liberty with which the poems are treated, they are inevitably mixed up with more recent elements and transmuted, often profoundly. Thus, epics which sing of bygone days always archaize in a higher or lesser degree. Examples have already been given and need not be repeated. It ought only to be noted that the measure of archaizing is proportionate to the vigour and force of the epic tradition and the weakness of the cultural environment. Thus epic poetry referring to the past presents a medley of old and recent elements.

This is so in respect of language also. Even the language archaizes, but is on the other hand constantly rejuvenated because in daily life the poets speak the language of their age. The poems may change language provided that during a certain time people use two languages, as, e.g. in the Frankish empire and the Russia of the Varägs. A new form of verse may be introduced more suited to the taste, as the assonance was exchanged for rhymes in the *chansons de geste* and the alliteration for rhyme in Teutonic poetry. The language of living epic poetry is constantly renewed, but when epics deal especially with a past age restrictions are imposed by the stock expressions and the typical descriptions, in which archaic words and forms are preserved. The bylinas contain not a few enigmatical elements which cannot be explained from Russian, and in the " Kalevala " epics are found diverging forms, and Swedish loan-words which are not used elsewhere ; some words are even misunderstood by the singers. Three-fifths of their lexicon is not in use in everyday speech. Evidently these phenomena do not so much belong to epics concerning contemporary events, as to traditional epics referring to a past age, and relying upon a strong epic tradition, whilst the cultural environment is rather feeble. Lastly, it may be noted that a certain dialect mixture sometimes occurs in Bosnian epics owing to the travels of the minstrels.

3. Conclusions Concerning the Greek Epics

When we at last turn to Greek epics the conclusions will come by themselves. Even Homer sings of great deeds of a past age whose glory impressed living men so much that they often profess themselves to be inferior to the heroes of bygone days. It is to be presumed that Greek epics also originated in describing contemporary events and praising living men as is the case elsewhere in epic poetry ; the idea that the heroes should be mythical figures and their deeds myths is now mostly discarded. This Heroic Age cannot be that age which immediately preceded and is partly contemporary with the composition of the extant poems, which from its art is called the Geometric, for this was an age of petty states and petty feuds ; the locally different styles of ceramics and of fibulas prove that life was cantonal, and we know that the Phoenicians had the mastery of the sea. Still less can it be the period intervening between this age and the downfall of Mycenaean civilization about 1200 B.C., for this is the darkest and poorest period of Greek history ; the exhaustion and feebleness which are characteristic of the material civilization indicate that it was the same in other respects.

Historical circumstances compel us to seek the origin of Greek epics in the glorious Mycenaean Age. From the examples quoted it is easy to understand that the epics which originated in this age were preserved throughout the subsequent dark and impoverished centuries, but an idea of the epics in this time cannot be recovered by an analysis of the extant poems ; such an analysis can at most proceed to unravel the immediately preceding stage, the epics from which the extant poems were formed. To get an idea of the origin and development of Greek epics in pre-Homeric times we must use the analogies quoted, but there is a means to test how far and in what manner they may be applied, namely, the Homeric information concerning the minstrels.

Minstrels are mentioned or hinted at in the Iliad more often than is generally supposed. Only one is mentioned by name, Thamyris, and this in the " Catalogue of the Ships," [1] but Apollo and the Muses act as minstrels chanting at the banquet of the gods, and Helen refers once to epic songs.[2] In the description of Achilles' shield a minstrel sings at the dance,[3] and in the last book they are fetched to sing dirges over the dead Hector.[4] Once we find a hero, Achilles, dispelling his boredom by singing the praise of men.[5] There

---

[1] *Il.*, ii, v. 595.　　　[2] *Il.*, i, vv. 604, and vi, 358, respectively.
[3] *Il.*, xviii, v. 604.　　　[4] *Il.*, xxiv, v. 720.　　　[5] *Il.*, ix, v. 186.

have always been gifted dilettanti, and it appears that minstrels played a great part at this time.

In the Odyssey minstrels are very conspicuous and take up an honoured position; they are court minstrels, and their songs are the usual delight after the meal. When leaving for Troy Agamemnon entrusted his queen to a minstrel.[1] Odysseus shrinks from killing Phemios who only by constraint sang for the suitors.[2] The minstrels knew a number of chants (οἶμαι) from which they would choose one when giving a performance of their art.[3] The eighth book especially is very much concerned with the minstrels' art, and relates the contents of not less than three songs which Demodokos recited in the Phaeacian court. Two refer to the Trojan cycle, one treating the quarrel of Odysseus and Achilles, the other the story of the wooden horse and the conquest of Troy; the third is of quite a different character, the well-known pleasant story of Ares and Aphrodite. It appears that a fixed cycle, the Trojan cycle, existed, but that occasionally other subjects were treated.

There are some precious hints in regard to the epic technique. Phemios says once that he has taught himself and that a god has implanted chants of all kinds in his mind.[4] This is a close parallel to the words of a Kara-Kirgize minstrel: " I can sing all songs, for God has implanted the gift of singing in my heart. He inspires me with the words without any need for me to seek them. I have not learnt from anybody, but the words stream forth from within me."[5] That is to say, he has learnt the epic technique, not the poems which he recites, and he is able to apply his art to every subject.

On the other hand, another passage proves that at a certain time a certain chant was popular; it is said that the fame of the song concerning the quarrel of Odysseus and Achilles reached the heavens.[6] This can only be understood as meaning that a song which a minstrel had composed on this subject had gained a far-reaching fame, and this is only possible if others tried to reproduce it. We must, of course, understand not a reproduction word by word but a reproduction such as is

[1] Od., iii, vv. 267.
[2] Od., xxii, vv. 330.
[3] Od., viii, vv. 480 ; xxii, v. 347.
[4] Od., xxii, vv. 347.
[5] Radloff, op. cit., p. xvii.
[6] Od., viii, vv. 73.

usual in epic poetry, i.e. a number of variants on this subject
were chanted by several minstrels.

This proves that there was a certain tendency towards
fixing the chants, and other circumstances point in the same
direction. The minstrels' art had become a profession, he is
a craftsman put on a level with the physician and the blacksmith. It may be that regular teaching had begun, if Phemios
is taken to contrast himself with others who had acquired
their art in this manner. At any rate, somewhat later we find
singers' schools, for the Homeridae were either such, if Homer
is taken to be their fictitious ancestor, or a family of minstrels
in which the art was inherited. The rhapsodists were their
heirs. The minstrels would spend their time wandering around.
Thamyris was on his way from King Eurytos in Oichalia when
to his misfortune he met the Muses. A later poet, Hesiod,
tells that he went to Chalkis in order to sing at the funeral
games of Amphidamas.[1] At this time at least, and probably
earlier, epic performances took place at festivals also.

Scholars have pointed to the difference between the Iliad
and the Odyssey in regard to the minstrels and have sought
for an explanation. Although minstrels are not absent from
the Iliad, the difference is notable and important, for it proves
that the self-assertion of the minstrels had risen to a high
pitch at the time when the Odyssey was composed, and this
may be understood from the fact that at this time a singers'
craft had been developed, at least in a certain sense. This is
of importance for the understanding of the genesis of the
Homeric poems.

At this point it will be convenient to make a survey of
the genesis and development of Greek epics. They originated
in the Heroic Age of Mycenaean times, in praise of contemporary men and events, and developed an epic technique of
the same kind as we find elsewhere. They survived through
the succeeding dark centuries limiting themselves as usual
to a certain cycle of men and events, and singing the glory
of bygone days. With the aid of the epic technique they preserved not only their memory but certain archaizing features,
in spite of an inevitable accommodation to a new environment, to the development of language, and to a new dialect,

---

[1] Hesiod, *Opera*, v. 654.

as they wandered from one tribe to another. Epics on other subjects, amongst which the War of the Seven against Thebes may be especially mentioned, may also have existed, but they passed into the background.

At the time at which the genesis of the Homeric poems commenced, we must presuppose the existence from olden times of a nebulous mass of songs with countless variants centring around the Trojan war. These songs had, as epics are wont to do, wandered from their first home and come to Asia Minor; how far they were preserved in the mother country we cannot tell. It is to be noticed that at this time the standard of wealth in Greece commenced to rise, whilst the aristocracy preserved its social and political privileges; a fact witnessed to by the Dipylon vases depicting the expensive funerals of the noblemen. This applies even more to Ionia, which during this time was ahead of the mother country. The activity of the Greeks rose anew, they commenced to sail the sea and to oust the Phoenicians.

This prepared the ground for a renascence of epics, but according to my conviction the salient point was the appearance of a great poet who infused new life and vigour into epic poetry, putting the psychology of his heroes in the foreground and planning a comprehensive composition under this aspect. Therefore Greek epics excel all other epics. He formed a school. When Homer made Achilles' wrath the theme of the Iliad, others followed taking up similar subjects. The fame of the epos on the quarrel of Odysseus and Achilles is said to have reached the heavens, and there is a hint at a quarrel between Odysseus and Aias, and the quarrel of the two Atreidae is related by Nestor.[1] This great poet mastered the epic technique; he had heard and learnt many older songs and used them freely in composing his poem on the wrath of Achilles, but owing to the fluctuating state of the traditional mass of epics and the minstrels' freedom in treating them, it appears to be a hopeless task to find out the older parts through a literary analysis, and this is furthermore proved by the different results put forward by scholars who have tried to do so. Even in the " Kalevala " no one has succeeded in distinguishing the old epics from Lönnroth's additions, although,

---

[1] *Od.*, xi, v. 544, and iii, vv. 136, respectively.

as we now know from his own papers, he worked more as a philologist than as a poet.[1] Certainly larger or smaller parts have also been added later on to Homer's poem.

For I should like to call this great poet, the author of the Iliad, Homer. The old question whether the art of writing was known at this time seems to me to be almost irrelevant ; it was perhaps known, but was certainly not used to write down an extensive poem. The example of the Atchinese poet Dokarim proves that even a long poem may be kept in the memory of an unlettered minstrel. We should only be abandoning the old idea that the poem was repeated word for word. We would do better to remember what is said of Dokarim : " This does not prevent him from giving himself, at each recitation, licence to modify, add, or omit as he thinks fit, or from filling up gaps from his really subtle poetic vein, whenever his memory fails him. Just as a literate poet reads his works again and again, and by the free use of his pen makes it conform more and more to the canons of art, so does our bard by means of incessant recitation. When the poem is written down, sundry faults and irregularities and overbold flights of imagination come to light which, though a listener may overlook them, are not to be endured in a written poem." And it is added that the copyist gives himself licence to make all the necessary corrections and that subsequent copyists or reciters take the same liberty.[2]

The great success gave fresh vigour to epic poetry and a kind of minstrels' craft came into existence, as we see in the Odyssey. Greek activity increased, as the colonization in the Mediterranean attests, so also did wealth, as is proved by the monuments of the Orientalizing period. Another great genius appeared, the poet of the Odyssey, whose latest elements refer just to the Orientalizing period and the age of colonization. This poem is connected with the old Trojan cycle, but in fact it is even more concerned with contemporary interests and events, though, owing to their nature, they have been wrapt in a veiled form of fable ; I mean the adventures of merchants and colonists during their sea voyages such as are told by Odysseus in the court of the Phaeacians. Even the plot of the Odyssey has a modern note ; therefore there is no hope

[1] See above, p. 193.   [2] Snouck Hurgronje, op. cit., pp. 100.

of rediscovering Odysseus' palace on Ithaca.   The Odyssey
consequently represents in a certain sense a revival of the
first stage of epics, such as took place, e.g. in France and Bosnia
and other countries, although it has very marked peculiarities,
is connected with the old epics, and has inherited their epic
technique with all details of this epic tradition ; consequently
it abstains from mentioning living men.

Thus the answer of the problem proposed in the third
chapter will be at hand.   Owing to the epic technique and
tradition elements from the Mycenaean Age, in which epics
first were created, were preserved down to the age in which
epics underwent a renascence, were fixed into two great poems
and ultimately written down.   Literary analysis may show
with more or less probability that some parts of these poems
are earlier, others later, but this difference falls very far short
of the difference between the earliest and the latest elements
in the poems.   A reference to something belonging to the
Orientalizing period proves that this part is composed in this
period, but it does not in any way prove that the elements of
which this part is composed all belong to that period.   Thanks
to the epic technique and tradition, elements from the earliest
time belong to the epic stock expressions and typical descriptions and may thus be embedded in the very latest strata.
These elements cannot be reached by literary analysis, they
are recognized by the fact of their belonging to an older stage
of civilization, as is especially apparent in the archaeological
instances quoted.

There exist other elements of this age also, and moreover
the whole background of the Iliad refers originally to this
same age.   These elements are freely mixed up with elements
from later times.   To unravel them is a difficult task ; it
requires a fine sense of history and a measure of tact and
common sense.   In spite of the difficulties and the uncertainty
of the subject it is too important to be put on one side.   We
will try to find out the conceptions of state organization from
the olden times which underlie the epics.

CHAPTER VI

STATE ORGANIZATION IN HOMER AND IN THE MYCENAEAN AGE

HOMERIC research has been compared to a methodically conducted excavation of an old mound in which the later strata are first removed and so on until the old layers are reached. Similarly, it is said, the relative age of the layers in the Homeric poems can be determined by the latest elements embedded in them. This is the fundamental idea underlying what I styled the patchwork hypothesis, whether the patchwork came into existence by adding later poems to an old kernel or by sewing together earlier and later poems. If on the other hand Greek epic poetry developed in the manner which I have described, this simple and striking comparison will not apply, but we ought rather to compare Greek epic poetry to a dough which was constantly rekneaded and rehandled and of which new forms were continually being fashioned. In kneading the dough new and contemporary elements were added to the old ones. This explains why very early elements were embedded in very late chants. A passage reflecting Mycenaean conditions or describing Mycenaean objects does not prove that its surroundings are old, nor is an admitted late date of a certain part of the Homeric poems any argument against the assumption that a passage found in it may refer to earlier and even to Mycenaean conditions if for other reasons this is likely.

To take an example. I stated that a passage in the seventh book of the Odyssey in which it is said that the goddess Athena leaving Scheria went to Marathon and Athens, the city of wide streets, and entered the strong house of Erechtheus reflects Mycenaean conditions, because during this age the cult of the city goddess was the house cult of the king and the goddess had her shrine in the palace of the king.[1] It

---

[1] In my *Minoan-Mycenaean Religion*, p. 418, referring to *Od.*, vii, vv. 80.

was objected that this passage is found in a very late part. I may readily concede that, but the objection is not valid. For the date of the composition of a certain poem does not admit any inference as to the age of other elements incorporated into it. Its own age is, of course, determined by the latest elements contained in it, giving the *terminus post quem*. If, e.g., the Phoenicians are mentioned it cannot have been moulded into its present form before the appearance of the Phoenicians in the Aegean, but it may include very much earlier elements, even of Mycenaean origin. The most evident example of the body-shield is found in the sixth book of the Iliad which is one of the latest, and the graphic description of the boars' tusks helmet is read in the lay of Dolon which is admittedly very late.

Consequently from this point of view no objection whatever can be made in principle, if a passage which is found in any late part is referred to Mycenaean conditions. It may be objected that this is the method which was applied by certain scholars who in their unreasoned desire, awakened as it was by the great discoveries of the Mycenaean background of Homer to take the Homeric poems as mainly Mycenaean were induced to suppose that Mycenaean conditions were described everywhere in the Homeric poems. In opposition to such overhasty and uncritical methods, if they are to be called methods, we have tried to justify the possibility of referring isolated passages and elements embedded in late poems to a much earlier age. Thus they are severed from their surroundings and these have no bearing upon their date. The method applied by the analytical school of dating the facts appearing in a certain poem according to the latest element contained in it is found to be deficient. Consequently we must rely upon other criteria. It lies in the nature of things that cases, in which archaeology affords means of dating, are rare, so rare, in fact, that these cases have been disposed of by taking them to be heirlooms and survivals without any intrinsic importance for the age of Greek epics. We have tried to prove that on the contrary they are most important testimonies to the long transmission of Greek epics through the centuries, and we have to make out the consequences of this point of view, for it will apply not only to objects, but to many other elements included in the Homeric poems.

There is one side of life in which we may especially hope to discover through this method elements handed down from the Mycenaean age—the state organization,[1] for though undeveloped this is closely bound up with the background of epics, and is therefore likely to be preserved through the epic technique, although not without alterations and misunderstandings. It may be expected to be so in Greek epics also, because it is the rule in other epics that the old social and political conditions are retained and form the background of the epics, in spite of later and profound changes in the life of the people. Other epics centre around a chief figure, a king or a prince, and this figure is often depicted as an overlord of vassals, and he is often treated not too reverently. The similarity was often noted between Charlemagne in the *chansons de geste*, Vladimir the Great in the *bylinas*, and Agamemnon in the Iliad. The former comparison was especially advanced by Andrew Lang.[2] He describes the Homeric society justly as a loose feudalism of princes ruled by an overlord who ruled by undisputed divine right, but was often both weak and violent, being subject to gusts of arrogance as well as to abuse of his vassals. This similarity is due to the similarity of cultural conditions, the aristocratic and even feudalistic organization of the state and society which is peculiar to the Heroic Age, i.e. the age in which epics originate.

Analogies are useful but they may be misleading, especially if they are pressed too hard. The political conditions of the Middle Ages which Lang especially takes into account are not the best comparison, being much more sophisticated than the more primitive Homeric society. The chief value of analogies is to show what is possible and what may be reasonably expected ; they do not prove anything in special or specified details. In trying to discern the Mycenaean elements in the Homeric descriptions of the state and the social organization, more reliable proofs are wanted, but the

[1] I put forth the subject-matter of this chapter in a lecture delivered before the Prussian Academy : " Das homerische Königtum," *Sitzungsberichte der preussischen Akademie der Wissenschaften*, 1927, pp. 23.

[2] Andrew Lang, *Homer and his Age*, pp. 51 ; *The World of Homer*, p. 21.

external criteria being absent we must rely upon internal criteria. Thus the task is extremely difficult and delicate. Our main method will be the same as that which in philosophy is called the criterion of reality, viz. the reasonable connection of phenomena with each other agreeing with our other experience of reality. In applying this method a great measure of tact and sound common sense is required, and above all, one-sidedness and attempts to carry through preconceived opinions must be strictly avoided.

1. THE KINGSHIP

State organization and social conditions in the Homeric poems have been very often and fully treated. Every comprehensive history of Greece and every handbook of constitutional antiquities has a section concerning them, and there are many treatises and papers especially devoted to them.[1] The leading idea of these treatises is commonly to grasp the historical development such as the author conceives it, whether he tries to deduce a development from a monarchical to an aristocratic form of the state as depicted in the Homeric poems themselves according to their earlier or later date, or tries to trace a development according to certain general principles which are taken as generally granted, viz. from the family organization and the patriarchal kingship to a more sophisticated, aristocratic organization of society and state. Neither of these methods can be admitted as sound ; their arguments are apt to be too much *a priori*. The first one is opposed to the view of the development of epic poetry which we consider to be well founded, and the second, tracing a line of development from intrinsically primitive conditions to those of the early historical times, overlooks the fact that a highly developed culture existed in Greece in the Prehistoric Age and that its state and social organization was probably developed accordingly.

---

[1] It is hardly necessary to quote the former,—they are well-known works. Only the latest exhaustive survey may be mentioned : G. Busolt, " Griechische Staatskunde," *Handbuch der Altertumswissenschaft*, iv, 1, 1, 3rd ed., 1920, pp. 317. Of earlier treatments I mention A. Fanta, *Der Staat in der Ilias und Odyssee*, 1882 ; L. Bréhier, " La royauté homérique et les origines de l'Etat en Grèce," *Revue historique*, lxxxiv, 1904, pp. 1, and lxxxv, 1904, pp. 1 ; C. W. Westrup, *Le roi de l'Odyssée et le peuple chez Homère*, Paris, 1930.

The most stimulating of recent treatises is that due to an able Homeric scholar, the late Dr. Finsler.[1] His starting-point is the political conditions prevailing in the Greek cities of Asia Minor in the earliest Historical Age, i.e. the age before the tyrants appeared and broke the aristocratic form of government and society. His result is consequently that the conditions depicted in the Homeric poems apply to the aristocratic, political, and social organization of the Ionian towns in the beginning of the Historical Age. If there are any differences these are said to be due to the poetical treatment of the subject. The position of Agamemnon is said to be that of a commander-in-chief of the allied Greek troops before Troy.

The picture given by Finsler is one-sided, since his deductions are founded exclusively upon the conditions prevailing after the overthrow of the old kingship which we know to have existed everywhere in Greece. As a matter of course, the conditions prevailing before the Homeric Age must also be taken into account if a correct result is to be attained. It is an implicit recognition of this fact that Finsler acknowledges that a few remnants of earlier tradition are still left in Homer,—the kingship bestowed by the gods upon the house of the Atreidae and its heir Agamemnon, and the Asiatic despotism of the Trojan king. Our concern is to inquire into the true bearing of these facts which Finsler counts as insignificant survivals.

The most important passage is the description of Agamemnon's sceptre.[2] Agamemnon arose in the assembly of the army carrying the sceptre which Hephaistos himself wrought. Hephaistos gave it to Zeus, the king, and Zeus gave it to Hermes, and Hermes to Pelops, driving the horses, and Pelops gave it to Atreus, the shepherd of the people. At his death Atreus left it to Thyestes, rich in sheep, and Thyestes left it to Agamemnon to carry and to rule over many islands and all Argos. It is acknowledged, even by those who share

---

[1] G. Finsler, " Das homerische Königtum," *Neue Jahrbücher für das klass. Altertum*, xvii, 1906, 313 ; and *Homer*, 2nd ed., pp. 203. Finsler develops the ideas of Wilamowitz, briefly hinted at in " Staat und Gesellschaft der Griechen," *Kultur der Gegenwart*, ii, 4, 1, p. 54. Appropriate criticism of certain points will be found in Busolt, loc. cit., pp. 317.

[2] *Il.*, ii, vv. 101-8. Cp. Calchas' words, *Il.*, i, vv. 78.

the opinion that the political conditions depicted in the Iliad chiefly refer to a later age, that these lines describe older conditions in which a hereditary kingship with a power of its own existed.[1]

These earlier times must be the Mycenaean Age, for it is unthinkable that such a kingdom, including all Greece and many islands, existed in the dark and poverty-stricken intermediate age during which was developed the cantonal seclusion of the Greek provinces which we find in the beginning of the Historical Age. Consequently the question arises whether we are able to know anything of the kingship and its rights in the Mycenaean Age. Those scholars who take the description of state organization and social conditions in Homer to reflect those of the beginning of the Historical Age may argue that their one-sidedness is necessary, because nothing is known of the conditions of the pre-Homeric times nor of the Mycenaean Age. This is, however, not quite the case in the present time.

To begin with, the pre-Homeric kingship is the Mycenaean kingship in the old geographical, as well as in its modern archaeological significance. That needs no discussion. The extremely rich and precious finds prove that the princes of Mycenae not only possessed the mountain fortress of Mycenae but extended their dominion over much larger areas. The princes of the neighbouring fortresses Midea and Tiryns cannot have been independent of them during the time of the flourishing of Mycenae, or the city would have been cut off from the sea. In making this statement I have not so much the treasures of the shaft-graves, the city wall, the palace, and the bee-hive tombs in mind as the roads radiating from Mycenae in all directions. They prove that Mycenae was the seat of a central power. In number and size the bee-hive tombs of Mycenae are very much superior to those found in other places. The so-called tomb of Atreus is the largest and most impressive cupola of the history of architecture before the Pantheon in Rome was built a millennium and a half later. Consequently prominent historical scholars have long ago recognized that Homer's description of the power of Agamemnon as an overlord ruling many islands

[1] Except Bethe in the paper quoted above, p. 249, n. 1, pp. 228.

and all Greece, corresponds to the actual state of things in
the Mycenaean Age, and have taken the other kings to be
his vassals, as Homer depicts them.[1]

There is, of course, no tradition independent of Homer,
except myths to which we shall recur in the next chapter,
showing what were the position and the rights of the king
in the Mycenaean Age. In trying to make a picture of it
we must needs add inferences from archaeological and historical circumstances, and analogies from other kindred peoples
of whom more is known. It is extremely important to use
the right analogies which are in agreement with the given
circumstances, and those are the most valuable which are
taken from peoples related by racial kinship to the Mycenaean
Greeks. For in this case it may be taken as highly probable
that they not only present analogies but that old institutions
of common origin have been preserved.

In view of the imposing constructions at Mycenae, the
power of the Mycenaean king has been compared with that
of the Pharaohs, but what little we know of the conditions
is enough to prove that this comparison with the old highly
civilized and organized culture state of Egypt is misleading.
I have called the Mycenaean Age the Greek Viking Age
because it was an age of migrations and expeditions on sea,
and I gave the evidence above.[2] This is quite permissible,
but it is necessary to 'remove a common misunderstanding
of the nature of such an age, viz. that the expeditions of such
tribes seeking plunder and land are spontaneous outbursts
and wholly incoherent and unorganized raids of small tribes
and bands. A very graphic description of such petty raids
and settlements in the Aegean by Greek bands during the
Mycenaean Age is, for example, given by Gilbert Murray.[3]
But such a description cannot be true generally speaking,
even if small disconnected undertakings existed, and besides
the great immigrations and expeditions, a constant infiltra-
tion of Greeks continued to reinforce their number and fighting
power. For such small bands would easily have been dealt

[1] E.g. Ed. Meyer, *Geschichte des Altertums*, ii, pp. 169 and 188 ; Walter
Leaf, *Homer and History*, p. 191, etc.
[2] Above, pp. 108.
[3] Gilbert Murray, *The Rise of the Greek Epic*, 3rd ed., pp. 67.

with by the settled population whom they attacked. A certain measure of organization is necessary for such wanderings and expeditions, and if it does not exist, it is created by the force of circumstances.

We find such organization among the Teutonic tribes who overthrew the Roman Empire as well as among the Vikings who founded their dominions in Western Europe and in Russia.[1] In regard to the kingship there is a notable difference between the western Teutonic tribes who were for long sedentary in western Germany, and those tribes who undertook far-reaching wanderings and played the most conspicuous part in breaking up the Roman Empire. The kingship was much more strongly developed among these tribes than among the more sedentary tribes, and this strengthening of the kingly power was called forth by the need of an organization for the wanderings and military expeditions.[2] People are apt to think that the Viking expeditions were disconnected raids, and such there were, but that is not the whole truth. The Vikings would not have been able to achieve such far-reaching results and to found large settlements and states if they had not been backed up by the state and military organization of the Scandinavian kingdoms, upon which they relied. The conquest of England by Canute the Great was but the largest of the Viking expeditions. In Sweden, and especially in its centre, the provinces around the lake of Mälarn, a naval organization existed. From this tract came the chieftains who founded the Russian Empire of Kieff, the ancestors of Vladimir the Great.

The analogy is at hand. Conditions were similar in the Greek Viking Age in which the invading Greeks conquered the Greek provinces and islands, and undertook large expeditions towards the south-east. A close resemblance exists between the old Teutonic and the Homeric kingship which

---

[1] The analogies are set forth by H. M. Chadwick, *The Heroic Age*, pp. 367.

[2] Concerning the two types cp. Chadwick, loc. cit., pp. 377. He says that the main feature of the Heroic Age with both peoples was the development of an irresponsible type of kingship, resting upon military prestige, the formation of kingdoms with no national basis, and the growth of relations between one kingdom and another through marriage alliances, etc.; cp. p. 442. The word " irresponsible " is too much. Genseric was a kind of tyrant who broke with national customs to a certain extent.

is explained partly by the similarity of life and of historical
circumstances, but is partly due to the common origin of
the Greek and the Teutonic races. The kings of the Swedes
and of the Burgundians were held responsible for the luck
of their people whether in the matter of victory, weather,
or good crops. It is related that the Swedes sacrificed
their king if the crops failed, and the Burgundian kings
were deposed if the luck of the war or the crops failed.[1]
Even among the Anglo-Saxons and other peoples kings were
deposed, though the reasons are not specified. There is a
faint trace of this very primitive conception in a passage
in Homer,[2] in which it is said of a king, who, fearing the gods,
rules over many and mighty men, maintaining right, that
the black earth bears crops of wheat and barley, the trees
are laden with fruit, and the sheep bring forth and fail not,
the sea gives fishes, and the people prosper under him. The
old idea has been deflected and modernized by the reference
to the righteousness of the king as the cause of the abundant
supply, but at the bottom there is the old primitive conception of the power of the king to influence the course of
Nature and the luck of his people [3] which has been so brilliantly
exposed by Frazer.

The old Teutonic kingship was hereditary within a certain
family; the king was, however, not necessarily succeeded by
his eldest son, but that member of the family was elected
who seemed best able to fulfil the duties of the king. Sometimes two brothers were made co-regents. The chief duty
of the king was that of a leader in war. His power was but
small in peace, and waxed accordingly when wars were frequent, as they were in the stormy age of the great migrations
of the peoples. The king was surrounded by a council of
the most prominent men, and at his side there was the army
assembly which possessed considerable rights. It is the oldest
form of the popular assembly. Even in peaceful times the
Scandinavians attended the popular assembly armed. Among
the Scandinavians the jurisdiction was in the hands of special
men called *lagmän*, who knew and kept the old laws which

---

[1] *Ammianus Marc.*, xxviii, 5, 14.   [2] *Od.*, xix, vv. 109.
[3] H. Meltzer, "Ein Nachklang des Königsfetischismus bei Homer,"
Philologus, lxii, 1903, pp. 481.

were handed down orally, and who " spoke " law in the popular assembly.

The position of Agamemnon in the Iliad is quite similar. The kingship is his by hereditary right, he is the leader in war, and at his side are the council of the elders and the army assembly.[1] We are, however, able to adduce not only these analogies but also a similar state of things in the Historical Age, among certain Greek tribes who had preserved old customs and rights long ago abandoned by other Greeks. These were, of course, relics inherited from olden times, survivals of the genuine Greek kingship handed down from time immemorial. The old kingship had been preserved in backward Macedonia, which was long untouched by the Greek civilization for good or for evil. That is recognized, but it must also be realized that the Macedonian king was a leader in war, and that he had at his side the council of the elders and the army assembly which acted as a popular assembly. It did so during the campaigns of Alexander the Great and even after his death. The army assembly made Philip Arrhidaios king at the side of the son of Alexander; it elected the commanders after the murder of Perdikkas, and it has even been asserted that the Ptolemies found the basis of their power in the ratification of the army assembly.[2]

The Spartan kingship was in fact very similar. The Spartan kings were hereditary leaders in war. Their power was slight in peace and almost unlimited in war. The much-discussed double kingship at Sparta is to be explained by the analogy of the Teutonic co-regents mentioned above. It has occurred especially in Sweden, but among other tribes also, that two brothers were invested with the kingship; there are several historically known instances of this, even in the beginning of the Middle Ages. We have only to add that the double kingship being continued to the heirs of the

[1] The neglect of these circumstances and their significance is the initial flaw in the recent paper in which Bethe defends his well-known standpoint, " Troia, Mykene, Agamemnon und sein Grosskönigtum," *Rhein. Museum f. Philologie*, lxxx, 1931, especially pp. 228.

[2] Cp. K. J. Beloch, *Griechische Geschischte*, 2nd ed., iv, 1, pp. 380. F. Granier, " Die makedonische Heeresversammlung," *Münchener Beiträge zur Papyrusforschung*, xiii, 1931.

brothers became a rule, as tradition says.[1] In earlier times the kings convoked the popular assembly, which essentially was the army assembly, for it consisted of those who were not excluded from army service because they were incapable of contributing to the common meals.

In the light of this old state of things in which the popular assembly was the assembly of the men doing field service, the hold which the slogan πολιτεία τῶν τὰ ὅπλα παρεχόντων had on the Greek mind may be better understood. The restriction of the right of attending the popular assembly to those who risked their lives in battle was always considered to be characteristic of the πάτριος πολιτεία, the constitution of the ancestors, and this seemed a self-evident principle to many. Even long after democracy had been established, this principle was one of its most powerful adversaries.

In Homer, Agamemnon is the war-leader and the king. There is no reason whatever to separate these two functions as Finsler does. This separation is the weakest point of his instructive paper, because it is made only in order to get rid of such facts as are contrary to his opinion. If Agamemnon was but the elected commander-in-chief of the allied Greek troops before Troy, his position would, to take examples from historical times, be that of Dionysios of Phocaea who was elected commander-in-chief of the Ionian fleet sometime before the battle of Lade, or that of Xenophon who conducted the march of the Ten Thousand from Mesopotamia to the Black Sea. The power of these elected commanders was apt to break down for slight causes. The Ionians disobeyed Dionysios with disastrous effects, and Xenophon's

---

[1] I set forth this explanation in my papers: " Studien zur Geschichte des alten Epeiros," *Lunds Universitets Årsskrift*, N.F., Avd. I, vi, No. 4, 1909, pp. 69 ; and " Die Grundlagen des spartanischen Lebens," *Klio*, xii, 1912, pp. 337. The double kingship is found among the Molossians also. The striking similarity between certain features of the kingship in Homer and in Sparta induced Finsler, *Homer*, 2nd ed., pp. 217, to assume a Spartan influence in Homer, without considering the preliminary question whether this similarity did not depend on tradition handed down from of old. His assertion that the Atreidae appear as co-regents in Homer is wholly unwarranted. Agamemnon is clearly the leader, but it is only natural that Menelaos is placed by his side being his brother and the war being waged on his account.

command came to an end, as soon as the most pressing needs were relieved by their arrival at the sea. Agamemnon's power was evidently much more securely founded.

The command in war was essential to the old kingship. Only later, during that development which led to the weakening and final abolition of the kingship, was it taken from the king and entrusted to other officials. For example, it is related that the polemarchos was put at the side of the king in Athens earlier than any of the other archons. The institution of this official is attributed to mythical times. There is a trace of this development in the Odyssey in a fictitious narrative of Odysseus,[1] who passes himself off for a Cretan and says that the Cretans asked him and Idomeneus to conduct their ships to Troy. This is a sign of a late date of this passage and does not apply to the old background of the epics.

The king appears in the Iliad as a leader in war, just as the Spartan and Macedonian kings were. He was no Pharaoh nor was he a king by right of divine standing like the Hellenistic kings and the late Roman emperors, a conception which was inherited by the European monarchs of later ages. But Zeus who gave him the kingship protected him,[2] just as he gave their lots to men and protected their rights. He who was the protector of moral life and laws ought especially to protect the man whom he had made the ruler of men according to the laws. If the Greek kingship had once been founded upon the belief in the religious position and magic efficiency of the king, this idea had receded into the background, pressed back by the urgent needs of a war-leader in this stormy age.

Nor was the administering of justice any essential part of the king's power.[3] The king is never represented as a judge in Homer, except for the above-quoted passage,[4] if the words εὐδικίας ἀνέχῃσι are to be referred to judicial functions. In certain cases the popular assembly administers justice in a somewhat rough and ready manner reminding us of lynch justice; this is due to the primitive and

[1] *Od.*, xiv, vv. 237.
[2] The τιμὴ ἐκ Διός; τιμὴ δ' ἐκ Διός ἐστι, φιλεῖ δέ ἑ μητίετα Ζεύς, *Il.*, ii, 197.
[3] Cp. Bréhier, loc. cit. (above, p. 215, n. 1) ; Busolt, op. cit., pp. 330.
[4] *Od.*, xix, v. 111 ; cp. above, p. 220.

undeveloped conditions.[1] In several places judges are mentioned and they are twice called by a special name .δικασπόλοι. In a passage in the Nekyia they seem to be a class identified with the noblemen.[2] This is, of course, a late development in which the nobility monopolized the courts, and to this later time belongs also a striking simile in the Iliad,[3] which foretells the cry of Hesiod for justice against the crooked judgments of the gift-devouring noblemen. The most detailed reference to court and justice is a scene in the description of Achilles' shield.[4] The judge who is surrounded by elders is here called ἵστωρ, "he who knows," i.e. knows the prescriptions of law. The administration of justice was undeveloped, and it seems that in their quarrels people applied to a man who was known for his knowledge of the traditional decrees of the law. Hence he is called ἵστωρ. This resembles not a little conditions in Scandinavia, where a certain man in every province was recognized for the same knowledge, the *lagmän*. He recited to the assembled people the decrees of the law which he kept in his memory, and administered justice in their meetings. Similar old conditions may be the reason why the judges in old Persia were independent of the king and could be deposed only for flagrant breach of their duty. On the other hand, the popular assembly had the right of administering justice, especially in cases where a man had acted against the public welfare. Such are the cases mentioned above. The judicial power of the Macedonian army assembly agrees with this principle. The little we know of it suggests that cases of high treason were referred to its judgment. In this judicial power of the popular assembly the starting-point is found of a far-reaching development.[5]

---

[1] Cp. *Od.*, xvi, vv. 424 ; xxii, vv. 216 ; and the words of Hector to Paris, *Il.*, iii, v. 57. Fine imposed by the assembly, *Od.*, ii, v. 192. R. J. Bonner and Gertrude Smith, *The Administration of Justice from Homer to Aristotle*, I, 1930, p. 26, call justly the Homeric assembly the medium of community self-help.

[2] *Od.*, xi, v. 186.   [3] *Il.*, xvi, vv. 384.   [4] *Il.*, xviii, vv. 497.

[5] The passage in the Nekyia, *Od.*, xi, vv. 568, presenting King Minos carrying a golden sceptre and seated on his throne and administering justice to the dead seated and standing around him, is justly recognized as a reminiscence of the fact that the Minoan civilization was highly developed even in regard to law and justice. This appears also in the often-repeated tale that Minos received his laws from Zeus himself.

Homer proves that the kingship was an old time-honoured institution protected by Zeus and by divine law. The sign of this power is the sceptre given by Zeus himself. With this in his hand Agamemnon appears in the assembly of the army,[1] and the same idea is met with elsewhere. It is true that Agamemnon is sometimes treated with little respect and even contemptuously, but on the other hand other passages show that the reverence for the king was deep-rooted. The aged Nestor warns Achilles not to quarrel with the king who bears the sceptre, for he, to whom Zeus has given the glory, has received a far greater honour than others.[2] Diomedes acknowledges that Zeus has given a far greater honour to Agamemnon than to other men because of the sceptre, but he adds that Zeus has not, however, given him strength and valour.[3] Some verses farther on Nestor uses words which would become a real courtier : " Most noble son of Atreus, Agamemnon, king of men, with thee will I end and with thee begin, for thou art king of many peoples and upon thee Zeus has bestowed the sceptre and the privileges that thou shouldst take counsel for them. Therefore especially it behoves thee both to speak and to listen and to perform whatsoever some other may say whose heart hath prompted him well." [4] And lastly there is the much-quoted verse : " A multitude of masters is an evil thing, let there be one master." [5] There is no reason whatever to restrict these words to the position of commander-in-chief ; they refer clearly to the king whose chief duty was the military leadership. All these passages show a kingship implying great and real power, and great and special honour.

We have noted that the kingship comprising the leadership in war as its chief duty was hereditary among the Teutons in Macedonia and in Sparta. Agamemnon's kingship is also hereditary, he had received it from his forefathers whose sceptre he bore. The hereditary principle was so deep-rooted that the throne when empty was given away with the hand of the queen-dowager. That is known from the myth of Oedipus and from the Odyssey, where the young

---

[1] *Il.* ii, vv. 101.   [2] *Il.*, i, vv. 277.
[3] *Il.*, ix, vv. 37.   [4] *Il.*, ix, vv. 96.
[5] *Il.*, ii, v. 204 : οὐκ ἀγαθὸν πολυκοιρανίη, εἷς κοίρανος ἔστω.

noblemen woo Penelope in order to get the kingship. Then it is objected that there existed a son of Odysseus, who might claim the kingship by hereditary right. But the hereditary right was among the Greeks as well as among the old Teutons subject to a restriction, which was self-evident to a people who gave themselves a king in order that he should command them in war. He must be able to fulfil his kingly duties himself. They were never capable of the idea of a regency during a king's minority. If we take this into consideration, the state of things in Ithaca is wholly clear and consistent. The hereditary right of Telemachos is recognized, even by the foremost of the suitors, Antinoos himself,[1] but because the young prince is not of such an age as to be able to exercise the functions of a king, it is necessary at once to procure another king, if Odysseus should be dead, and the way to the throne is laid open by the hand of the queen with which it is given away. Thus a nobleman will be able to possess himself of the kingship by marrying the queen. Hence the reply of Telemachos shows a certain amount of resignation. Although he does not cede his hereditary right, he himself takes the possibility into account that he may be put aside.[2] The cause of the ambush laid by the suitors to Telemachos on his return is precisely this hereditary right and the fact that he soon will come of age. He is a youth, and will soon be a man capable of exercising the kingship. His resolution to go to Pylos, carried through in spite of obstacles, makes the suitors aware that this time is drawing near. There is really *periculum in mora*, if they wish to possess themselves of the throne. Hence their attempt to get rid of the heir by assassination.

2. THE ARMY ASSEMBLY

At the side of the king was the army assembly. What a prominent part it played in the camp before Troy is well known, especially from the first book of the Iliad. It is not to be understood as an occasional institution, an assembly of

---

[1] *Od.*, i, v. 387 : ὅ τοι γενεῇ πατρώιόν ἐστι.

[2] *Od.*, i, vv. 391. The same idea is behind the words, xv, v. 533 : ὑμετέρου δ᾽ οὐκ ἐστι γένευς βασιλεύτερον ἄλλο. The comparative hints at the possibility that the kingship may be transferred to another family.

the allied troops before Troy, like certain instances from the
Historical Age of Greece, in which we find army assemblies
of a wholly occasional character, e.g. that which Lysander
summoned after the battle of Aigospotamoi in order to con-
demn the Athenian captives, or that which was formed by
the Ten Thousand during their march from Mesopotamia to
the Black Sea. The assembly which the Athenian mariners
instituted on Samos in 411 B.C. in order to check the conservative revolution at home, posed as the popular assembly
of the Athenians. These late examples are, however, a re-
crudescence of a much older state of things in which the
assembly of the armed men was the regular popular assembly.
It is the oldest form of popular assembly, and we find it in
Macedonia, in Sparta, although its true nature is a little
veiled by later development of state institutions, and among
the old Teutonic peoples. The army assembly in Homer is
not, as it is in the above-mentioned examples, an occasional
creation in order to draw up an organization of the allied
troops and their leaders, but is founded on old customs.

This is proved by the king's relation to it. The king
summons the army assembly in order to deliberate on important matters, e.g. his proposal to abandon the war and to
go back home, the peace proposals of the Trojans, etc. The
assembly gives voice to its opinions by cries, but the decision
belongs to the king alone. He turns Chryses off in spite
of the applause with which his request is greeted by the
assembly. This power is acknowledged by old Nestor in
the words already quoted.[1] If the king shares the opinion
of the assembly, he may refer to it, as he does when Idaios
brings the offer of the Trojans to give back the treasures
but to keep Helen.[2] He says to the herald: "You hear
the word of the Achaeans yourself, Idaios," but adds the
kingly sanction: "to me also it is pleasing."

Except this we know next to nothing of the rights of the
assembly. Only one thing is clear, freedom of speech was
inherent in the nature of this institution. But what might
happen to a commoner who ventured obloquy is well known
from the famous episode of Thersites. This is only natural,

---

[1] Above, p. 225. [2] *Il.*, vii, vv. 406.

for the chiefs were the representatives of their contingents and spoke in their name. Further, the mode of fighting gave prominence to the chiefs and the noblemen who possessed horses and chariots. In this respect conditions were similar to those of feudal Europe in the Middle Ages. The noblemen played the most prominent rôle both on the battle-field and in the assembly. They spoke and fought for the people. The people were accordingly little more than a chorus both in the assembly place and in battle. How old these conditions are we cannot say. They can only have come into existence after the horse had been introduced and brought about a revolution in the art of fighting. The horse was unknown in an earlier age, but known during the Mycenaean Age. It was probably introduced by the immigrating Greeks.[1]

Two other points must be noted. Old age prevents a man from being prominent on the battle-field but not from giving his counsels in the assembly and the council of the chiefs. Here, on the contrary, his experience and eloquence may be held in high esteem. Here he has a chance of gaining fame and influence, as old Nestor did. This is nowise contrary to an undeveloped society; we may think of the high esteem in which eloquence is held by the American Indians.

Further, the assembly is summoned not only by the king but by others also, e.g. by Telemachos or by Achilles.[2] The first example may be excused by the abnormal state of things on Ithaca, but not the second. We do not know whether this was so from the beginning; or if it is a sign of incipient decay of the king's power. It has been pertinently observed that the people may have daily assembled in the *agora*, as the Athenians did,[3] and that the Greeks had a natural instinct to resort to the place of assembly even without special summons when something happened to the community;[4] so an assembly might come about without being summoned formally.

[1] Above, pp. 79.

[2] *Od.*, ii, v. 6 ; *Il.*, i, v. 54.

[3] G. Calhoun in the *Proceedings of the Classical Association*, xviii, 1921, p. 93, n. 2.

[4] R. J. Bonner and Gertrude Smith, *The Administration of Justice from Homer to Aristotle*, i, 1930, p. 7.

3. VASSALS AND RETAINERS

If the king is the leader in war, he must possess the right and power to summon his subjects to follow him, and so it is in the Iliad. The plot of the story is founded on this right, for only a later age, which did not understand this right of the king, invented the story that Tyndareos took an oath of Helen's suitors to help the one who was chosen to avenge any wrong which might be done to him because of his wife. In the last book of the Odyssey [1] it is stated that Odysseus was fetched by the Atreidae to the war, and according to the Cypria he tried to escape his duty by a ruse. The presumption is that he was bound to follow Agamemnon's call, being his vassal.

This duty to take the field is mentioned in some passages of the Iliad. It is told that Polyctor's sons cast lots which of them was to take the field,[2] and that Echepolos from Sicyon bought himself free by giving to Agamemnon a costly horse.[3] If anybody tried to escape his duty it might be enforced; it is said that the Achaeans compelled Euchenor from Corinth to follow by imposing a fine.[4] It has hardly been noticed how remarkable this information is. If the war against Troy was waged by a league, a town might take part or not according to its own wish, and if it took part, it elected its contingent itself; the league had no right to pick out individuals in an allied town. In the quoted passages, we find on the contrary, a supreme authority compelling a man from Corinth and another from Sicyon, and we may reasonably add, from other towns also, to take the field. This authority is in one passage said to be that of the Achaeans, but it must be supposed that this is only a vague phrase.[5] The authority was originally the king as is said in the passage concerning Echepolos who gave a costly horse to Agamemnon in order to be released from taking part in the war. I do not think that this is to be understood as bribery, but that the duty of personal service might be exchanged against some other tribute according to the king's discretion.

---

[1] *Od.*, xxiv, vv. 115.
[2] *Il.*, xxiv, v. 400.
[3] *Il.*, xxiii, v. 297.
[4] *Il.*, xiii, v. 669.
[5] Cp. the phrase quoted below, p. 230, n. 1.

The king was surrounded by vassals and each of these commanded his own troops. That is the immediate impression given by a reading of the Iliad, but certain peculiar features appear on a closer inspection of certain passages. The vassals are sometimes called " kings " in the Iliad, in the Odyssey this name belongs to all members of the nobility. Agamemnon was, in fact, a King of Kings, a Great King, though he is never called by this name. In regard to the position of the vassals it is natural that they spoke on behalf of their troops in the army assembly, as was noted already, and that the king summoned them to deliberation and took their counsel in all matters of importance. Hence they are called γέροντες, seniors, but this word does not necessarily imply old age. The king was free to summon such vassals as he liked, but this liberty was, of course, rather strictly limited by the power of the individual vassals. If he neglected some, open or secret opposition followed.

These deliberations are often mentioned, and were regularly connected with meals and wine-drinking, which the king was expected to offer. The official character of the banquets is testified by such expressions as these: " the foremost of the Argives mix the wine of the seniors "[1] or " the chiefs of the Achaeans drink at public expense in the house of Agamemnon and Menelaos."[2] The duty of giving such banquets was, of course, imposed not only upon the Great King but also upon the other kings who were each surrounded by their retainers and had to entertain them. Its obligatory character is illustrated by the state of things in Ithaca where the young noblemen, i.e., the king's retainers, ate and drank in his house during his absence. This was, of course, abnormal, but there must be some reason even for an abnormality. During the king's absence, the retainers took of their own accord the right which was due to them, and misused it grossly.

The character of these meals is, however, subject to different opinions, and we must enter a little more closely into the matter, because they are important for our understanding of Homeric state organization. Finsler has tried to show

---

[1] *Il.*, iv, v. 259 ; cp. viii, vv. 161.
[2] *Il.*, xvii, vv. 248 (δήμια πίνουσι).

that in the Homeric Age there existed societies which had common meals.[1] Such societies of classes and ages are well known from primitive peoples, but they belong to an undeveloped stage of primitive democracy.[2] Where a stronger government or power of chieftains is established, these societies are dissolved or remodelled. This happened at Sparta where the educational and military system is based upon the age classes.[3] The Dorians were at the time of their immigration certainly a backward tribe, and from a general point of view it is not very likely that such associations and age classes had any importance in the Homeric society. There is nothing in Homer to prove their existence except the common meals, and these are to be understood in another way.

Homer has two words for meal, εἰλαπίνη and ἔρανος.[4] The latter is a meal to which every partaker brings his contribution. Such were the Spartan *syssitia*.[5] The expenses of the meals of the Cretan ἀγέλαι were defrayed from common property. In Homer, on the contrary, the meals are always

---

[1] Finsler in the *Neue Jahrbücher für das klass. Altertum*, xvii, 1906, pp. 313.

[2] H. Schurtz, *Altersklassen und Männerbunde*, 1902 ; H. Webster, *Primitive Secret Societies*, 1908.

[3] See my paper, " Die Grundlagen des spartanischen Lebens," in *Klio*, xii, 1912, pp. 309.

[4] The ἔρανος is barely mentioned twice, *Od.*, i, v. 226, and xi, v. 415. Its nature is to be inferred from the later use of the word.

[5] Finsler, *Homer*, 2nd ed., i, p. 217, finds a trace of the Spartan *syssitia* in the passage, *Od.*, iv, vv. 621, in which it is related that the guests of the king (δαιτυμόνες) came to the house of the king bringing sheep, wine, and bread which their wives had sent. But the *syssitia* were not given in the king's house. In the following section it is stated that the king gave meals to his retainers. We should realize the source whence the means came. At an earlier period the subject indigenous population may have brought them as tithes (cp. below, p. 237) ; they came in fact from the king's reservations ; but as the conquerors and the conquered became fused into one, they were brought by the subjects indiscriminately. The verse, *Il.*, ix, 73, πᾶσά τοι ἔσθ᾽ ὑποδεξίη, πολέσιν δὲ ἀνάσσεις, refers to the gifts brought by them. They were obligatory gifts corresponding to the duty of the king to entertain his people, a widespread custom of a certain cultural stage. The development of property conditions resulting from the more peaceful conditions in the end of and after the Mycenaean age (cp. below, pp. 271) quite naturally brought it about that the subjects at one time brought supplies to the king and were entertained by him. This is the state of things described in the passage in question. In regard to the difference between tithes and gifts see Busolt, op. cit., p. 325, n. 2, but not all passages quoted by him in this connection are relevant.

offered and prepared by a single person ; they are consequently no common meals of classes. From a formal point
of view, Moreau is right in stating that these meals were
given by private persons,[1] but that is true only formally
and not in reality. For the person who gave the meals was
the king, and to give meals was a duty to him as well as a
necessity, for through them he honoured and fed his men.
The meals were the means by which the king maintained
touch with his vassals and retainers, and thereby their obligatory character is explained. Moreover, they were the means
by which the king fed and entertained his personal retinue,
the warriors who formed his personal surrounding and on
whom his power chiefly rested. This retinue is to be compared with the *hird* of the old Scandinavian and Teutonic
kings ; the Romans called its members *convivae regis*, the
king's table companions. Exactly the same expression is
used once in the Iliad where Hector's brother-in-law, Podes,
is called his " comrade and dear table-companion." [2]

The correctness of this view is proved by an inquiry into
the real significance in Homer of the often-recurring words
" friend " and " servant " (ἑταῖρος and θεράπων). It has been
contended that the word " friend " connotes the members
of the alleged societies or clubs of young noblemen which
were mentioned above. We note that in Macedonia the same
word denotes the men who constantly surrounded the king
at meals and in war, and from whom he selected his helpers.
We will now see what a " friend " is in Homer.

It is decisive that " friends " and " servants " are identical.
Patroclos, who very often is called the dearest friend of Achilles,
says himself that Pelias called him his servant,[3] and also
another friend of Achilles, Automedon, is called his servant.[4]
Both words are at the same time used of the same person.
In one passage it is told that two servants followed Achilles,
Automedon and Alkimos, whom he honoured most among
his friends after Patroclos' death.[5] In another place it is
said that Aias' servant Lycophron was killed, and a few lines

---

[1] F. Moreau, " Les festins royaux et leur portée politique d'après l'Iliade
et l'Odyssée," *Revue des études grecques*, vii, 1894, p. 133.

[2] *Il.*, xvii, v. 577.　　　　　　　　[3] *Il.*, xxiii, v. 90.

[4] *Il.*, xvi, v. 865.　　　　　　　　[5] *Il.*, xxiv, vv. 573.

farther on, speaking of the same man, that his faithful friend
was killed.[1] Patroclos exhorts the Myrmidons, who are said
to be the friends of Achilles, calling them his servants.[2] I
am afraid that the translation of θεράπων by " servant "
may be misleading for us who think of a class distinction
between servants and friends according to later conditions,
which, moreover, already begin to appear in the Odyssey.   A
" servant " attends to a hero, they take the weapons of
Menelaos and they take care of his horses ; Poseidon himself does the same service to his brother, the king of the gods.
The " friends " do the like humble services, e.g. they skin
the sacrificed animal and divide its flesh. It is characteristic
of a certain cultural stage that the personal entourage of a
chief perform such services, that they are his friends and
his servants at the same time. What a so-called servant
is in reality, is shown by a tale of Nestor.[3] When Lycurgos
grew old he gave his weapons which he had taken as plunder
from the slain Areithoos and thereafter always worn, to his
servant Eurythion. This man is mentioned also as the most
prominent hero in the war of the Pylians with the Arcadians.

It appears that " friends " and " servants " denote the
same men only from a different aspect. They are the personal
attendants of a king, they eat at his table, they perform all
kinds of services for him and they surround him in the battle.
Most prominent among them is his chariot-driver. He was
a most trusted man, on whose skill the life and luck of the
hero in the battle depended. It is characteristic of the part
played by servants in battle that when Idomeneus has slain
Phaistos his servants strip the slain of his weapons.[4] In
this light, the stock expressions applied even to such heroes
as Pelias and Neleus, " Ares' servants " or " servants of the
great Zeus," [5] will be better understood. These " friends "
and " servants " being the personal entourage of the great
and the petty kings, are in all respects to be compared with
the *hird* of the kings of the Teutonic tribes in the age of the
great migrations and of the Scandinavian kings in the Viking
Age. In later Greece we find nothing similar except in backward Macedonia, where the old kingship and old conditions

---

[1] *Il.*, xv, v. 431, and v. 437.   [2] *Il.*, xvi, vv. 269.
[3] *Il.*, vii, vv. 133.   [4] *Il.*, v, vv. 43.   [5] *Od.*, xi, v. 255.

lingered on late into the Historical Age. Such an organization, if the word may be used, is characteristic of a stage
of society but little developed, and is found especially in the
Heroic Age of wandering peoples and in the Viking Age of
Scandinavia, which was but the continuation of the migrations of the Teutonic tribes. We may confidently take it as
belonging to the Viking Age of Greece too, the Mycenaean Age.

The power of the king was especially based on this retinue,
and the more retainers his wealth permitted him to entertain,
the greater was his power. A mighty vassal with a numerous
and valiant retinue may have a strong position even against
the king. And the power of the Great King also was ultimately based upon his personal retinue. As always happens
under similar conditions the interests of the king and the
vassals clashed, for the former strove to assert his power
over the vassals and these to extend their independence.
That is self-evident, even if we had not the illustrations in
Homer of the self-assertion and obstinacy of the Achaean
chiefs. The position of these vassals, their command of their
retinues who were devoted to them personally made it possible
for them to assert their independence, and their position was
strengthened by the fact (which is always implied in the
myths), that their dominions were hereditary, as was the
kingship. Thus it is not surprising that chiefs are sometimes
called " kings " in the Iliad. There may have been among
these chiefs, men who were princes by origin as well as others
who had received dominions as their part of the plunder—
we shall recur to this topic later. They belonged perhaps
to old families of petty kings, and the Great King may have
been chosen from among them, as happened among the
Teutonic tribes. The hereditary principle was the rule, and
was applied even to vassals whose dominions were given
them by the king.

Consequently the relation between the king and his vassals
was not always amiable. Achilles goes far in showering
abuse upon Agamemnon, and others also permit themselves
to say harsh words to him. The Homeric image of the great
king has irreverent features. This is so in other epics in
which a Great King appears, in the *chansons de geste* and in
the *bylinas*, and is to be explained from the similarity of

conditions. The epic songs were chanted at the courts of the vassals who tried to assert themselves and their valour against their overlord, and in a certain sense were hostile to him. Hence the lack of respect for the overlord which colours epics both in Greece and elsewhere.

From the hints in Homer we are thus able to piece together a picture of the state organization during the Mycenaean Age, consistent with the conditions which for other reasons we may surmise obtained during this stormy age, and which we find among other peoples under similar circumstances. A hereditary king who was the chief leader in war ruled over a number of vassals whose position was also hereditary, and who had to go to war with their troops under his command. Both the king and the vassals were surrounded by retinues ; the bond uniting the vassals to the king was loose, and the vassals strove continually to assert their independence.

4. THE ORGANIZATION OF THE CONQUERED COUNTRY AND ITS BREAKDOWN

If we take the state of things and some hitherto little understood Homeric passages into account, we shall be able to get some idea of the manner in which the immigrating Greeks took possession of the Greek lands. This question is unavoidable but has never really been broached, either because the idea prevailed that it was impossible to attain a well-founded opinion, or because it was fancied that the Greeks immigrated in wholly unorganized swarms, of which one possessed itself of one town and another of another town accidentally and without any coherence. The latter view is due to the typical splitting up of Greece in independent cities of the Historical Age. As remarked above such a process is unlikely, because disconnected bands would have been easily dealt with by the indigenous population. Now that we know of the great expeditions to the East, now that Hittite documents have revealed the existence of a great Achaean kingdom in the Mycenaean Age, we have to revise our conceptions of the prevailing conditions. We have to acknowledge the existence of some organization, though an undeveloped one, of a central power invested in the Great King, and we have to interpret accordingly the hints preserved in Homer from this age.

The advantage gained by the wars, and indeed their chief aim was plunder. We know how the plunder was distributed ; the king got the largest part, after him the noblemen, e.g. Achilles got especially selected parts, the people divided the rest.[1] During that time in which the immigrating Greeks possessed themselves of the Greek land, the plunder consisted not only in implements, herds, and slaves, but in towns and rural districts also. This period lasted several centuries ; new Greek tribes invaded the country constantly, and after some time the indigenous population which they conquered was at least partly Greek also. It seems that we know nothing of the manner in which the Greeks possessed themselves of the country except for two words : κλῆρος, lot, and τέμενος, selected part of land. These words show that special parts were selected for the chiefs and the gods and that the rest was divided among the people by lot.

Homer gives, if rightly understood, a very simple answer to questions which are important in this respect. There is a much-discussed passage [2] in which Agamemnon promises to give to Achilles, if he will let himself be appeased, one of his daughters in marriage and seven towns situated in Messenia. In the Odyssey [3] Menelaos says that he had wished to evacuate a neighbouring town of his own in order that Odysseus might settle there with his family, people, and belongings. It has been said that the former passage presupposes the Spartan conquest of Messenia, and both have been explained by a reference to the vast possessions of the Spartan kings who are said by Plato to be the wealthiest men in Greece. This is very ill considered, for a Spartan king never had power to give away a town as dowry, or to evacuate a town and to give it to whom he pleased. Certainly the Spartans settled the inhabitants of Asine in Argolis at Asine in Messenia, but for this there were political reasons, namely, the controversy between Argos and Sparta. It was an affair of the state and not of the kings.

Such an explanation is evidently impossible in regard to

[1] *Il.*, i, vv. 125 and 166.
[2] *Il.*, ix, vv. 144.   [3] *Od.*, iv, vv. 174.

a third passage.[1] To the exiled Phoinix Peleus gave great wealth and many people, and settled him in the extreme district of Phthia as ruler of the Dolopes. We conclude that these towns were the private possessions of the king, who had the right of giving them to whom he pleased, because he had received them as his part of the plunder when the land was conquered.

The passage concerning the seven Messenian towns also gives the answer to the question how the indigenous population was dealt with, for it is clear that it was not wholly exterminated. Agamemnon says that these towns are inhabited by people, rich in sheep and oxen, who will honour Achilles as a god with gifts and under his sceptre pay rich dues.[2] That is to say that the old population remained but must pay tithes to their new lords. But part of the land was certainly confiscated and distributed by lot as $\kappa\lambda\hat{\eta}\rho o\iota$ among the common people of the conquerors.

There are further consequences of these passages. It has never been asked in what manner the immigrant Greeks ruled the land which they had conquered, probably because of the general opinion that the Greeks immigrated in scattered bands, and that one band settled in one town and another in another. Because the king received the greatest part of the plunder, the inference is warranted that he received the greatest part of the conquered land also, and Homer shows that a number of towns with their inhabitants were among his private possessions. The only manner in which he was able to rule these towns was in handing them over to chiefs or to his " friends " or " servants " as fees ; they ruled them as his vassals. Among the immigrant Greeks there were certainly lesser chiefs also who received towns as their share of the plunder. Whether the town was given over to a " friend " or to a chief the result was the same, the establishing of a vassal in a certain town. His position was, of course, hereditary like that of the king.

It may seem that I have drawn far-reaching conclusions from the passages quoted, but I think that the explanation is sound and consistent with what is known from similar historical epochs and it is confirmed by—a myth. I mean

---

[1] *Il.*, ix, vv. 480.   [2] *Il.*, ix, vv. 154.

the myth about the division of the world between the sons of Cronos, which of course, is copied from human life. Zeus got as his share the heavens, Poseidon the sea, and Hades the underworld, but the earth and Olympus remained common to them all, just like a *temenos*,[1] but Zeus had the supreme rule because he was the eldest brother. The myth of the return of the Heraclidae into the Peloponnese tells of a similar division of the conquered country. The three brothers divided it in three parts and cast lots for them, but the story of the deceit of Cresphontes is probably a Spartan invention in order to justify their conquest of Messenia. It may be inferred that Temenos as the eldest brother received the most valuable portion, the old country of Mycenaean civilization, Argolis. In the next chapter we shall see that in other details also the state of the gods is copied from the Mycenaean state just described.

This is the state organization of which scattered passages in Homer give evidence, if it is worth the name of an organization, for it is a kind of loose feudalism, but it is wholly consistent with the conditions which we have reason to suppose existed in the Mycenaean Age, and it resembles the kind of state organization which we know from other similar historical epochs, and these epochs were also those in which epics were created. We find a king whose chief function was to lead in war ; at his side were the army assembly and a council of chiefs. The chiefs were vassals commanding their troops. Both king and vassals relied especially upon a personal retinue, their " friends " or " servants," their *hird*, to use the old Scandinavian word, whom they fed at their table. The king was only able to control the conquered districts by appointing to rule over them men whom he trusted, vassals who while they commanded their own troops were bound to appear with them whenever the king bade. Thus they spoke for their men in the army assembly, and the king asked their counsels in all matters of importance. That these conferences were held during a meal is a sensible concession to human propensities and the existing circumstances.

The coherence of this loose organization depended very

[1] *Il.*, xv, vv. 185.

much upon the king's energy and the resources in men and wealth belonging to him personally. We have dwelt upon the fact that the vassals strove to assert their independence and were often refractory ; it is amply testified in Homer and occurs everywhere in similar conditions. There was yet another serious disadvantage. This organization was only good for war. So long as great wars were undertaken the duty of the vassals to take the field was effective, the leadership of the war-king a necessity, the vassals had to obey him in the war operations, and plunder was taken by which the king was able to enrich himself and his vassals. But the stormy age of the great wanderings passed away. The reason for this was no doubt partly to be found in the exhaustion supervening after such great exertions. Crete was pillaged and impoverished, its flourishing culture was gone, nothing more was to be obtained from it. The great expeditions towards the East led in the long run to such great losses that they contributed more to exhaustion than to enrichment. The Mycenaean civilization broke down and merged into the poor sub-Mycenaean and proto-Geometric Age. The archaeological finds from this age are the best testimonies to the great poverty of the age intervening between the Mycenaean and the early Historical Ages. The graves are very poorly furnished, the decoration of the pottery extremely poor, and hardly a house even from the Geometric period has left enough to enable us to trace its ground-plan, so poorly were they constructed.

We do not know the precise date of the Dorian invasion which is passed over by Homer, but it took place at some time in the intermediate age, perhaps rather at its beginning than towards the end. It resulted in the débâcle of the older civilization. It is to be observed that the Dorians possessed themselves only of provinces and islands already inhabited by Greeks, and that in contrast to the earlier invasions, they did not conquer land inhabited by an earlier indigenous population.

The Geometric Age shows a striking contrast to the Mycenaean Age. Late Mycenaean art, especially ceramics, is everywhere the same and local varieties very slight, so that it has become customary to speak of a Mycenaean *koinē* of art, as of a *koinē* of language in the Hellenistic Age. On the other hand, during the Geometric period, art shows very marked local differences. Each province, each island has its easily recognizable and characteristic variety of Geometric decoration of ceramics. Only rarely are vessels found imported from other places ; in Attica they are even wanting. The same is the case with the fibulas. They were invented in the late Mycenaean period, and in the Geometric period very marked local varieties came into existence.[1] These archaeological facts, the marked local varieties of the Geometric period contrasting with the *koinē* of the late Mycenaean period, reflect historical and cultural conditions, the cantonal and static life of the early historical epoch as contrasted with the uniform civilization of the late Mycenaean Age, conditioned by the common enterprises and the common leadership uniting the migrating tribes of these times. These bonds had been severed with the downfall of the Mycenaean organization and civilization. Every city cared for itself only and looked no farther afield than to its nearest neighbours. The wars were petty feuds and plunderings of neighbours, or perhaps piratical expeditions undertaken by private persons.

This is the end of the epoch of the great exertions and wanderings as we know it from archaeological facts and from some scanty historical information. These conditions give the background for the decay of the Greek kingship. The cessation of the great war expeditions was decisive. For with them the great kingship ceased to have any reason for its existence. The bond, almost the only one uniting the vassals with the king, the duty to take the field, was severed. When the vassals lived each in his town without being summoned to do military service for the king, and when they undertook only petty feuds and plundering expeditions against their neighbours on their own initiative, they were, in fact, independent rulers. When the exhausted Greeks were thrown back upon their own country and had to turn to peaceful work and everyday needs, the organization of the great empire, which was fit for common war expeditions only, had no means of keeping in obedience vassals who were scattered

---

[1] This is the result of Blinkenberg's fundamental work quoted above, p. 76, n. 1.

over many cities. The personal power of the Great King was not sufficient to impose his authority upon them ; he sank to be one of many kings, and his power and wealth survived in epic tradition only.

Within each town a kindred process took place. The vassals, who might be called petty kings, were surrounded by retainers, " friends " and " servants." As the vassals became independent petty kings, these retainers developed into a nobility and directed against them the same claims as they had done against the Great King. Hence the word " king " came to be attached to all noblemen. But the town was too small, in fact an inseparable unity, to be divided into independent parts. Consequently the nobility strove to retrench the king's power until he became only one of the many " kings," a *primus inter pares*. This state of things is drawing near in Ithaca and in Scheria it is reached. King Alcinoos is the thirteenth of the kings, the president of an aristocratic council. So the aristocratic state of the early Greek Age came into being, but Homer preserves, among other relics handed down from the Mycenaean Age, the memory of a Great King residing at Mycenae who ruled many islands and all Greece, and of his peers who strove successfully to assert their independence.

5. Social Conditions in Post-Mycenaean Times

I cannot end this chapter without making some further remarks. The breaking down of the king's power and the building up of an aristocracy, was, of course, a much more complicated process than appears in our exposition which has been mainly concerned with the kingship. It had an economic aspect too. Since property, with the exception of slaves, cattle, weapons, and jewellery was chiefly landed, it would be of fundamental importance to know the prevailing conditions in this respect and their development. Unfortunately our knowledge is even more insufficient than is believed. We stated above that the Greek immigrants received allotted parcels of land ($\kappa\lambda\tilde{\eta}\rho o\iota$). The assumption that these were held in fee from the king [1] is not warranted.

---

[1] U. Kahrstedt, *Griechisches Staatsrecht*, i, 1922, pp. 12.

In Homer personal property is the rule. It is an old assumption that Homer mentions landed property as communal [1] and that this property was redivided from time to time, but the passage adduced as evidence [2] can be interpreted otherwise.

The pasture land was certainly of very great importance for the development of property and social conditions. Generally prevailing custom leads us to suppose that its use was common to all. Consequently there were here ample opportunities for the powerful and wealthy man to oust the weaker. We may think of the description of the large herds of cattle and sheep belonging to Odysseus. The problem does not, however, end here. What of areas of pasture ground broken up and cultivated by individuals? For cultivated land was certainly enlarged at the expense of the pasture grounds when the population was on the increase. It seems that the garden of Laërtes was such a plot of land which had been broken up and cultivated by him, and if this is so, the question arises whether we may infer from the word κτεάτισσε [3] that this area by its cultivation became private property. If this is so, there was an opportunity of adding to landed property, because there was plenty of cheap labour. This suggestion is uncertain, but it is to a certain extent borne out by comparing the legal institution of ἐμφύτευσις, well known in a later age. It implied that a man appropriated a plot of land by breaking it up and cultivating it. This form of ownership must be of ancient origin. [4]

There was another kind of land which, in Homer, is called τέμενος. [5] Commonly one *temenos* is mentioned, but one

---

[1] See e.g. H. J. Rose, *Primitive Culture in Greece*, 1925, p. 180.

[2] *Il.*, xii, vv. 421. It is uncertain whether the word ἐπίξυνος signifies " communal " ; it may signify simply " common," viz. of disputed ownership, and the quarrel may be one of the quarrels concerning boundaries common among farmers.

[3] *Od.*, xxiv, v. 207.

[4] It seems to occur in the very interesting Locrian law from about 500 B.C., published by Papadakis in the *Ephemeris archaiologike*, 1924, pp. 120, and treated by Wilamowitz in the *Sitzungsberichte der preussischen Akademie der Wissenschaften*, 1927, pp. 7.

[5] See especially the full treatment by F. Moreau, " Les finances de la royauté homérique," *Revue des études grecques*, viii, 1895, pp. 287. A. Andréades, " Les finances de l'état homérique," *Revue des études grecques*, xxviii, 1915, pp. 377.

passage [1] shows that the king might have more than one *temenos*. The word is very well translated by Kahrstedt "reservation." [2] Such reservations were put aside for the gods and for the kings. In regard to the king's reservations we might assume that they comprised originally such areas as were not divided into lots (κλῆροι), and assigned to individuals, and that they included both cultivated and uncultivated areas, which the indigenous population was allowed to keep by paying tithes to the king. Here the kings are taken to be the petty kings also, and that they possessed such *temene* is proved by the passage concerning the Messenian towns.[3] As the indigenous population and the immigrants became fused into one, the causes underlying this difference were obliterated and changes in property came about. The general tendency was probably a levelling up of the old differences in regard to the landed property of the common people. The effects were certainly far-reaching, but our means of following them are insufficient.

The reservations of the kings remained and were distinguished from his personal property.[4] In certain Homeric passages we hear that a reservation was given to a hero on account of peculiar merits.[5] It should be observed that such a reward in land is always given by the people and not by the king. The king did not, of course, like to retrench his land and his revenues, but he was unable to resist a proposal to give part of the reservation to a man of merit, for it was, in fact, undivided common land. The right of the people to dispose of that seems not to have been forgotten. Finsler inferred with probability from a passage in the Odyssey that the nobility used these conditions in order to divide the rest of the reservations among themselves.[6] Thus the basis of the king's power in the petty states was withdrawn. The noblemen appropriated reservations to themselves, and only those given to the gods remained.

The manner in which landed property was divided and

---

[1] *Od.*, xi, v. 185.

[2] Cp. the etymology, i.e. " separated area "; τέμενος τέμνειν, *Il.*, vi, v. 194 ; xx, v. 184.

[3] Above, p. 236.   [4] See Moreau, loc. cit., pp. 288.

[5] *Il.*, ix, vv. 574 ; xx, vv. 184 ; vi, v. 194 ; cp. xii, vv. 310.

[6] *Od.*, vii, v. 149 ; Finsler, *Homer*, 2nd ed., p. 201.

possessed laid the foundations of the social conditions prevailing during the time of aristocratic rule. There is, however, an important circumstance which is generally overlooked,
—the great number of the vagrant population which is especially marked in the Odyssey. The famous words which Achilles
says to Odysseus in the underworld [1] are very often quoted
in order to illustrate the cheerless Greek conception of the
other world, but hardly in order to show the unhappy conditions of the *thetes*. These *thetes* are, of course, not to be
taken in the later technical sense of the word as it is used
in the Athenian class organization of the state. There they
were a political class, in Homer they were plainly free labourers.
Eurymachos invites Odysseus who is disguised as a beggar to
collect thorns and to plant fruit-trees on a distant field.[2]
The Odyssey shows what kind of people sought such work,
runaway slaves or the great mass of the vagrant population
who were compelled to earn a beggarly pittance.[3] Such men
are called μετανάσται, immigrants, and Achilles complains to
the embassy that Agamemnon has treated him as a despised
metanastes.[4] These men were employed especially in agriculture. *Thetes* only are mentioned as agricultural labourers
in Homer, whilst he often mentions slaves as herdsmen.
This is very easily understood, for agriculture is a seasonal
work, and thus it is more economical to use free labour which
could be dismissed as soon as the work was ended, whilst
slaves had to be fed continuously. Hence Hesiod gives the
pitiless counsel to drive the *thes* out of the house as soon as
harvest is over.[5]

There were apparently plenty of such vagrant, beggarly
people, and their condition was clearly one of extreme poverty.
In the intervals, when work was not to be had, nothing was
left to them but to beg for food. During the epoch of the
great wars and migrations, men carved out their livelihood
either by war or by emigration. But when the large expeditions ceased many were unable to find a place and a
plot of land in the peaceful conditions and sank down to

---

[1] *Od.*, xi, vv. 489. [2] *Od.*, xviii, vv. 357.
[3] Quoted from Finsler, *Homer*, 2nd ed., p. 190, where more is to be found
concerning this matter.
[4] *Il.*, ix, v. 648. [5] Hesiod, *Opera*, v. 602.

the proletariat.   As conditions became more established, they were forced to settle down either for good or for bad.   This is the origin of the great mass of the lowest free population, the *thetes*.   This state of things must be taken closely into account in order to understand the desperate social needs of the early Historical Age, so vividly portrayed by Hesiod.

6. CONCLUSION

There is a people which is usually thought to be sharply contrasted to the Greeks in political organization, although it sprang from the same common stock, and the differences are due to different development.   I mean the Iranians.   In the early times in which we have the first scanty information concerning the Medes in Assyrian documents, it seems that minor chiefs existed among them, but later we meet a Great King, a King of Kings, at the head of the Medes as well as of the Persians.   Agamemnon was, in fact, such a King of Kings, although this name is never bestowed upon him.   Herodotus' tale of how the great kingship of the Medes was created [1] is more a romance or historical tale than actual history.   In any case it is certain that the great and glorious kingship sprang from more modest origins.   This creation of a great kingship has its foundation in the historical necessity for taking up the contest against the organized states in the valley of Euphrates and Tigris; its power and greatness was a consequence of the great conquests, and its continued existence depended on the necessity of ruling the conquered peoples and countries.

If it were asserted that the great kingdom of the Greeks may have been capable of a similar development, I should not be prepared to deny the possibility.   But circumstances did not allow it.   The sea called men to piracy and far-off expeditions, but at the same time it severed the cohesion of the conquered countries and hindered the formation of a great empire.   Moreover, the peoples were undeveloped and little accustomed to political organization in contrast to the peoples of the East.   The premises necessary for holding together the conquests were wanting.   Nor had the early

[1] *Herodotus*, i, 96 *et seqq.*

Greeks the civilization or the means necessary for maintaining
their rule. The Persians learned and took these over from
Babylonian culture and Assyrian state organization with
which they were in close and enduring connection. For
whatever may be said of the methods of the Assyrians, it
is being more and more justly recognized that they were
pioneers in developing a strong and efficient organization of
the state and of the countries conquered by them. The
Persians have, according to their more primitive standpoint,
relaxed this organization.

I have emphasized strongly that the period after the
breakdown of the Mycenaean civilization is the poorest and
darkest epoch in all Greek history except for the Stone Age,
but it ought to be added that it was of fundamental importance. During this time the foundations of the future history
of Greece were laid. The indigenous population and the immigrant Greeks became fused so as to form the historical
Greek people, the social conditions and the conditions of
property were developed and fixed, and finally that form of
state came into being in which the political life of the Greeks
was vested until the downfall of Greek civilization. We call
it by the Greek word *polis*. For the *polis*, with all ideas and
institutions attached to it, is the result of a historical development. The foundations were laid when with the breakdown of the great kingship the vassals became independent
kings, their interests became limited to their immediate surroundings, and consequently the cities cared for themselves
only and considered their neighbours to be their natural
foes. The petty feuds constantly carried on compelled the
people to retreat within the walls of a city. Thucydides
knows that in earlier times the settlements were dispersed
over the countryside.[1]

It is common to blame the narrow-mindedness of the
polis. Through law and customs the *polis* exercised a keen
and sometimes harsh rule over its citizens, the idea of the
absolute independence and self-sufficiency of the *polis* made
the Greeks incapable of forgetting their internal feuds, and
of building up a political organization comprising all Greeks
and corresponding to the position of importance which they

[1] *Thucydides*, i, 5.

occupied with regard to culture in general. But this price had to be paid in order to achieve something which was still greater. The idea of the *polis* created the self-consciousness of the Greeks and compelled them to concentrate themselves on themselves. So when they came into contact with other peoples they realized at once the peculiar character of Greek manners and culture. This concentration and this self-consciousness brought about an unwillingness to receive foreign ideas and manners which could not be fitted in with the peculiar Greek ideas and manners. This was fundamentally necessary for the creation of the peculiar Greek culture as opposed to Oriental culture.

The historical fate of the Persians led to expansion in contrast to the self-concentration of the Greeks. The consequence of their great empire and rule over other peoples was that their original character was almost submerged in the manifold and powerful influences of foreign cultures and peoples. In its later days the Persian kingdom appears almost as an Oriental despotism. This has obscured the great qualities of the Persians which were an inheritance from their Aryan origin, their loyalty to their king, their open-mindedness, their righteousness, and their humanity.

In spite of the splitting up of Greece in independent *poleis* there existed a common bond which united the Greeks as opposed to other peoples, and they were thoroughly conscious of it. The common bond was firstly language, not the various and differing dialects spoken in daily life, but the epic language which was heard and understood everywhere. In the beginning it was taken over by other kinds of literature as well as the epics, and it influenced them continuously and strongly. Secondly, it was the world of the gods which comprehended gods and men under the rule of the father and king of gods and men, and thirdly, the heroic mythology which provided the stepping-stones for art and literature. But all these uniting factors were created before the splitting up of Greece, they are a heritage from the age of the great Greek kingdom of Mycenaean times. Although this age and this kingdom very soon came to an end in prehistoric times, they are fundamental conditioning factors of Greek history and culture.

CHAPTER VII

MYTHOLOGY IN HOMER

THE fact that the mythological centres are always at the same time centres of Mycenaean civilization, and conversely that the great centres of Mycenaean civilization have always cycles of myths attached to them, proves that the cycles of heroic myths in their outlines go back to Mycenaean times. There are two exceptions, Mycenaean sites with unimportant or no myths attached to them, viz. Midea and Gla, but an explanation is found in the fact that these sites were abandoned early and were not inhabited during the succeeding ages, so that they were forgotten. More relevant is another fact, namely, that some of the cities, which were rich and important in the Mycenaean Age, were utterly unimportant in a later age, so that it is inconceivable that this later age should have attached a wealth of myths to these cities. This concerns precisely Mycenae and Tiryns. The proof given by the identity of Mycenaean and mythological centres is strikingly corroborated by the close correspondence between the mythological importance of a city and its importance in the Mycenaean civilization. The mythological importance of a city is, so to speak, a function of its importance in the Mycenaean Age; small, if the city was only a small one, increasing in proportion to the Mycenaean finds in various places, and great, if the place was a great centre of Mycenaean civilization.

These are the general principles on which is founded the view that the formation of the mythological cycles in their main outlines took place during the Mycenaean Age. I have discussed the evidence in another book,[1] surveying the Mycenaean remains and the myths, and I have tried

---

[1] In my *Mycenaean Origin of Greek Mythology*, 1931.

to show that elements and conditions inherent in some myths must with more or less probability be referred to the Mycenaean Age. Here I have to discuss the Trojan cycle of myths in order to inquire into the problem whether this cycle too in its main outlines goes back into the Mycenaean Age. This discussion is bound up with peculiar difficulties, because the stage of the myth is laid outside Greece and because, attracted by its great fame, additions clustered around this myth more than around any other ; it was, moreover, embellished by poetical inventions.

I have set forth the reasons why I cannot adopt such a seemingly logical method as certain scholars do, arguing from the localization of certain heroes in the mother country, that the Homeric poets built up a complex and intricate cycle upon scarce and meagre mythical data.[1] The decisive reason is, however, the well-founded opinion that the main outlines of the mythological cycles were handed down from former times and that they were the store on which the poets drew.

If these principles are taken as granted and made the starting-point of an inquiry into Homeric mythology, it appears that we must rely chiefly on general principles and on intrinsic probability for our analysis of the Trojan cycle. We are concerned with the main outlines and must generally leave details on one side.

1. THE TROJAN WAR AND ITS LEADERS

The existence of the city of Troy is the fundamental fact and the central point of the myth ; Troy is not accidental to the myth, as is, e.g., the castle of Etzel in the " Nibelungenlied ". Consequently common opinion recognizes the destruction of the sixth city of Troy as the underlying historical fact. It cannot have been the conquest of Troy by the Aeolian colonists which may have taken place c. 700 B.C., for this is much too late, nor is there any evidence for a destruction of Troy at that time. The attempt to account for the myth in another manner was criticized above [2] and found to be a failure. Here we come to the positive side of the

---

[1] Cp. above, pp. 44.   [2] Above, pp. 45.

question. Archæological evidence proves that the sixth city
of Troy was a mighty and wealthy city, flourishing contemporaneously with the late Mycenaean Age, that it had connections with Mycenaean Greece, importing and imitating
Mycenaean pottery, and that it was destroyed by fire and
violence at the end of this age.[1] At a time which roughly
coincides with the end of the Mycenaean Age and the destruction of the sixth city, Thracian tribes, viz. the Phrygians, emigrated to Asia Minor. They crossed, of course,
the straits, and it is possible to conjecture that they destroyed
Troy. On the other hand, we know that precisely at the
same time, Greek tribes made warlike expeditions oversea,
even attacking the Delta of the Nile. That the Greeks knew
Troy and its riches is proved by the imported Mycenaean
objects found at Troy. There is undeniably another possibility, viz. that the Greek Vikings, incited by the wealth
of the city, chose it as a goal of an attack.

It has been said that this attack was a vain attempt by
the Greeks to gain a foothold in the Scamander valley.[2] If
this view is right the attack failed, the city was not taken,
and the myth of its destruction is a later addition. This
view is determined by the idea that the Greeks went colonizing
as they did in a later age. There is nothing to warrant such
an idea. The Greeks may primarily have sought plunder,
and when they had sacked and pillaged the city they may
have retired, allowing the site to lie unoccupied. We have
the choice between the two possibilities mentioned ; neither
of them is strictly demonstrable, but when we find that the
great cycles of myths generally go back to the Mycenaean
Age and that the chief personages mentioned in the Trojan
cycle are connected with the same age, there will be no doubt
that the common opinion is right, assuming that the destruction of the sixth city of Troy by a Greek war party is the
historical fact underlying the Trojan myth. The coincidence
of the Homeric description of Troy with the ruins and with
the landscape, which has been very vigorously discussed, is
generally speaking of less value ; for it is hardly possible
to decide to what extent these descriptions depend on old

---

[1] Cp. above, pp. 111.   [2] Above, p. 44.

tradition or are due to later minstrels who knew the site of Troy at first hand.

The simple fact that a war was fought in a certain place is no myth, even if the war took place in bygone days. A few chief personages, and especially a leader, are wanted to make up a myth. The leader is essential to all such myths, even if he is not the hero most extolled. For example, in the cycle of the War of the Seven against Thebes, Adrastos is more firmly bound up with the myth than any other hero,[1] and the same is true of the leader of the expedition of the Argonauts, Jason. The leader of the Trojan war is the King of Mycenae, Agamemnon. Attempts have been made to show that Agamemnon is the shadow of a god who was venerated at Sparta, but Agamemnon's divinity is a late invention. Another opinion holds that Agamemnon belongs to Asia Minor because his descendants are found there. But if the kings of Cyme and the family of the Penthelidae on Lesbos traced their descent back to Agamemnon, they did only what, e.g., the royal families of Lydia and Macedonia did, ennobling their pedigree by attaching it to a famous Greek hero. Agamemnon exists in the myth only as King of Mycenae, the foremost of the Mycenaean cities in wealth and power.[2] I see no reason to doubt that the name is that of a historical king of Mycenae. He represents evidently the bloom of Mycenaean power, which belongs to the beginning of the late Mycenaean Age, but the destruction of Troy took place some two centuries later. I do not venture to express any opinion as to whether the historical Agamemnon belonged to the one or to the other of these periods. Myths and epics very often combine persons and events from widely differing ages.

Whilst Agamemnon commands his troops himself, the King of the Trojans is an old man who does not take part in the war. His name, Priamos, is un-Greek, and attempts to refer it to Greek stems have failed.[3] Hence the inference seems to be warranted that Priam belongs to the old stratum

---

[1] See my *Mycenaean Origin of Greek Mythology*, p. 113.

[2] A detailed discussion, op. cit., pp. 45. Cp. above, p. 49.

[3] E. Kalinka, " Das trojanische Königshaus," *Archiv für Religionswissenschaft*, xxi, 1922, pp. 18. I do not enter upon the genealogy which seems to me to be late invention.

of the myth. Some traces of Oriental customs seem to have
been preserved in his character. Attention has been called
to his harem. He has fifty sons and many daughters.[1] It
is objected that Greek princes had concubines and that heroes
have children by many women,[2] but these connections were
irregular, whilst the polygamy of Priam seems to be quite
regular.[3] That is, however, of less importance ; the important facts are his name and his characterization as an aged
man, which can but belong to an ancient myth.

The only other Trojan hero with an un-Greek name is
Paris. His character has been transformed by the epic poets
who put his love affair in the foreground. It is generally
admitted that the man who slew Achilles was no weakling
but a valiant warrior, and so he is sometimes described in
Homer also. The remarkable thing is that he has a double
name and is called Alexandros also. With Paris-Alexandros
we come to a complication of the myth, the story of the cause
of the war, the carrying off of Helen. Helen was a pre-Greek
vegetation goddess who in historical times was venerated
especially at Sparta. A few traces of her are preserved in
other provinces also. A Minoan sacred myth told of the
rape of the vegetation goddess by the god of wealth, i.e. the
grain supply stored in subterranean silos.[4] This myth was
preserved in various versions of which one only retained its
sacred character, the rape of Kore by Pluton, whilst the
others were metamorphosed into heroic myths, the rape of
Persephone, of Ariadne, and of Helen by Theseus, and finally
the rape of Helen by Paris-Alexandros.[5] For the Greeks
did not understand the religious significance of the myth
of the rape, but thought it to be one of the common tales
of the carrying off of a fair woman. This pre-Greek myth
was grafted on to the myth of the Trojan war, and thus the
double name of the robber can be explained. Alexandros,

[1] Cp. Finsler in the *Neue Jahrbücher für das klass. Altertum*, xvii, 1906,
p. 398.
[2] By Drerup, *Homerische Poetik*, i, p. 145, n. 1.
[3] Kastianeira who bore Gorgythion to him is said to be wedded (ὀπυιομένη),
Il., viii, v. 304.
[4] This explanation of the myth, given by F. M. Cornford, " The 'Απαρχαί
and the Eleusinian Mysteries," in *Essays and Studies to W. Ridgeway*, 1913,
pp. 153, evidently hits the mark.
[5] See my *Mycenaean Origin of Greek Mythology*, pp. 75 and 170.

the name of the robber in Greek myth, was identified with the Trojan prince Paris.

Helen was venerated especially at Sparta. Her temple at Therapnae, the Menelaeion, is built on a Mycenaean site. Consequently she was localized at Sparta and when made a princess she was given as spouse to the King of Sparta, Menelaos. Menelaos' connections with the Mycenaean Age are not so certain as those of his brother Agamemnon. It may be objected that he owes them to his being the husband of Helen, just as he probably owes his connection with the vegetation cult to this fact,[1] but on the other hand, there is no reason why his connection with Helen and with Agamemnon should be later. He is probably the representative of the princes ruling Mycenaean Laconia. As the woman carried off was not said to be the wife or the daughter of the Great King himself, the most obvious way of giving a cause for the great war was to give her over to some person with whom the Great King was closely connected, viz. his brother who at the same time was his vassal. The fact that Laconia is a vassalage of the Great King residing in Argolis is in perfect consistency with the relative importance of the two provinces in the Mycenaean Age.[2]

The name Aineias seems to be Greek,[3] or Thracian.[4] The etymology of the name of Aineias' father, Anchises, is unknown. The myth seems, however, to be of Oriental origin. The myth that he was the beloved of Aphrodite, and that she bore him a son is so current that it is too little observed that Greek goddesses do not associate themselves with mortal men. Thetis did so, but she was a nymph who was promoted to be a goddess by the poets, and nymphs do sometimes associate themselves with men. The instance of Tithonos or Kleitos and Eos [5] and of Endymion and Selene are not comparable ; Tithonos is moreover attached to the Trojan royal

---

[1] The temple of Helen was called Menelaeion ; his well and plane-tree near Caphyai, *Pausanias*, viii, 23, 4.

[2] See my *Mycenaean Origin of Greek Mythology*, p. 69.

[3] Wilamowitz, *Homer und die Ilias*, p. 83; objections by K. Meister, Die *homerische Kunstsprache*, p. 156.

[4] L. Malten, " Aineias," *Archiv für Religionswissenschaft*, xxix, 1931, pp. 41.

[5] Kleitos, the cousin of Amphiaraos, *Od.*, xv, v. 250. Concerning Tithonos see an interesting paper by J. Kakridis, *Wiener Studien*, xlviii, 1930, pp. 25.

house, and the myth of Endymion is late. The love affair of Aphrodite with Anchises is localized on Mount Ida in Asia Minor and this localization gives the clue. The myth is a Grecized form of the myth of Magna Mater, who sometimes is called the Idaean Mother, because she was venerated on Mount Ida, and of her paramour.[1] In the Homeric hymn describing the meeting of Aphrodite and Anchises the same sensualism prevails as in the myths of Magna Mater. The consort of this great mother goddess is sometimes said to be her lover and her son at the same time. This was unintelligible to the Greeks and they split the figure into two persons. So the sacred myth lost its religious significance and was incorporated into heroic mythology. The poets who cast about for Trojan heroes, thought Aineias fit to be made such an one because he belonged to the neighbourhood. It is, of course, uncertain when this remodelling of the old sacred myth took place. It may be very old, for the cult of Magna Mater in Asia goes back into very ancient times. In the Minoan religion there was a kindred goddess, although the often repeated assertion that she had a paramour is not sufficiently founded.[2]

The chief hero of epics is very often not the king but some other hero. This fact is associated with the jealousy of the vassals of the king, and as the kingship was weakened and the vassals gained the upper hand, the forms of the myths were determined by their taste. That is true especially of the Iliad whose actual hero is Achilles. His myth is evidently old, for it is bound up with the folk-tale motif that his mother was a sea nymph who was won by his father, wrestling with her in spite of her metamorphoses, but who soon abandoned her husband, returning to the sea. She rises from the sea to assist her son. The localization of the myths of this cycle is fixed but in a certain respect subject to doubt. Peleus is connected by name with Mount Pelion in southeastern Thessaly. His dominion comprises in Homer Phthia

---

[1] This view is hinted at by G. Kaibel in the *Nachrichten der Gesellschaft der Wissenschaften zu Göttingen*, phil.-hist., Kl., 1901, p. 498 (Ἀγχίσης a Grecized form of Ἀγδιστις or Ἀγγιστις), and Wilamowitz, *Homer und die Ilias*, p. 83, n. 1, and developed at length by H. J. Rose, *Classical Quarterly*, xviii, 1926, pp. 11.

[2] See my *Minoan-Mycenaean Religion*, pp. 344.

in southern Thessaly and the Spercheios valley. Achilles
himself promises to offer his hair to Spercheios after his
return. This can only be explained if the people whose
heroes were Peleus and Achilles occupied both southern
Thessaly and the Spercheios valley. This district was, however, once inhabited by the Minyans according to the myths,
but Achilles is no Minyan. The conclusion is that one people
ousted the other, and I have tried to show that the Minyans
were the earlier inhabitants who were ousted by the Aeolians
to whom Achilles belonged.[1] The Achilles myth belongs consequently to a comparatively late period of the Mycenaean
Age. The folk-tale motif denotes the great antiquity of
the myth, whilst the Mycenaean remains in southern Thessaly
prove more for the Minyans than for the Myrmidons. The
Achilles myth is probably of Mycenaean origin. It was
grafted on to the tale of the Trojan war, and by this grafting
the true Trojan cycle was first created. It was continually enlarged. The myths not mentioned in the Iliad, the wedding of
Thetis and the judgment of Paris, were added in order to connect
the myths of Achilles with the prehistory of the Trojan war.

It is disputed whether the destruction of Troy was the
end of the old myth or not.[2] If the attack of the Greeks
failed, it must be a late invention added in order to smooth
over the failure. Mythology knows another great war that
failed, the War of the Seven against Thebes, and here the
failure was made good by another war, that of the Epigonoi.
There is, of course, no reason to apply this analogy to the
story of the Trojan war. It shows only that myths did not
shrink from telling of disasters in war. I stated above that
from a historical point of view there is no valid objection
against assuming that the old myth ended with the destruction of Troy. Hints in the Iliad show that this end was
known and the story told by the minstrel Demodokos in
the Odyssey [3] has some details also, although with one exception there is only a bare hint of them given. They are
known to us from the cyclic epics only. They were enlarged
by added scenes of ruthlessness and cruelty. In the narrative of Demodokos' song, the ruse by which Troy was taken

---

[1] See my *Mycenaean Origin of Greek Mythology*, pp. 156.
[2] Above, p. 44.   [3] *Od.*, viii, vv. 492.

is described, the wooden horse built by Epeios in which a number of warriors were enclosed. The device is strange but must have a meaning. The current interpretation is that the wooden horse was a battering-ram, for these were often provided with animals' heads and given animals' names ; [1] but then it is impossible that men should have been enclosed in the machine. There is a parallel in an old Egyptian story which has been overlooked and which tells how the city of Joppe was taken by a ruse, warriors being smuggled into the city concealed in big sacks or jars. They got out of these and seized the city with its inhabitants. The hero of the tale is a well-known officer from the reign of Thutmose III, and the papyrus containing the story is written about the time of Ramses II. [2] The story is so old that it may possibly have come to the ears of the Greeks in early times. The motif of taking a city by smuggling in warriors is the same. We do not, however, understand why the warriors should be concealed in a wooden horse precisely ; there may be a confusion with another motif.

2. MYCENAEAN HEROES AND HEROES CREATED BY THE POETS

The results of this survey do not amount to much more than what is advanced by the common opinion, viz. that the historical kernel of the Trojan cycle is a war against Troy undertaken by the Greeks in the Mycenaean Age under the leadership of the King of Mycenae. We stated, however, that the myth adduced as the ground of the war is also of Mycenaean origin, and that the myth of the chief hero of the Iliad, Achilles, is probably Mycenaean. Heroes other than the leader are not organically connected with the myth of the war. Just as in the myth of the War of the Seven against Thebes, or in the cycle of Heracles' Labours, the series is

---

[1] W. F. J. Knight, " The Wooden Horse," *Classical Philology*, xxv, 1930, pp. 358, interprets the horse as a magical device in order to reverse the protection of the deity of the wall.

[2] A. Erman, *Die Literatur der Ägypter*, 1923, pp. 216 ; G. Maspéro, *Les contes populaires de l'Egypte ancienne*, 4th ed., 1911, pp. 115. The plot is the same but the end different in the story of " Ali Baba and the Robbers " in the *Thousand and One Nights*.

like a string of pearls from which pearls may be taken and to which they may be added. If, however, the important heroes have Mycenaean connections, this will in a certain measure corroborate the view of the Mycenaean origin of the cycle.

The foremost hero of the Iliad next to Achilles is Aias, but there are two personages with this name. Many scholars think that these were originally one hero who has been split into two,[1] whilst others reject this opinion as impossible.[2] For our purpose we need not enter upon this question. The one Aias is the Telamonian who is localized on the island of Salamis and who, according to a myth told by the cyclic epics, killed himself, when the weapons of Achilles, after his death, were awarded to Odysseus. This Aias is especially connected with the Mycenaean body-shield which is worn by him and most graphically described.[3] His patronymic is thought by many to refer to the baldric of the shield (τελαμών) and only by a misunderstanding to have been taken to be a patronymic. This suggestion may be judged on its own merits.[4] The fact of Aias' special connection with the body-shield remains and proves his Mycenaean origin. I cannot see why his localization in Salamis should be rejected.[5] Some Athenian myths may be better understood if Aias was firmly established in Salamis.

The other Aias is the Locrian, the son of Oïleus, who is described as a prominent hero and an excellent runner. He wears a linen corslet and his troops use bows and slings. This Aias violated Cassandra according to a myth told in the cyclic epics and often represented in archaic art. The Odyssey describes graphically how he was shipwrecked because of the hatred of Athena and, boasting that he would escape in spite of the gods, he was cast into the deep sea by Poseidon.[6]

---

[1] This view was proposed by C. Robert, *Studien zur Ilias*, pp. 406 ; *Griechische Heldensage*, pp. 1037.

[2] Wilamowitz, *Die Ilias und Homer*, p. 49, n. 1.

[3] *Il.*, vii, vv. 219 ; cp. above, p. 172.

[4] It seems a little strange that he should have been named after the baldric and not after the body-shield itself.

[5] There is a Mycenaean necropolis on Salamis, though the finds are unimportant and late ; Fimmen, *Die kretisch-mykenische Kultur*, p. 9.

[6] *Od.*, iv, v. 499.

This characterization recalls such heroes as Capaneus and Tydeus, rough and reckless men but valiant fighters, of whose ruthlessness the humanized Homeric poetry disapproved,[1] and it is certainly a heritage from olden times. But it is uncertain if it applies to the Locrian Aias because this characterization is absent from the Iliad and appears only in the relatively late passage of the Odyssey and in post-Homeric myths.[2] If we take the Locrian Aias to be a reckless and valiant knight-errant of the Mycenaean Age, such as the Aetolian Tydeus, we have to assume that the poet of the Iliad changed and humanized his character.

The cycle of Odysseus is post-Mycenaean, for the story of his return is a novel, and his adventures on the sea are sailors' stories. As a mythical figure he is old and goes back probably into the Mycenaean Age,[3] but he had no cycle of his own from former times. His prominence is due to the poet, who characterized him as the wise and cunning man, and to his localization in the islands of the West. Thus he became a figure suitable as a rallying-point for stories of sea adventures.[4]

Diomedes is one of the most valiant heroes, in fact a part of the Iliad is especially devoted to his praise and he performs greater deeds than any other hero, wounding even gods. Robert justly points out his curious relations or rather lack of relations, to Achilles.[5] The two are never brought together, and when Achilles reappears on the stage Diomedes disappears. The only passage where they seem to know of each others' existence is the epilogue to the embassy to Achilles where Diomedes gives voice to his disapproval of the attempt at reconciliation.[6] On the other hand, his deeds are hardly inferior to those of Achilles and are parallel to his. He hits Hector so hard that he faints, and he is wounded

---

[1] Cp. my *Mycenaean Origin of Greek Mythology*, pp. 116.

[2] His grandfather is called by the descriptive name Ὀδοιδόκος, " the Highway man," in Hellanikos. See *Stephanus Byz.* s.v. Καλλίαρος, compared with Lycophron, *Alexandra*, v. 1150.

[3] This is proved by the varying and unexplained forms of his name ; see my *Mycenaean Origin of Greek Mythology*, p. 96.

[4] Loc. cit., p. 99.

[5] C. Robert, *Die griechische Heldensage*, pp. 1059.

[6] *Il.*, ix, vv. 696.

in the heel by Paris' arrow.[1] Both fight with Aineias and
in both cases Aineias is saved only by the interference of a
god.[2] In one passage [3] Diomedes hurls almost as harsh words
against Agamemnon as Achilles does, but in the review of
the troops he answers him meekly and reprimands his comrade
Sthenelos for rebuking the king.[4]

The great poet who composed our Iliad made a masterly
use of this parallelism, contrasting the self-assertion and
obstinacy of Achilles with the loyalty of Diomedes to his
suzerain and to the gods. But this is a part of the poet's
art, a humanizing of the old stuff which is characteristic of
Homer. Such an artful composition was certainly foreign to
the old epics. Homer has taken up two parallel personages
which he found in earlier epics and used them in his way.

Robert ends by saying that Diomedes and Achilles are
parallel figures excluding each other, and that it is possible
to conceive of an Iliad in which Achilles and Hector were
wanting, and Diomedes among the Greeks and Paris and
Aineias among the Trojans were the chief heroes. But he
becomes afraid of his venture and adds that the problem
lies in obscurity. The observation is just, and the conclusion
seems to be justified. In the "Catalogue of the Ships" Diomedes is made king of Argos, occupying almost the whole
province to the exclusion of Agamemnon. Leaf has well
shown the fancifulness of this picture.[5] In the Iliad, Diomedes lives in Argos, because his father, the Aetolian Tydeus,
marrying the daughter of Adrastos, settled there ; he is described as a wealthy man but not as a king or a prince.[6] In
the late lay of the games there is a vague expression that
he ruled among the Argives.[7] From this hint the Argive
kingdom of the famous hero was construed. His partaking
in the sack of Thebes is mentioned.[8] We see that the Iliad
pictures Diomedes as one of the retainers of Agamemnon ;
he can hardly be called a vassal, because he possesses no
city of his own. That was attributed to him later. We
have seen that the myth of Achilles was only later grafted

[1] Il., v, vv. 297 ; xi, vv. 369 resp.
[2] Il., v, vv. 311 ; xx, vv. 318 resp.
[3] Il., ix, vv. 32.
[4] Il., iv, vv. 370.
[5] W. Leaf, Homer and History, pp. 232.
[6] Il., xiv, vv. 110.
[7] Il., xxiii, v. 471 : μετὰ δ' Ἀργείοισιν ἀνάσσει.
[8] Il., iv, v. 406.

on to the myth of the Trojan war, and if we take these circumstances into consideration, it appears that Robert's conclusion is amply justified.   It may be added that many think
that the character of the lay of Diomedes is especially old-
fashioned.[1]   There was an Argive stage of the Trojan cycle
before the Achilles myth was incorporated into it, and in
this form of the cycle Diomedes was the foremost hero.   He
and Achilles could not be associated, and Diomedes was too
important to be relegated to the second plan ; they had to
be separated as they are in our Iliad.   This line was kept
even by late minstrels, e.g. the author of the " Doloneia ".   It
follows that Diomedes, being one of the earliest heroes of the
cycle, goes back into the Mycenaean Age.   But I should not
venture to ascribe such a great antiquity to the parts of the
Iliad in which Diomedes plays the foremost part, although
they are old to be Homeric.   There was probably a double
tradition of the Trojan war, one celebrating Diomedes and
another praising Achilles, which ultimately were fused into
one.

Two others of the " Epigonoi " appear in the Iliad, Sthenelos,
a son of Capaneus, the true comrade of Diomedes, and Euryalos,
a son of Mekisteus.   This is significant for the time at which
the mythology supposed the Trojan war to have taken place ;
it came after other celebrated mythical events as far as they
are mentioned.   This was the result of the introduction of
heroes from other cycles into the Iliad.

This applies even to the Pylian cycle, although this cycle
refers to a late period of the Mycenaean Age.[2]   Large parts
of an epos telling of the wars of the Pylians, and especially
of the exploits of Nestor, were incorporated into the Homeric
poems by being put into the mouth of Nestor.   This is the
reason why Nestor is represented as an aged man ; though
not unfit for war, he is especially valued as a counsellor and
narrator, and as such he is wonderfully characterized.   The
dominion of Nestor, of which Pylos is the capital, corresponds
to the Mycenaean settlements on the western coast of the
Peloponnese.   The Pylian epos celebrated the struggle of this
Mycenaean dominion against the tribes pressing on from the

---

[1] Cp. below, pp. 267 and 274.
[2] Cp. my *Mycenaean Origin of Greek Mythology*, pp. 87.

north and the east.   As this dominion existed in the Mycenaean
Age only, the Pylian cycle goes back into these times.

Among the Trojan allies there are a few interesting heroes.
The peoples allied with the Trojans are with one exception
strictly limited to north-western Asia Minor and Thracia.   The
Phrygian Empire and the Maeones of Lydia loom in the
background only, and the Carians are barely mentioned.[1]
This is a very reasonable limitation to the countries bordering
on Troas.   It is probable that these peoples were introduced
only after the Greeks had learned to know them in the beginning of the colonization of north-western Asia Minor, and
that their own battles with the Thracians, Paeonians, Paph-
lagonians and other tribes were incorporated into the myths
of the Trojan war.

It is not an idle question to ask why the Trojans have
allies.   They might have fought the war with their own forces.
The answer is plain if we turn to the remaining and the most
important allies of the Trojans, the Lycians.   The Lycian
heroes, Sarpedon, Glaucos, and Pandaros, play a most prominent part in the Iliad.   The geographical situation gave no
clue as to why the Lycians should be introduced as allied
with the Trojans.   On the contrary it ought to have prevented it, for the Lycians live far off in the south of Asia
Minor.[2]   In order to explain why the Lycians, in spite of
geography, appear in the Homeric poems as the foes of the
Greeks, we may begin with the observation that the stage
of another famous myth, the adventures of Bellerophon, is
laid in Lycia.   The Mycenaean date of this myth is proved
by a representation of the Chimaera on a glass plaque from
the bee-hive tomb at Dendra,[3] and the introductory scenes
of the cycle are enacted at the court of the old Mycenaean
city Tiryns.[4]   The reason why the Greeks as early as in the
Mycenaean Age told of mythical events taking place in Lycia,
is evidently because they waged war in Lycia during the

---

[1] Loc. cit., pp. 57.

[2] The localization of Pandaros at Zeleia on the river Aisepos which flows
from Mt. Ida, *Il.*, iv, vv. 85 and 103 ; xii, v. 21 ; ii, vv. 824, is a desultory
attempt to comply with the customary localization of the Trojan allies;
loc. cit., p. 58.   Concerning Leaf's explanation, see above, p. 25.

[3] A. W. Persson, *The Royal Tombs at Dendra*, p. 65.

[4] *Il.*, vi, vv. 150.

Mycenaean Age ; we know that they made repeated attacks on southern Asia Minor, and voyaged along its coast.

The myths of the Lycian heroes contain the reminiscences of the intercourse of the Greeks with the Lycians, as the Bellerophon myth implies. Not only did they fight in southern Asia Minor, but even carved out principalities for themselves, as the Bellerophon myth implies. In this myth connections between Lycia and Argolis appear ; the Argive hero Diomedes appears in the Iliad as the guest-friend of the Lycian hero Glaucos in a famous passage in which they recognize each other and exchange armours. Glaucos is the grandson of Bellerophon who received half the kingdom of Iobates with the hand of his daughter. Sarpedon is still more extolled, and one of the foremost champions on the Trojan side. He is a son of Zeus, he performs valiant deeds in the battle at the ships and he kills the Rhodian hero Tlepolemos.[1] It is generally said that this is a reminiscence of the fights between the Rhodians and the neighbouring Lycians introduced into Homer. That seems probable, but there is no apparent reason for supposing that Tlepolemos represents the Dorian colonists of Rhodes who made attacks on Lycia. He may as well belong to Mycenaean times in which the Greeks made repeated attacks on the southern coast of Asia Minor. Rhodes was in this age an important centre with a numerous population, as the rich finds of Mycenaean cemeteries and vases prove. If this view is right, Tlepolemos' affiliation to Heracles is a later invention ; the Dorians of Rhodes appropriated him, just as the Dorians of the Peloponnese appropriated Heracles in order to justify their claims on the country.

In the Iliad Sarpedon is slain by Patroclos. The Homeric poet transfers the heroes whom he borrows from other cycles to his own purposes. Sarpedon was so great a hero that he was thought to be the worthiest adversary of Patroclos before Patroclos himself met his death. The description of Sarpedon's death [2] is very remarkable, because the gods interfere in a manner with which their interference in the lay of Diomedes only can be compared : Zeus would like to spare his son, but gives him over to his fate on the rebuke of Hera. He lets raindrops of blood fall in honour of his son. The

---

[1] *Il.*, v, vv. 628.　　　　[2] *Il.*, xvi, vv. 419.

dying Sarpedon asks Glaucos not to allow the Achaeans to despoil him. Glaucos' bravery is vain, but Zeus orders Apollo to wash Sarpedon's body, and to let Sleep and Death bring it to Lycia. It seems not unlikely that this really old-fashioned description is taken over from an old epos, celebrating the fights with the Lycians. For the most probable explanation of the great rôle played by the Lycian heroes, is that the fights of the Lycians and the Greeks in the Mycenaean Age were chanted in epics, of which fragments were incorporated into the Iliad, just as fragments of the Pylian epos were incorporated into it. The Lycian heroes being adversaries of the Greeks, the only means of introducing them into the Trojan cycle was to make them allies of the Trojans. Thus they became their first allies ; later others were added, but in these additions geography was taken into account.

These are the most prominent heroes of the Iliad, and they can all with more or less probability be proved to go back into Mycenaean days. It is another question as to when they were annexed to the cycle of the Trojan war, but the view that this cycle was formed in outline during that age is undeniably strengthened by the fact that its chief heroes are of Mycenaean origin. The other heroes, even Idomeneus, do not play the same rôle, and generally there is no sufficient clue to show whether they belong to the Mycenaean Age or not. Some of them are probably taken over from old myths, others not. Many are certainly poetical inventions, and some words may be added concerning this subject.

The Homeric poets invented names freely, borrowing from the common supply of Greek personal names. The names referring to towns or tribes make up an unusually large number, about one-fourth. In certain cases they only name a person after his home, e.g. Chryses, Chryseïs, Briseïs, etc., but very often they are quite arbitrary. Many Trojans have names referring to Greek localities.[1] It must be conceded that, generally speaking, the case is the same with the Greeks. But the significance of this fact ought not to be over-estimated. If the prince of Cnossos, Idomeneus, kills

---

[1] H. Roer, *De nominibus heroum propriis quae in Iliade inveniuntur ab ethnicis derivatis*, Dissertation, Münster, 1914. W. Meyer, *De Homeri patronymicis*, Programm, Göttingen, 1907.

Phaistos, whose name is that of the second great city of Crete, it seems too much to deny that Phaistos really is the eponymous hero of the city,[1] although a new genealogy is invented for him, saying that he is a son of the Maeonian hero Boros from Tarne. But the value of the fact is slight. The poets knew a rich supply of myths, but they treated these little-known myths very freely.

It was observed that except Priam and Paris the Trojan heroes have good Greek names.   That is to say that the names were invented by Greeks and probably are poetical fictions.   For genuine tradition certainly knew very little of Trojan heroes, whilst there was a rich supply of Greek heroes to be found in the myths.   Hence the necessity arose of inventing Trojan heroes in order to vary the narrative and to create adversaries for the Greek heroes.   With this statement we enter upon the difficult question as to the extent to which the personages of the Homeric poems are created by the poets.

The outstanding problem in this respect concerns the Trojan champion Hector.   His name is a Greek personal name.   A king of Chios was so called.[2]   It seems to be a descriptive name, derived from $\check{\epsilon}\chi\epsilon\iota\nu$, " to hold," and its sense is well explained by the Homeric phrase : " for only Hector guarded Ilios." [3]   Scott has in a very suggestive chapter [4] argued that Hector is an invention of the poet's, and his arguments seem very striking.   The opinion that Paris was the original champion of the Trojans, who was superseded by Hector, is shared by many scholars.[5]   Scott thinks that Paris, who is derived from tradition, was for moral reasons unworthy to be the great leader.   Homer tried to repress him, but in spite of this he is no weakling.   Hector was substituted for him as the protagonist of the Trojans. Hector receives high praise in general terms, but the events of the Iliad give no warrant for assigning him a high place as a warrior.   When he appears in the battle he is almost

[1] E. Drerup, *Homerische Poetik*, i, p. 306.
[2] The fifth king of Chios, *Pausanias*, vii, 4, 9 ; cp. Wilamowitz, *Sitzungsberichte der preussischen Akademie der Wissenschaften*, 1906, pp. 52.
[3] *Il.*, vi, v. 403 ; cp. Platon, *Cratylos*, p. 393 A.
[4] Scott, *The Unity of Homer*, pp. 205.
[5] Cp. above, p. 252.

always defeated. Hector does not slay any Greek leader except Patroclos, and even in this event his rôle is singularly restricted. Scott thinks that these circumstances are to be explained by the supposition that Homer invented a Trojan champion but was not able to invent outstanding achievements, for these were given by tradition. Consequently the contradiction arose of a leader and hero to whom no great deeds were attributed.

The distinguishing feature of Homeric poetry is the humanizing of the old and sometimes rough myths. Hector is the greatest and most sympathetic personage of the Iliad from a human point of view, and the spell of his personality may be understood, if he is a free creation of the poet's mind, a creation into which he was able to put his own heart and his own sentiments without the restrictions which old myths imposed upon him. This view is, of course, subjective, but I concede that it appeals very strongly to me.

The further inference is that Patroclos too is a creation of the poet's. Although Patroclos is a central figure in the Iliad, he is not an important mythological figure. His existence is bound up with the motif of the wrath of Achilles. This wrath was, at a certain time, very popular in epic poetry. The subject of wrath or jealousy ($\mu\hat{\eta}\nu\iota\varsigma$ or $\nu\epsilon\hat{\iota}\kappa\circ\varsigma$) is often hinted at in Homer, e.g. the quarrel between Odysseus and Aias, that between the Atreidae, and that between Odysseus and Achilles which Demodokos chanted. This motif is less mythological than psychological, and I cannot but think that for psychological reasons, it was made the leading idea of the Iliad, and that the great poetical progress consisted precisely in this. We do not know when the motif was originally created,[1] but once it had been invented, fresh inventions of the kind were made. If this is right, it seems to be probable that the motif of wrath, or at least its development into the pivot of the plot, belongs to that stage of epic poetry which may be called Homeric. Only in this stage Patroclos has a real existence. Consequently it is not only Scott who takes him to be an invention of the poet's,[2] but Wilamowitz

[1] It is hardly safe to say that the Meleagros myth was the first instance of this kind ; cp. above, p. 18.

[2] Cp. above, p. 34.

also is inclined to think that his death was but an effective
poetical motif.[1] Some old myth may perhaps have spoken
of such a quarrel, and another of a secondary person with
the name of Patroclos, but if they did exist, they were unimportant. Only a poetical genius could have created the
character and story of Patroclos as they were current in all
later ages.

3. THE GODS AND THE STATE OF THE GODS

From the men we turn to the gods, for there is not only
a heroic but also a divine mythology in Homer, a side of the
conception of the gods which is essentially not religious,
although it has affected religion also. Religion comprises
the relations of the gods with men, mythology their relations
with each other, and especially the systematization of the
gods into a state under the overlordship of Zeus. This idea
of Olympus where the gods dwell ruled by their king Zeus,
was imposed by Homer upon the minds of all later ages.[2]
Its model was admittedly taken from the conditions of human
life, and we find a similar pantheon in other countries, in
Egypt and in Babylonia. Here the systematization of the
gods under one supreme god was due partly to cosmological
and theological speculations, partly to the political prevalence
of a certain city. As one city subjugated the other cities
of the country or became its capital and the seat of the king
and the government, the local god of this city became the
overlord of the gods of the other cities and the head of the
pantheon. So Marduk, Assur, and Amon attained to their
supreme position. Amon was, moreover, identified with the
sun-god Re, to whom old cosmological systematization of
the gods had given the supreme place.

In Greece these conditions were absent. Only very faint
traces of a cosmology appear in Homer, it was elaborated
by Hesiod. There was no city which subjugated the other
cities so that its god was able to become the ruler of a pantheon. The comprehension of the gods under the rulership

---

[1] Wilamowitz, *Die Ilias und Homer*, p. 335.
[2] For a fuller discussion of this subject see my *Mycenaean Origin of Greek
Mythology*, ch. iv.

of a supreme god came about in another way. The god who by virtue of his nature was the fittest for the ruling position was made the overlord of gods and men, Zeus, the weather-god, the rain-giver and the thrower of the thunder bolt.

Our ideas of Olympus are determined by Homer's descriptions, and the attempt has been made to show that this idea was developed with the development of Homeric poetry. It is asserted that the descriptions of the interference of the gods in the battles and the Olympic scenes belong to a late stage of the development of Homeric poetry, and that the gods are more independent in the early parts of the poems.[1] The interference of the gods is, however, most prominent in the lay of Diomedes, which is generally considered to be very old. If the Olympic scenes are cut out, little would remain. These scenes may, however, have been enlarged later. The salient point is that even in the admittedly early parts Zeus controls fate. A Mycenaean vase picture (fig. 56) shows a man holding a balance in front of a warrior and a chariot with two men.[2] It can be but Zeus taking the scales of destiny in order to determine the fate of the combatants, a famous scene of the Iliad which is described twice and hinted to in two passages [3] in words proving that it was an old and worn idea. It comes consequently down from Mycenaean times. Zeus was the supreme ruler.

What this implies will be made clearer through the following observations. Olympus is everywhere the common dwelling place of the gods, only in two passages does Zeus alone dwell on Olympus.[4] This idea is expressed in fixed and often repeated phrases and verses. The gods are twice called " the Olympians," more frequently " the Heavenly Ones," and in

---

[1] G. Finsler, *Homer*, 2nd ed., pp. 220 ; and *Die olympischen Szenen der Ilias*, Programm, Bern, 1906. Cp. Wilamowitz, *Die Ilias und Homer*, pp. 316 and 284.

[2] I wish to acknowledge my debt of gratitude to Mr. E. Sjöqvist who has sent me a photograph of the vase and kindly given me the permission to publish it. It was found during the Swedish excavations in Cyprus in the upper burial stratum of the chamber tomb No. 17 at Enkomi. This stratum which contains a rich tomb furniture consisting of several gold and ivory objects, etc., is dated by Mr. Sjöqvist to *c.* 1300 B.C.

[3] *Il.*, viii, vv. 69, xxii, vv. 209, and xvi, v. 658, xix, v. 223 resp.

[4] *Il.*, xiii, v. 243 and xvi, v. 364. In both passages he is the weather-god.

prayer men turn themselves towards the heavens. The heavens and Olympus are identical, because lightning and rain come down from the heavens as well as from the mountain around which the clouds gather, the peak of Zeus. No single god is called an Olympian except Zeus alone, who is "the Olympian One." The name of the Olympian Ones applies to the gods as a collective body. This is but natural. For Zeus alone dwells originally on Mount Olympus as the weather-god, the cloud-gatherer and the thrower of lightning. The other gods dwell in the places where their works are visible, Poseidon in the sea, Artemis in forests and on meadows, Athena on the acropolis. Zeus has lifted them up to his dwelling place on Mount Olympus or in the heavens, and this idea is so ingrained and prevalent that it cannot possibly be doubted that it is much earlier than Homer. It follows, and this is the salient point, that the gods were in the remote past subordinated to Zeus, for this subordination is the reason why they had to dwell in the same place as Zeus. Zeus is the Olympian One, the ruler; the other gods, the Olympian Ones, are his subjects or in a certain sense, his court. In this subordination of the gods under Zeus, the Olympic state of the gods is contained *in nuce* and this idea is much older than Homer.

The model of the monarchical rule of Zeus is not found in Ionia of historical times, where there was nothing but lack of political unity and unified government, a great number of kings and princes, one in each town, before the kingship was abolished. The model is often sought in Thessaly, but the political institutions of Thessaly do not bear out this suggestion. There was an overlord, the *tagos*, but his position was not hereditary, he was elected for lifetime from one of the various ruling families of the cities and in case of need only. He had not the same name or power as the old kings or Zeus, the king of the gods. More specious is the reason that Mount Olympus is situated in Thessaly. Even Homer describes Olympus as the Thessalian mountain, although it may be doubted whether he always has this mountain in mind, whenever he mentions Olympus.

There are several mountains in Greece called Olympus, and still more in Asia Minor. The assumption that their

FIG. 56.—ZEUS WITH THE SCALES OF DESTINY:
CYPRO-MYCENAEAN VASE FROM ENKOMI

names were all borrowed from the famous Thessalian mountain is improbable, and in the case of the sanctuary of Olympia
the assumption of a borrowing would lead us into insur-
mountable difficulties, especially as Hera seems to be earlier
than Zeus at this place. On the contrary the name Olympus
is one of the many pre-Greek words which the Greeks took
over from the indigenous population.[1] It had simply the
significance " mountain," just as Ida has the significance of
a forest-clad mountain, and it was used as a name of various
mountains, but was ultimately applied to the Thessalian mountain especially because of its Homeric fame. This coincides
perfectly with the original character of the weather-god Zeus,
who dwells on the loftiest mountain peak in the neighbourhood, around which the clouds gather and from which thunder
and rain break forth. Thus we are not compelled to ascribe
the origin of the idea of the mountain of the gods to Thessaly.
It was a common Greek idea, for Zeus dwelt everywhere on
some mountain peak.

The conception that the gods dwelt on Olympus as the
subordinates of Zeus is pre-Homeric, and we do not find
its model in the political conditions of the Historic Age. Consequently it goes back to the Mycenaean Age, and there we
find the missing model. This is the rule of the Great King
as it was described in the previous chapter. The Great King
of Mycenaean times had the same full power as Zeus, and
the political institutions are the same, whilst in a later age
they altered rapidly. On Olympus there was monarchical rule,
on the earth, a republic after the overthrow of the kingship.

Undue attention has been directed towards the quarrels
and the strife between the gods, their refractoriness and their
stubbornness, their attempts to delude Zeus by guile, the
pride of Zeus in his strength, and his threats. The Ionian
minstrels delighted in these pictures, sometimes tainting
them with burlesque. Due attention ought to be paid also
to the great veneration and respect shown by the gods to
their king. They recognize his rule as self-evident and on
many occasions they obey his orders without any opposition.
When Zeus enters the assembly of the gods, no one dares

[1] C. Theander in the periodical *Eranos*, xv, 1915, pp. 127.

to remain seated but all arise to greet him.[1] The reason
of this overwhelming power of Zeus is not only his strength
but also a moral fact : he has inherited the kingdom of the
heavens as the eldest son of Cronos.[2] But the right of the
eldest son was later superseded by the folk-tale motif which
made him the youngest son of his father. The sons of Cronos
divided the world among themselves, just as the sons of
Aristomachos divided the Peloponnese.[3] The realm is considered as a possession of the ruling family, and this idea is
unthinkable in historical times but natural in the Mycenaean
Age, in which the king gave away towns at his pleasure.
The myths and even the story of the Olympians are full of
strife and contentions in the ruling families. Such quarrels
may certainly have occurred in the stormy age of the wanderings of the peoples. Zeus possessed himself of the kingdom
by an act of violence against his father, and other gods tried
to deprive him of it. The myth that Hera, Poseidon, and
Athena tried to chain Zeus but that Thetis injected fear
into them fetching the hundred-armed Briareos,[4] resembles
strikingly, if the mythological colouring is disregarded, a
story telling of an attempted revolt in a kingly family which
was quelled by calling upon foreign aid.

More important for our purpose is the political organization of the Olympic State. Zeus has full power by right
of inheritance, as has Agamemnon. The other gods appear
as his retainers whom he summons to counsel or to meals,
just as Agamemnon summons the chiefs. Just as the war-
king summons the army assembly, so Zeus summons twice
an assembly of the gods, in which even the lesser gods, the
rivers and the nymphs of the springs and the meadows, take
part.[5] Poseidon once performs for his kingly brother the
service of unharnessing his horses ; [6] his relation to Zeus
is that of a " friend " or " servant," as the Iliad calls the
retainers of the king. Of course there are other servants
on Olympus too, e.g. the Horae.

On the other hand, the gods could be conceived as the
vassals of the supreme god, since they ruled each over his

[1] *Il.*, i, v. 534.   [2] *Il.*, xv, v. 166, and v. 204.
[3] *Il.*, xv, vv. 186.   [4] *Il.*, i, vv. 399.
[5] In the beginnings of books viii and xx.   [6] *Il.*, viii, v. 440.

domain, and this conception got the upper hand, since it agreed with the inclination of the poets to favour the vassals in opposition to their suzerain. When Zeus sends a message to Poseidon to desist from helping the Greeks, Poseidon says, just as an obstinate vassal would, that Zeus ought to be content with the third part allotted to him ; [1] he is of the opinion that Zeus ought to allow his vassals to act according to their pleasure. But he obeys when Iris reminds him of the protection afforded to the eldest brother by the Erinyes, i.e. the moral laws. The current motif of the strife or the wrath, which was beloved by the Homeric poets, favoured the broad and picturesque description of the so-called Olympic scenes.

These scenes partly bear the stamp of a later age in which the nobility ruled the state, but it is doubtful whether the conditions of this period formed the model for the description of Olympus in its essential outlines. The conception of the cloud-capped mountain peak on which the cloud-gatherer dwelt formed an important contribution to the picture. The gates of the City of the Gods were clouds which the Horae opened and shut. Zeus is seated on the highest peak when he desires to be alone. Otherwise the City of the Gods is depicted as a human city. It is surrounded by a wall with gates. Zeus has a magnificent palace in which the gods assemble for meals and for meeting in counsel, and it is surrounded by the dwellings of the other gods. The picture corresponds to the conditions at the beginning of the His- torical Age of Greece, in which every city had a king whose house was built on the acropolis and was surrounded by the dwellings of the noblemen, but it corresponds also to the conditions of the Mycenaean Age, in which the stately palace of the king was also built on an acropolis and surrounded by the dwellings of his retainers. There are other houses besides the palace on the acropolis of Mycenae and Tiryns, and the great number of graves with rich contents is a proof of a well-to-do population. Even the picture of the City of the Gods may go back into Mycenaean days. The idea arose spontaneously, as soon as the gods were transferred to Olympus as the subjects of their king Zeus. Some traits borrowed

[1] *Il.*, xv, vv. 194.

from the imaginary idea of the Fields of the Blest are applied
to the description of Olympus in a passage in the Odyssey.[1]

The fact that the idea of Olympus and the State of the
Gods is copied from the Mycenaean state is very important
from a historical and religious point of view, but it has no
bearing on the question of the age of the Trojan cycle. As
we have seen that the underlying fact, the destruction of
Troy, is probably historically true, and that all the prominent heroes go back into the Mycenaean Age, the opinion
is well founded that the Trojan cycle also belongs to the
myths which in their main outlines go back into this age.
The great cycles of myths are mentioned or at least hinted
at in Homer, as well as many other myths. It is evident
that many more myths and details of myths were known
than those which are told. It is very characteristic that the
ship " Argo " is said to be on the lips of all men in the only
passage where the myth of the Argonauts is hinted at.[2] A
survey of the myths recorded in Homer would be of great
interest for the history of the development of the myths,
but even if most of these myths have come down from the
Mycenaean Age, it would not contribute to the elucidation
of the question here discussed, because the time of their incorporation into the Homeric poems must be left undeter-
mined. It may have taken place at any late period, however
ancient the myths may be.

4. Homer's Use of the Myths. The Similes

There is, however, another point to which attention should
be drawn, the curious attitude of Homer to the myths. We
are accustomed to think of the contents of the Homeric poems
as myths. That is true, but only with certain important
restrictions. The leading idea of the Iliad, the wrath of
Achilles, is not conspicuous among the myths. Its importance lies on the psychological side, and it is not without
reason suspected to be a poetical invention. If Hector too,
and perhaps Patroclos, are creations of the poet's, or even
if from third rank figures barely mentioned in the myths,
they were made the principal actors in his drama—and this, at

[1] *Od.*, vi, vv. 42.   [2] *Od.*, xii, v. 70 : 'Αργὼ πᾶσι μέλουσα.

least, seems to be certain,—the plot and the main part of
the Iliad have very little to do with traditional mythology.
It is certain that some parts of the poems in which we seem
to feel the poet's pulse beating, and which are the most
charming, are poetical fictions, e.g. the meeting of Hector
and Andromache and Priam's visit to Achilles. The poet
uses the traditional mythological material, but as his background only. He does not relate myths for the pleasure of
story-telling, but he creates something new on the basis of
the myths, freely rehandling them, and, adding to them the
description of men with flaming passions and keen sorrows
who act and suffer. This psychological characterization is
not inherent in the myths, it is an achievement of the poet's
and in this his real greatness lies. The traditional myths
must have grown old before it was possible to handle them
so freely and to infuse such a different spirit into them.

Homer's curious attitude to the myths appears also in
another little noticed fact. I have said that he does not
relate myths for the pleasure of story-telling, although we
commonly think of myths as the contents of his poems. The
statement is especially true in the sense that the poet does
not himself narrate the myths, but that he always puts them
into the mouths of personages introduced by him.[1] It would
seem that epic poetry should provide ample occasions for
mythological digressions, but the references to myths which
the poet gives in his own words are limited to the bare statement of genealogical relations. In the whole Iliad there is
only one mythological digression told by the poet himself,
the passage concerning the origin of the two Thessalian heroes
Menestheus and Eudoros.[2] In the Odyssey there are apparently more digressions, but two of these are so closely
connected with the subject-matter that they can hardly be
called digressions, the story how Odysseus while hunting a
boar received the scar which made his nurse recognize him,[3]
and the story of the bow, the gift of Iphitos, by means of
which vengeance on the suitors was brought about.[4] There
remains one real mythological digression, that referring to

[1] Cp. my *History of the Greek Religion*, pp. 173.
[2] *Il.*, xvi, vv. 173-92.   [3] *Od.*, xix, vv. 392-466.
[4] *Od.*, xxi, vv. 11-41.

the seer Theoclymenos and his family.[1] All other myths, which do not directly pertain to the plot of the poems, e.g. the myths of the return of the heroes and their fate after their return, are put into the mouths of personages introduced by the poet. He makes even the minstrel Demodocos sing of the love affair of Ares and Aphrodite.

Generally speaking, the myths are not told for the love of story-telling and for their own sake, but if the poet puts them into the mouth of his personages he does so with a special intention. Myths are told as examples, warning or exhorting, deterring or comforting ; and when a man prays, he adduces some myth as a reason why the gods should grant his prayer. If old Nestor so often relates the exploits of his youth, it not only serves to depict his character, but the stories are intended to exhort or to warn his comrades.

We see that Homer relates the traditional myths not for their own sake but because of their impression upon men's conduct. It is not the events, but their psychological effects which interest him. With this another fact is in agreement, namely, the modification of the old, crude myths in an anthropomorphic direction. Old myths told of real combats between the gods ; such are hinted at, but the late poet who chose a battle of the gods as his subject [2] did not dare to let the gods really come to blows with one another notwithstanding the magniloquent opening. The old-fashioned appearance of the fifth book depends merely on the fact that the gods interfere much more actively than elsewhere and are even wounded by a hero. This book is moreover richer in mythological allusions than any other. Old myths were still more free in this respect ; it is related, for example, that Idas used his bow against Apollo to protect his bride Marpessa from the advances of the god. This myth is mentioned only in passing ; [3] elsewhere Homer always adduces the contest of a mortal with a god as a deterrent example. The gods do not have intercourse with men except for fabulous peoples, such as the Ethiopians and the Phaeacians. Nor do men receive gifts from the gods except for the altogether special case of the weapons which Hephaistos

---

[1] *Od.*, xv, vv. 225-55.　　　　[2] *Il.*, xx, vv. 31-74 ; xxi, vv. 385-513.
[3] *Il.*, ix, vv. 558-60.

makes for Achilles. Elsewhere gifts of the gods are heir-looms from past generations, given to earlier heroes and inherited by the Homeric heroes.

The Homeric poet has widened the gap between men and gods—in earlier myths they were on a more equal footing—just as he softened the brutal characterization of the old myths. He knows that his heroes are not so strong as those of olden times and says it often, but they are more human. He has humanized and anthropomorphized the myths, and this is his great achievement, the new and original feature of Homeric poetry. If he sometimes recurs to the old crude motifs, they readily acquire a burlesque character,[1] and this is due not only to his lack of understanding of the early myths, but also to the fact that he had lost any respect for them on account of their absurdities; consequently he reacted, turning them to the ridicule.

It may sound astonishing, but mythology was really out of date with Homer. He used it because he had taken it over as traditional, but he deflected it to other purposes than the telling of mythical stories. The new aspect of life appears in the similes which Homer loves to introduce. Comparisons are seldom taken from mythology and they are applied to women only.[2] Long ago, in a short but striking paper,[3] Platt tried to show that Homer drew his similes from what was ready to hand, beginning with the observation of Aristarchos that the use of the trumpet, of boiled meat, and of riding on horseback occur in similes only, and differ from heroic customs. Since that time a vigorous discussion concerning the similes has been carried on. Winter pointed to the life-like and vigorous descriptions of animal life in certain similes and found their parallels in the works of Minoan art which were prompted by a similar spirit, other similes are duller and are consequently thought to be later.[4] His

---

[1] W. Nestle, " Die Anfänge einer Götterburleske bei Homer," *Neue Jahr-bücher für das klass. Altertum*, xv, 1905, pp. 161 ; K. Bielohlawek, " Komische Motive in der Homerischen Gestaltung des griechischen Göttermythus," *Archiv für Religionswissenschaft*, xxviii, 1930, pp. 106.

[2] *Od.*, vi, vv. 162 ; vv. 102 ; xviii, vv. 193 ; xix, vv. 518 ; xx, vv. 66.

[3] A. Platt, " Homer's Similes," *Journal of Philology*, xxiv, 1896, pp. 28.

[4] In Gercke and Norden, *Einleitung in di klass. Altertumswissenschaft*, 1st ed., 1910, ii, pp. 161.

conclusion was that the similes which correspond to the Minoan art go back into that time. They disagree completely, he thinks, with the Geometric art to which nature is foreign. Winter seems, however, not to have found his interesting arguments convincing ; for he has withdrawn them from the subsequent editions.

I have referred above [1] to Evans' comparison of certain similes with works of Minoan art, which tends in the same direction. I am, however, afraid that the underlying principle of the correspondence between the description in a literary work and the representation in works of art is questionable. The description of a poet may, even if it explicitly refers to a work of art, be inspired not by this work but by his own keen and vigorous observation of nature and life. In drama, for example, the graphic descriptions are intended to replace the lack of decoration of the stage. This is well known in regard to Shakespeare, and the same is certainly the case with the Greek drama. This is the reason of the failure of the repeated efforts to prove that the stage in the age of the great Greek dramatists was decorated so as to imitate reality. Stage decoration was certainly slight and strictly conventionalized. I may also point to the fact that primitive peoples give vivid and graphic descriptions of their very primitive paintings and carvings which others would hardly recognize as representing real beings and things.

The question of the similes has been treated by Fränkel in an exhaustive and, according to my opinion, convincing manner.[2] Comparisons are, he thinks, very old, and there are typical comparisons from which extensive similes were developed. They do not aim at a concrete description but at arousing a certain sentiment. It would seem that the poet had a number of images ready at hand which he uses, but on the other hand the variations are almost unlimited. Fränkel supports Platt's opinion that the world of the similes is very different from the archaizing world of Homer and much more modern, but he points to the fact that Platt passed over such similes as point in another direction. Consequently

---

[1] Above, p. 28. Cp. H. L. Lorimer, " Homer's Use of the Past," *Journal of Hellenic Studies*, xlix, 1929, pp. 150.

[2] H. Fränkel, *Die homerischen Gleichnisse*, 1921.

Fränkel recognizes the correspondence between certain similes and Minoan works of art, but he attributes much of this similarity to *Wahlverwandtschaft* not to *Blutsverwandtschaft*. He comes near the opinion I have expressed above, but he admits, however, that reminiscences of this earlier civilization may to a certain degree have been preserved in the similes. If there are any, they were but fragments, for in the similes the poet draws from the life, which the conventionalized style of epics prevented him from doing elsewhere. In the similes he incorporated the most recent elements of life and civilization and gave a free hand to his keen observation of nature and life. The similes tend to replace mythology which had become somewhat outworn and old-fashioned.

The fact that the kingship of Zeus on Olympus is modelled after the pattern of the Mycenaean great kingship has a bearing on the Mycenaean date of the myths, because it shows that the earthly as well as the heavenly organization of the state given as the background of the Homeric poems is derived from Mycenaean times. Our last comments seem, however, to have little to do with the connection of Homer with the Mycenaean Age, but they are, perhaps, not without a certain interest in this respect. The fact that Homer does not tell myths for their own sake but that he deflects mythology to side purposes, dressing it up in a psychological garb, freely embellishing the plot with his own inventions, and telling the myths as examples of warning or exhortation only, and that he loves to talk in similes, in which he was able freely to refer to the conditions of his own times, unbound by the rigid epic conventionalism, these facts show that at the time when the Homeric poems were composed, mythology on the one hand was rigidly binding as the subject-matter of the poems, but that on the other hand it was somewhat old-fashioned and outworn. This state of things can only have come about through a lengthy development, in which the myths were chanted until the poets became somewhat tired of story-telling, and the inspiration of a great poetical genius turned in another direction. This agrees with the fact that hints in Homer prove that the great cycles of myths were already formed in their main outlines, although there may have been many variations in details. Consequently mythology is much older than Homer.

These considerations do not say how old mythology is, only that it was very old in the age in which the Homeric poems were composed. This is to a certain extent a confirmation of the view that the myths, and especially the great mythological cycles, were handed down from an age which was long since past, from that age in which the great events took place and in which famous heroes lived and fought, the age of the great wanderings of the Greeks and of the mighty Mycenaean kingdom.

INDEX

A

Achaean dialect, 176.
Achaeans, 89, 91, 96.
Achilleïs, 6.
Achilles (*see also* wrath), 42, 254, 258.
Adrastos, 251.
Aeolic dialect, 163.
aeolisms, 163.
Agamemnon, 44, 49, 116, 156, 214, 216, 221, 222, 225, 234, 251.
agora, 228.
Ahhiyava, 103.
Aias, 257.
Aineias, 47, 49, 253.
Alakshandush, 105.
Albion, 186.
Alcinoos, 241.
Alfred the Great, 187.
Ali Pasha, 196 *n.* 1.
amber, 76.
Amon, 266.
analysis, 6, 211.
Anchises, 253.
Antaravas, 102.
Antenoridae, 46, 50.
anthropology, physical, 84.
Antinoos, 226.
Aqaiwasha, 106.
Arcadian dialect, 175.
Arcadians, 89.
Argonauts, 113, 117, 272.
Ariadne, 252.
Asine, 79, 80, 85.
assembly, army, 220, 221, 222, 224, 226, 238.
— of the gods, 270.
— popular, 221, 222.
Assuva, 105.
Assyrians, 149, 246.
Athenians, 50, 91.
Attarissiyas, 104.
atticisms, 5, 161.
Attila, 186.
Automedon, 232.

B

bards, 186.
Bechtel, F., 9, 20, 168.

Bédier, J., 190.
Bellerophon, 261.
Beloch, K. J., 91 *n.* 1, 141.
Belzner, E., 32 *n.* 1.
Bentley, R., 8.
Beowulf, 186, 189.
Bérard, V., 14, 25.
Bethe, E., 11, 13, 16.
Blegen, C. W., 67.
blind singers, 201.
Blinkenberg, Chr., 124.
boars' tusks, 77, 138.
— tusks' helmet, 77, 138.
Bowra, C. M., 35.
breaks in civilization, 63, 68, 83.
Bréal, M., 4.
Briareos, 270.
bucchero, 84.
Buck, C. B., 61.
Buckelkeramik, 45.
burial customs, 152.
burlesque character of myths, 269, 275.
Busolt, G., 42.
Byblos, 100.
bylinas, 192, 205, 234.

C

Canute the Great, 219.
Caphtor, 107.
Capys, 47.
Carians, 261.
Cauer, P., 5, 18, 42, 142 *n.* 1.
Cephallenes, 116.
Chadwick, H. M., 59, 185, 187.
chansons de geste, 189, 234.
Charlemagne, 187, 191, 214.
Chimaera, 261.
choric lyric, 200.
Chryses, 227.
Cilicia, 97.
Cinyras, 125.
city of the Gods, 271.
classes, 231.
Clothar, 190.
Cnossos, 93, 95.
colonization, Mycenaean, 97.
Colophon, 99.
communal property, 243.

279

compilation theory, 35, 50, 53.
co-regents, 43, 220, 221.
council of elders, 220, 221, 230.
cremation, 154.
Cresphontes, 238.
Crete, 93, 107.
Croiset, M., 19.
Cronos, 270.
Crusius, O., 48.
cuirass, 125, 142, 143.
cyanos frieze, 138.
Cypriot dialect, 175.
Cyprus, 90, 97, 104, 133.

D

Danaoi, 108.
Danielsson, O. A., 169.
Danuna, 106, 107, 108.
Dardanos, 47.
Demodokos, 207, 255.
Dendra, 80, 85, 155.
dialects, 86.
— Homeric, 160.
digamma, 8, 166.
Digenis Akritas, 196.
digressions, mythological, 273.
Diomedes, 225, 258, 262.
Dokarim, 197, 202, 210.
Dorians, 70, 90, 109, 157, 177, 231, 239, 262.
Dörpfeld, W., 21, 154.
Drerup, E., 31, 43, 54, 164.
dress, 75.
dual, 171.
duels, 47.
Düntzer, H., 179.

E

Echepolos, 229.
Edda, 186.
Egypt, 102, 132, 136.
Einhard, 187.
emphyteusis, 242.
Endymion, 253.
Epeios, 256.
Ephyraean goblets, 83.
epics of other peoples, 51.
— Abakan Tartars, 195.
— Atchinese, 196, 203.
— Bosnian, 194, 201.
— Esthonian, 193.
— Finnish, 193.
— French, 189.
— Greek, mediaeval and modern, 196.
— Kara-Kirgizes, 195, 204, 207.
— Ossetes, 196, 200.
— Russian, 192.

epics, Serbian, 194.
— Swedish, 192.
— Teutonic, 185.
— stages of, 187.
epithet, ornamental, 179.
Erechtheus, house of, 212.
Etagenperücke, 127.
Euchenor, 229.
Eumaios, 130.
Euryalos, 260.
Eurythion, 233.
Evans, A., 28, 57, 70, 121, 123, 151, 276.

F

Fate, 267.
feudalism, 198, 214, 238.
fibula, 76, 123, 240.
Fick, A., 9, 20, 65 n. 1, 131, 168.
Finsler, G., 18, 216, 222, 230, 231 n. 1, 243.
Forrer, E., 102.
Fränkel, H., 276.
" friends," 232, 237, 238.
Fürst, C. M., 84.

G

Geometric Age, 122, 239.
Glaucos, 262.
glosses, 181.
Great King, 245.
Grote, G., 11.
γύαλα, 143, 145.

H

Hague fragment, 190.
hair-dress, 127.
Harland, J. P., 69.
Hartel, F., 169.
Hector, 48, 264.
Helbig, W., 19, 143.
Helen, 252.
Heraclidae, 70, 238.
Heraion, Argive, 68 n. 1.
— on Samos, 99.
Herder, J. G., 12.
Hermanaric, 186.
Hermann, G., 11.
hero cult, 80.
Hesiod, 208, 244, 266.
Heusler, A., 31.
Hildebrandslied, 189.
Hildegaire, 190.
hird, 232, 233, 238.
Holland, L. B., 70.
Homer, 36, 210.